SWEET
Reason

SWEET Reason

Rhetoric and the Discourses of Modernity

SUSAN WELLS

THE UNIVERSITY OF CHICAGO PRESS

CHICAGO AND LONDON

SUSAN WELLS is associate professor of English at Temple University.

The University of Chicago Press, Chicago 60637
The University of Chicago Press, Ltd., London
© 1996 by The University of Chicago
All rights reserved. Published 1996
Printed in the United States of America
05 04 03 02 01 00 99 98 97 96   1 2 3 4 5
ISBN: 0-226-89336-7 (cloth)
　　　 0-226-89337-5 (paper)

An earlier version of chapter 5 has been published as "Narrative Figures and Subtle Persuasions: The Rhetoric of the MOVE Report," in *The Rhetorical Turn: Invention and Persuasion in the Conduct of Inquiry,* ed. Herbert W. Simons (Chicago: University of Chicago Press, 1990), 208–38. ©1990 by The University of Chicago. All rights reserved.

Library of Congress Cataloging-in-Publication Data

Wells, Susan.
　　Sweet reason : rhetoric and the discourses of modernity / Susan
Wells.
　　　　p.　　cm.
　　Includes bibliographical references and index.
　　1. Narration (Rhetoric)　2. Discourse analysis.　I. Title.
PN212.W45　　1996
808'.0014—dc20　　　　　　　　　　　　　　　　　　　　　95-46870
　　　　　　　　　　　　　　　　　　　　　　　　　　　　　　　　　　CIP

CONTENTS · · · ·

ACKNOWLEDGMENTS ● ● ● ●

● ● ● ● $\mathbf{M}$y work for this book was supported by a Faculty Study Leave and two Faculty Summer Research Grants from Temple University. I am very grateful for this aid.

Early drafts of some of the chapters have benefited from the comments of audiences. An early version of chapter 2 was read to the Temple University English Department Journal Club; of chapter 3, to the Champaign-Urbana Conference on Marxism and Critical Theory. Versions of chapter 5 were read at the Rhetoric Department Colloquium, the Penn State Conference on Rhetoric and Composition, the Conference on College Composition and Communication, and the University of Pennsylvania Graduate Lecture Series. Chapter 6 was read at the Gender and the Classroom Lecture Series at Cornell University.

I revised the manuscript at the Tokyo campus of Temple University. The faculty, students, and staff of TUJ have my continued affectionate gratitude. Students and faculty in the rhetoric program of the English Department at Penn State University, particularly Don Bialostosky and Jack Selzer, put me back in touch with the intellectual project of the book. I am grateful to Doug Mitchell, at the University of Chicago Press, to the Chicago referees, and to copyeditor Pamela Bruton for their generous work with this manuscript.

I am indebted to my colleagues at Temple University, particularly the members of the Cultural Studies Reading Group and the Literacy Research Group. I am grateful to Daniel O'Hara for accompanying me in the readings of Lacan's seminars. Frank Sullivan, Alan Singer, Lawrence Venuti, Arabella Lyon, Hugh Grady, James Bono, Stephen Mailloux, Susan Jarratt, and Jan Swearingen have read sections of this manuscript; their comments and suggestions, as well as their collegial friendship, have been invaluable. Susan Stewart's friendship and intellectual companionship sustained me in this work. Finally, loving thanks to my husband and best collaborator, Hugh Grady, and our daughters, Laura Rose and Constance.

Toward a Rhetoric of Intersubjectivity: Language and Narration

•   •   •   •   O utside the walls, Socrates meets Phaedrus, just come from visiting Lysias. Phaedrus has heard Lysias's latest speech, "in a way, a love speech,"[1] in which the beloved is tempted by someone who is not a lover. Socrates wants the speech immediately, and Phaedrus reluctantly agrees to summarize it, since he has not learned it by heart. And then, Socrates: "Yes, my dear, when you have first shown me what you have in your left hand, under your cloak. For I suspect you have the actual discourse. And if that is the case, believe this of me, that I am very fond of you, but when Lysias is here I have no intention of lending you my ears to practice on. Come now, show it."[2] Phaedrus reluctantly accedes. And from this gesture, much follows: Phaedrus's recitation of the concealed speech, Socrates' speech uttered from the concealment of his cloak, the two horses straining toward the forms, toward the beloved, the myth of Theuth, Ficino's musings, Derrida meditating on the good and bad seeds. With Phaedrus's gesture, I begin a series of reflections on the relations of desire and reason in what we read and write now. Phaedrus, concealing a text imperfectly conned and invoked repeatedly as "dear," carries the infection of writing, in the form of a fictional text that argues against desire. Many years later, Horkheimer and Adorno would identify the accents of Lysias's speech as those of instrumental reason. His text, of

1. Plato, *Phaedrus,* trans. H. N. Fowler (Cambridge: Harvard University Press, 1914), 1.
2. Plato, *Phaedrus,* 3.

course, changes as Phaedrus recites it to Socrates and becomes quite different again when Socrates transposes it, recants it, reflects on it. Socrates discerns the text for us, erotically hidden under Phaedrus's robe, and also identifies it as an alternative to, an improvement on, Phaedrus: he will not hear Phaedrus's dutiful précis, but Lysias himself. But Lysias was not really the importunate nonlover, any more than Phaedrus (or, in his turn, Socrates) was: he was a teacher of rhetoric working on a problem, a technician of language, like most of the probable readers of this book. His text, the written text, is an object that doubles and displaces those who read it or might want to read it and draws them, absent or present, into relation with each other. The text offers to satisfy both desire and reason. Desire, certainly: it is a beloved object, begged from the famous Lysias by the brilliant Phaedrus. It leads Socrates, he says, like fruit dangled before a hungry animal (only later will Socrates say that nothing of real value can be written). And now, before we hear the chillingly opportunistic speech of Lysias, it offers us reason, a reason especially appropriate to Socrates: a paradox, a proof that the least likely alternative is true, a reversal of accepted knowledge. There may even be transfer value to the cases of the poor lover, the old lover. Phaedrus yields up this desired speech in response to both entreaty and the plausible injunction that, since he is already bent on reciting the speech, he might as well do so at once.

I will return to the *Phaedrus* in chapter 4: it is a central text linking desire, rationality, and rhetoric. For now, note the geometry of this scene. Reason and desire are enacted as distinct but interdependent, underwriting each other as a system of exchanges, multiplying the discursive relations between Phaedrus and Socrates, Phaedrus and Lysias, Lysias and Socrates. And those multiple relations situate the text, prompting a rhetorical reflection both on the relations among the fictional speakers and on the work of the text for Plato, for Renaissance readers, for Derrida, for us. With Phaedrus's unfolding of the hidden scroll, the text's materiality is foregrounded. Finally, Phaedrus's gesture recognizes the complex, intersubjective grounding of discourse: Socrates does not want Phaedrus's speech, or even Lysias's, but Phaedrus reading Lysias; we will not hear Socrates monologically, but in rejoinder to Lysias, in a passionate speech to Phaedrus. Whatever the propositional content of the dialogue, it is situated in its discursive relations, the complex relations among writers and readers which support and constrain its textuality.

We read the *Phaedrus* as a philosophic text, assimilating it to disciplinary conditions that are distinctly modern.[3] The writing of modernity is differentiated: texts are oriented to varied discursive practices, including forms of reason, and their supporting intersubjective relations are deeply sedimented in such institutions as academic disciplines and professions and in practices of language and media. Our texts certainly do work, but the exchanges they manage are dispersed, acting for us at a distance. They inhabit a densely problematic and politically charged terrain. Sometimes we aspire to the rationality of a public sphere in which all speakers are equal, relations unimaginable to the *Phaedrus*. Sometimes we search abjectly for lost rationality, imagined as lost. Such complex relations require a new rhetoric, and theorists from Burke to Perelman to de Man have worked at constructing one.[4] This book joins that labor of construction, arguing that although it is fruitful to see rhetoric as epistemic, it need not therefore be defined as narrowly cognitive. Burke showed us how to read the close relation between trope and persuasion, between language as a material, bodily practice and as an articulated system of reason. We have yet to extend this work of reading to the discourses of modernity, to the texts of the sciences, the professions, of government and the academy. Modernity is a system of texts that we are only now learning to read.

But here we are at leisure: the stream runs at our feet, the willows bloom overhead, the breeze, the grass, the cicadas, all charm us, all are

3. We might begin to trace discussions of modernity and postmodernity with Jacques Derrida's "Signature Event Context," *Glyph I* (1977), and his reply to Searle in "Limited Inc abc, *Glyph II* (1977), which investigate modernity and the text. Another line of investigation can be traced to Max Weber's theory of modernity as shaped by an iron cage of rationality (Weber, "Science as a Vocation," in *From Max Weber: Essays in Sociology,* ed. and trans. H. H. Gerth and C. W. Mills [New York: Oxford University Press, 1974]). The line of investigation linking postmodernism with textuality can be continued through Jean-François Lyotard, *The Postmodern Condition: A Report on Knowledge,* trans. Geoff Bennington and Brian Massumi (Minneapolis: University of Minnesota Press, 1984). Hal Foster's anthology *The Anti-aesthetic: Essays on Postmodern Culture* (Seattle: Bay Press, 1983) includes essays approaching these questions from various perspectives.

4. See Kenneth Burke, *A Grammar of Motives* (New York: Prentice-Hall, 1945; reprint, Berkeley and Los Angeles: University of California Press, 1969); Chaim Perelman and Lynn Olbrechts-Tyteca, *The New Rhetoric: A Treatise on Argumentation,* trans. John Wilkinson and Purcell Weaver (Notre Dame: University of Notre Dame Press, 1969); Paul de Man, *Allegories of Reading: Figural Language in Rousseau, Nietzsche, Rilke, and Proust* (New Haven: Yale University Press, 1979); Paul de Man, "Semiology and Rhetoric," in *Textual Strategies,* ed. Josue Harari (Ithaca: Cornell University Press, 1979).

invested with stories. Our Phaedrus reaches under his robe for the manuscript. Our Socrates listens expectantly. Let us begin.

Borrowing from Burke's "key terms of dramatism,"[5] I suggest three terms for an intersubjective rhetoric: language, narration, and action. A rhetoric of intersubjectivity attends to language, since central problems of interpretation bear on the relation of the materiality of the inscribed text to the uncontainable proliferation of meanings. Narration locates the text in time—both in the lived time of reading, reception, and the coordination of action and in the textual time of reflection, reordering, and multiplied subject locations. Narration forms the intersection between the text as formal structure and the text as representation and social practice. Finally, action—because the discourses of modernity are themselves formed as social actions. They are contested in their production, their readings are contested, and their production is a central element in the work of social reproduction. These three terms are not meant to be exhaustive, any more than Burke's pentad was intended to be comprehensive. They will focus discussion of the discourses of modernity, suggest more than one way of reading those texts, forestall premature closure, and remind us that the text is not only a labor but a labor of language, with its own specificity and density.

The three terms *language, narration,* and *action* are necessarily entrained, one leading to the other. To reflect on language is to come to terms with the materiality of the signifier, especially as it plays its role in the formation of the speaking, reading, and writing subject. Unofficially since the *Phaedrus,* and officially since Quintilian, rhetoric has been a discipline forming subjects capable of a certain kind of linguistic agency. Almost alone among the disciplines of antiquity, it survives as an ordinary "school subject"—the composition class, which preserves scraps of the rhetorical wisdom of all the ages. Whether this pedagogical investment is seen as a permanent tendency toward vulgarization or as an admirable public service, it implicates rhetoric in a narrative of development. Within the boundaries of the individual text, a rhetoric that attends seriously to the materiality of writing, to its entrainment in relations of desire and displacement, will read in the discourses of modernity various narratives of power, knowledge, disclosure, and conversion. Power and desire operate within such narratives: to say so does not discredit the text but places it in time, as a situated act of writing and as an extension of the reader's attention and memory. Both the work of

5. Burke, *Grammar of Motives,* xv–xxii.

reading and the work of writing are actions: they are even
like any others. But reading and writing also suggest inte
other events, events that may have already been textualizec
and competing discourses. To analyze those relations, rela
textuality, returns us to the topic of language, since we must consider
quotation, doubling of meaning, and multiplied locations of the reading
subject.

My work of reading has sought the sponsorship of an unlikely pair of
theorists, Jacques Lacan[6] and Jürgen Habermas.[7] I have chosen them as

6. Lacan's massive work, which will eventually come to equal Freud's in its extent, is only now becoming available in any language. Lacan's seminars are being
published in English by Norton (New York) and Tavistock/Routledge (London) in
chronological series, edited by Jacques-Alain Miller, beginning with the seminars of
1953–54, *Freud's Papers on Technique,* trans. John Forrester, and of 1954–55,
The Ego in Freud's Theory and in the Technique of Psychoanalysis, trans. S. Tomaselli.
Both volumes were published in 1988; the third volume was published in 1992.
The seminar of 1959–60, vol. 7, *The Ethics of Psychoanalysis,* trans. Dennis
Porter, was published in 1992. The eleventh seminar was published as *The Four
Fundamental Concepts of Psycho-analysis,* ed. J.-A. Miller, trans. Alan Sheridan (New
York: Norton, 1978). The twentieth seminar is available in French as *Encore, 1972–
73,* ed. J.-A. Miller (Paris: Seuil, 1975). The seminar on "The Purloined Letter"
was published as "Seminar on 'The Purloined Letter,'" in *The Purloined Poe: La-
can, Derrida, and Psychoanalytic Reading,* ed. John Muller and William Richardson
(Baltimore: Johns Hopkins University Press, 1988). Other writings available in English include *Écrits: A Selection,* trans. A. Sheridan (New York: Norton, 1977),
Feminine Sexuality: Jacques Lacan and the École Freudienne, ed. Juliet Mitchell and
Jacqueline Rose (New York: Norton, 1982). The seminars are becoming available in
French in a series published by Seuil (Paris); the full collection of *Écrits* was also
published by Seuil (Paris, 1966). The standard introduction to Lacan's work in English is Ellie Ragland-Sullivan's *Jacques Lacan and the Philosophy of Psychoanalysis*
(Urbana and Chicago: University of Illinois Press, 1987); the introductions by the
editors of *Feminine Sexuality* are also very useful. Essays on the clinical practice of
the Lacanian School are included in Stuart Schneiderman's *Returning to Freud:
Clinical Psychoanalysis in the School of Lacan* (New Haven: Yale University Press,
1980). Attempts to apply Lacan to the analysis of literary texts are Shoshana Felman, *Jacques Lacan and the Adventure of Insight: Psychoanalysis and Contemporary
Culture* (Cambridge: Harvard University Press, 1987); Jane Gallop, *Reading Lacan*
(Ithaca: Cornell University Press, 1985); Robert Con Davis, ed., *The Fictional Father: Lacanian Readings of the Text* (Amherst: University of Massachusetts Press,
1981); and James M. Mellard, *Using Lacan, Reading Fiction* (Urbana: University
of Illinois Press, 1991). Mark Bracher, in *Lacan, Discourse, and Social Change* (Ithaca: Cornell University Press, 1993), articulates a political critique based on Lacan.
Sherry Turkle's *Psychoanalytic Politics: Jacques Lacan and Freud's French Revolution,*
2d ed. (New York: Guilford, 1992), gives an account of Lacan's career.

7. The works of Jürgen Habermas constitute a substantial body of texts ranging
from theoretical works on philosophical issues, works in social criticism, and extended controversies with such theorists as Gadamer to interviews and essays on po-

representatives of the central polarities of the argument: Habermas functions as the representative of universalism, rationality, and orientation to agreement and to coordinated action; Lacan, as the representative of desire, the unconscious, the necessarily excessive and exigent nature of discourse. I am not at all interested in finding an impossible

---

litical issues. The most important titles include *Toward a Rational Society: Student Protest, Science, and Politics,* trans. J. J. Shapiro (Boston: Beacon, 1970); *Knowledge and Human Interests,* trans. J. J. Shapiro (Boston: Beacon, 1971); *Theory and Practice,* trans. J. Viertel (Boston: Beacon, 1973); *Legitimation Crisis,* trans. T. McCarthy (Boston: Beacon, 1975); and two works that are central to my interests in this book: *The Theory of Communicative Action,* 2 vols., trans. T. McCarthy (Boston: Beacon, 1983); and *The Philosophical Discourse of Modernity,* trans. Frederick Lawrence (Cambridge: MIT Press, 1987). Recent translations include *Moral Consciousness and Communicative Action,* trans. Christian Lenhardt and Shierry Weber Nicholsen (Cambridge: MIT Press, 1991); *Postmetaphysical Thinking: Philosophical Essays,* trans. William Mark Hohengarten (Cambridge: MIT Press, 1992); and *Justification and Application: Remarks on Discourse Ethics,* trans. C. Cronin (Cambridge: MIT Press, 1993). Habermas's very early work *The Structural Transformation of the Public Sphere* has recently been translated by T. Burger and F. Lawrence (Cambridge: MIT Press, 1989); this early work is analyzed and critiqued in a collection of essays edited by Craig Calhoun, *Habermas and the Public Sphere* (Cambridge: MIT Press, 1992). Interviews with Habermas are collected in Peter Dews's *Habermas: Autonomy and Solidarity: Interviews* (London: Verso, 1986). A recent festschrift for Habermas is *Philosophical Interventions in the Unfinished Project of Enlightenment,* ed. Axel Honneth, Thomas McCarthy, Claus Offe, and Albrecht Wellmer (Cambridge: MIT Press, 1992). The standard summary of Habermas's work is still Thomas McCarthy's *The Critical Theory of Jürgen Habermas* (Cambridge: MIT Press, 1978), although important additional treatments include Seyla Benhabib, *Critique, Norm, and Utopia: A Study of the Foundations of Critical Theory* (New York: Columbia University Press, 1986); Peter Dews, *Logics of Disintegration: Poststructuralist Thought and the Claims of Critical Theory* (London: Verso, 1987); Martin Jay, *Marxism and Totality: The Adventures of a Concept from Lukacs to Habermas* (Berkeley and Los Angeles: University of California Press, 1984); David Held, *Introduction to Critical Theory* (Berkeley and Los Angeles: University of California Press, 1980); and John Thompson and David Held, eds., *Habermas: Critical Debates* (Cambridge: MIT Press, 1982). More recent titles include Zygmunt Bauman, *Intimations of Postmodernity* (London and New York: Routledge, 1992); Robert C. Holub, *Jürgen Habermas: Critic in the Public Sphere* (London and New York: Routledge, 1991); Axel Honneth and Hans Joas, eds., *Communicative Action: Essays on Jürgen Habermas's "The Theory of Communicative Action"* (Cambridge: Polity Press, 1991); David Rasmussen, *Reading Habermas* (Cambridge, Mass: Blackwell, 1990); Stephen K. White, *The Recent Work of Jürgen Habermas: Reason, Justice and Modernity* (Cambridge: Cambridge University Press, 1988); and Thomas McCarthy *Ideals and Illusions: On Reconstruction and Deconstruction in Contemporary Critical Theory* (Cambridge: MIT Press, 1993). The collection by Thompson and Held includes a bibliography of translated work available to them; the complete bibliography is Rene Görtzen's *Jürgen Habermas: Eine Bib-*

harmony between such different perspectives, although there are some surprising convergences between them; rather, the divergences between the two theorists identify points of tension and difficulty in the discourses of modernity.

Using the three terms, at first in tandem, I will read several texts representing some of the central discourses of modernity: the discourses of science, of the state, and of the university as it organizes knowledge and forms students. My selection is not comprehensive, although I have relied on Habermas's distinctions among cognitive-instrumental, moral-practical, and aesthetic-practical rationalities for my choice of published texts,[8] and on my most intense experiences of boredom and anger in the classroom for the student and institutional texts in the two pedagogical chapters. I will begin by examining the first two terms, language and narration, and then read a group of scientific texts under them, extending my reading of "high science" with an examination of the pedagogy of technical writing. Returning to the development of rhetorical terms, I will discuss action and consider how the three terms together form a rhetoric. Using all three terms, I will examine the documents that emerged from the MOVE catastrophe as examples of public discourse and then analyze a catastrophe in the classroom. The book ends with a reading of Montaigne's *Essais,* a text that demonstrates some of the relations among forms of knowledge that shape the discourses of modernity, their rhetorical address to readers, and the forms of subjectivity they suggest.

In reflecting on language, action, and narration, I repeatedly encounter the limits of Habermas and Lacan. Such limits emerge as necessary implications of each theorist's initial, productive choice. A refutation of Habermas or Lacan would be even less interesting than a harmony between them: both theories are singular raids on the impossibly complex discourses of modernity. Habermas's reduction of language to illocution and perlocution and Lacan's elision of propositional claims both have their costs, but for a rhetorical analysis, their productive power is more salient.

Schriften und der Sekundarliteratur, 1952–81 (Frankfurt: Suhrkamp, 1982). Rasmussen's *Reading Habermas* includes an extensive bibliography by Rene Grotzen.

8. Jürgen Habermas, "A Reply to My Critics," in *Habermas: Critical Debates,* ed. John Thompson and David Held (Cambridge: MIT Press, 1982), 249, contains a compact explanation of these domains.

Language

Language Is Unstable.

Many of our most convincing stories about the wanderings of language have come from Lacan. One of his best is about Freud's reading of the dream of the burning child.[9] Freud's text is given toward the end of *The Interpretation of Dreams:* a father is sleeping near his child's corpse while an old man watches over the body.

> After a few hour's sleep, the father had a dream that his child was standing beside his bed, caught him by the arm and whispered to him reproachfully: *Father, don't you see I'm burning?* He woke up, noticed a bright glare of light from the next room, hurried into it and found that the old man had dropped off to sleep and that the wrappings and one of the arms of his beloved child's dead body had been burned by a lighted candle that had fallen on them.[10]

This "moving dream" is told to Freud by a woman patient who will later "redream" it; she herself heard it first in a lecture on dreams. Freud reads here a story about desire and loss; Lacan reads one about desire and language.

Like Freud, like us, Lacan is touched by this dream, which he sees "suspended around the most anguishing mystery";[11] he uses it to trace out the "passion of Freud" for truth, a passion that links this dream to another story of warnings, ghosts, fathers and sons, delays—*Hamlet.* The dream incites the analyst's desire for truth, but only as a relation to something absent. Two lectures later, Lacan returns to the dream of the burning child and concludes that it is "an act of homage to the missed reality—the reality that can no longer produce itself except by repeating itself endlessly, in some never attained awakening."[12] The desiring unconscious is essentially oriented toward absence and lack; the father misses (longs for, avoids) meeting his dead son.

In Lacan's second reading, the dream represents a wish, which is very

9. Seminar 11, "The Unconscious and Repetition," in *Four Fundamental Concepts of Psycho-analysis,* 17–66.

10. Sigmund Freud, *The Interpretation of Dreams,* trans. James Strachey (New York: Avon, 1965); reprint of *Standard Edition,* vols. 4 and 5 (London: Hogarth Press and Institute of Psychoanalysis, 1975), 548.

11. Lacan, "The Unconscious and Repetition," 34.

12. Lacan, "The Unconscious and Repetition," 58.

different from fulfilling it. Since the dream both represents and discusses desire, it is performative; it does what it refers to. At its center, simultaneously fulfilling it and rupturing it, language emerges: the child's cry, *"Father, don't you see I'm burning?"* Here, where the dream intersects with the lived, the actual burning child, desire prompts speech, becoming material both as a terrifying loss of the already lost child and as an impossible utterance, a specific set of words impossibly uttered. Lacan comments, "This sentence is itself a firebrand—of itself it brings fire where it falls—and one cannot see what is burning, for the flames blind us to the fact that the fire bears on . . . the real."[13] The child's cry represents language by doing what language does: revealing and hiding in the same instant, like Lacan's unconscious, a gap or fissure that is always in the act of closing. The light of its flame hides what it burns.

Language Permits a System of Exchanges.

A wandering system can move among subjects. The system of language links speaker and listener, reader and writer, regulating and disrupting the relations among them in acts of interpretation and subversion, in searches for a common language that are also exercises of power.

In Lacan's interpretation of the burning child, he gives us a story that can be repeated and exchanged, constituted in the act of telling and being passed on. The dream, already repeatedly transmitted from lecturer to patient to Freud, also moves to Lacan, and then to us. Lacan himself redreams it in the seminar, framing his second discussion of the dream with two homologous stories of sleeping and waking. In one story, Lacan himself is awakened from a dream by knocking;[14] in reflecting on the incommensurable gap between himself asleep and awake, he is struck by an image of consciousness as something that befalls the subject, something organized in response to a call. Later in the same lecture, commenting on the *fort/da* game, Lacan proclaims:

> I, too, have seen with my own eyes, opened by maternal divination, the child, traumatized by the fact that I was going away despite the appeal, precociously adumbrated in his voice, and henceforth more renewed for months at a time—long after,

13. Lacan, "The Unconscious and Repetition," 59.
14. Lacan, "The Unconscious and Repetition," 56.

having picked up this child—I have seen it let his head fall . . . and drop off to sleep, sleep alone being capable of giving him access to the living signifier that I had become since the date of the trauma.[15]

The dream passes from Lacan to the child who stands in place of his son; in this transmission, all of the signifiers from the original narrative reverse. It is no longer a matter of the death of the son but of the absence of the father, nor of the father awakening but of the child going to sleep. We do not hear, "Father, don't you see?" but "I, too, have seen with my own eyes the child" and, under erasure, the repeated, "Father, don't go." But the underlying structure of the narrative has not changed, a structure that supports both language and the unconscious, a structure of delay, absence, division of the subject, and error: in sum, of desire.

For Jürgen Habermas, such exchanges are understood quite differently—as collaborations in search of a common understanding, attempts by subjects to orient their actions by a collective construction of knowledge. If something is exchanged in language, if some relation among speakers and hearers, readers and writers, is effected, all participants must hold something in common. It has been Habermas's project to define that "something in common" as a formal practice of rationality and to consider its political and philosophical implications. Speakers raise claims oriented to distinct elements of their world-concepts: the truth of propositions, the normative rightness of speech acts, or the intentions of speakers.[16] In discourse, these claims are expanded, justified, and modified: "Reaching understanding functions as a mechanism for coordinating actions only through the participants in interaction coming to an agreement concerning the claimed *validity* of their utterances, that is, through intersubjectively recognizing the *validity claims* they reciprocally raise."[17] All communication (although not necessarily all speech) raises validity claims of truth, rightness, and sincerity—the claim to represent reality, to take up discourse in good faith, and to express what one thinks. Habermas does not define these claims as transcendent orientations of the subject; rather, he reinterprets them as issues that can only be discursively redeemed. Readers and writers exchange, not only the wandering figuration of desire, but the power of the text to disclose the world, to regulate social life, to reveal interiority.

15. Lacan, "The Unconscious and Repetition," 63.
16. Habermas, *Theory of Communicative Action*, 1:99.
17. Habermas, *Theory of Communicative Action*, 1:99.

Such claims are verified formally, in the procedures and relations of discourse: Have all the concerned speakers been heard? Are all propositions open to criticism? Such formal constraints operate only counterfactually: we can identify specific limits or blockages to the language's possibilities for exchange; we cannot guarantee that any speech situation is unconstrained, let alone ideal. Habermas's formal constraints are not guarantees of what has been exchanged—meanings, relations—but they operate powerfully and critically.

Such power is gained at the price of an analytic reduction—for Habermas, a particularly costly reduction of language to proposition and illocution. But Habermas's reduction also locates rationality within the exchanges of language; without embracing foundationalism, it permits a universal understanding of rationality and therefore sponsors an ethics not limited to maneuvers of choice. For Habermas—and for the rhetoric I am working out in this book—the commonality of language offers the hope of a common rationality but does not in any way determine its positive content.

Language Is Implicated in Error.

So much for hope. Since language operates among subjects, since it is irreducibly mobile, it is necessarily implicated in error. For Habermas, the "ideal communicative community," in which all participants have full and equal access to all means of communication, is necessarily counterfactual, only experienced as a specific failure within the necessarily inadequate, provisional relations of actual communicative communities.[18]

Lacan's understanding of error is more insistent. In his analysis of the dream of the burning child, for example, Lacan makes errors, distorting the dream, using it to refute Freud's central idea—that the dream is a fantasy fulfilling a wish[19]—all the while declaring his fidelity to Freud. Error subdues the text to the laws of desire: it represents the analyst as a desiring subject who approaches the text. Error establishes a textual gap

18. For a fuller discussion of this topic, see Karl-Otto Appel, "Normatively Grounding 'Critical Theory' through Recourse to the Lifeworld? A Transcendental-Pragmatic Attempt to Think with Habermas against Habermas," in *Philosophical Interventions in the Unfinished Project of Enlightenment,* ed. Axel Honneth and others (Cambridge: MIT Press, 1992), 125–70.

19. Freud, *The Interpretation of Dreams,* 548.

between sleep and waking, between representation and consciousness, between quotation and source, so that desire, the unconscious, and the text are adumbrated as absence and error. Lacan entangles proposition with illocution, forming a tie that can be more fruitfully described as an infection or contagion of error than as an intersubjective argument.

Nor would Lacan be scandalized by the implication of analytic truth with error. The Lacanian subject reads herself out of error by making one more mistake; by stepping outside the inexorable chain of signification that binds her to endless representations—and deferrals—of the desired object. Fidelity to the text of the lived, to the intention of the writer, would merely implicate the reader within a narrative chain, unable to see its repetition as repetition, its coherence as a fragile structure of displacements, its hidden secret as a casually folded piece of paper. Once this series of connections has been broken, it is not crucial that the letter—any letter—be read: the referent of the signifying chain, like the analysand's recovered personal history, is nothing special, simply an instance of the "common lot."[20] The movement outside the signifying chain into the action of naming desire—rather than denying or displacing it—creates something new, generating a truth that might pay its debt to the text that prompted it by initiating another narrative chain, one that privileges acts of naming and desiring. Truth in reading is not, for Lacan, quite the same as propositional content: that "discourse of exactitude" is at best a useful prop, at worst simply a lure or pacifier. Truth is an act of the subject, a willingness to call something new from the displaced story by naming it. Truth is what stands in the place of love as the analyst's desire: it incites the production of the chain of signifiers reaching toward deferred disclosure and also prompts the repeated disruption of that chain by the desiring analytic reader.

For a rhetoric of intersubjectivity, then, error is not an embarrassment. Error redirects the reader's attention from the smooth unrolling of the text to its surface: whatever had been forgotten in an automatic act of reading is suddenly foregrounded, presenting itself as a demand, interrogating the reader, reorienting him from contemplation to the messy, almost involuntary, work of correction. (Who can keep from correcting typographical errors in library books?) Error reminds us that the text is a work undertaken by human beings; it returns the text to the necessarily limited time of its inscription. The reader, too, accedes to error, can only read in error. Unless the reader comes to the text as

20. Lacan, *Écrits*, 41.

desiring, nothing at all will happen. But the reader implicated in his own desire is at a bias to the text's own embodiment of (possibly) other desired others.

A refusal to be dismayed by error is not simply a shameless concession. It is also a recognition that, just as the text is only understood because its validity claims are open to a common investigation, the text's importance depends on being read by desiring subjects. Both in its most intense rationality and its most vagrant openness to misreading, the text as a location for reading and writing speaks of language as a common ground among readers and writers.

Language Is (Also) Material.

That commonality, for Lacan, can be located in precisely the materiality of language, in its syllables, words, and utterances, the signs of its dense contingency. We are reminded of Kristeva's reference to "the connections between the (glottal and anal) sphincters in (rhythmic and intonational) vocal modulations."[21] The material signifier incites a rhetoric of intersubjectivity to analyze its embodiment in particular forms, sounds, inscriptions, and systems of distribution, including especially the material practices that support the discourses of science and public policy.

In an early seminar, Lacan undertook a reading of the *Meno* as a way of reflecting on the nature of an *episteme* (here, a science, a reliable body of knowledge).[22] Much later in the year, Lacan returned to the dialogue, taking up the relation between representation, labor, and the real. The slave who "remembers" geometry sees no diamonds, no squares, but lines that Socrates has traced, eliding his own work in producing them as representations of the real, as demonstrative symbols: "It took a world of surveyors, of practical procedures, preceding the people who discourse so knowledgeably in the agora of Athens, in order that the slave no longer be what he could have been, living on the banks of a great river, in a wild state of nature, in a space of waves and sweeps on sand, on a perpetually shifting, pseudopial beach."[23] If at first the diagram traced in sand represented for Lacan an intervention by the master, inaugurating a knowledge implicit in the exigencies of lived ex-

21. Julia Kristeva, *The Revolution in Poetic Language* (New York: Columbia University Press, 1984), 29.
22. Lacan, *Seminar II*, 13–18 and 256.
23. Lacan, *Seminar II*, 256.

perience, it is now seen as a material practice, revealed as an object of labor, located in history, dependent on a range of discursive and productive practices. Both the aristocratic witnesses at the scene of instruction and its docile object, the slave who finds in Socrates' diagram a direct imprint of the real, forget themselves into the material inscription.

We can understand the materiality of language as an aspect of the erotics of the text or as a metonymy for the individual's accession to language. Or we can undertake a commonsense reading of the materiality of the signifier: since propositions do not beam from one mind to another in projected transparency, communication is carried in channels and organized in code.[24] The communication of meaning makes use of a preexistent linguistic code, modulates that code to spoken and written channels, and directs a message through institutional settings: it is an elaborated social practice.

But we can also go further. The materiality of language, like the persuasive force of rhetoric, is a scandal to certain kinds of reflection (a scandal: a place where it is easy to fall, a trap, a sign of stratagem and artifice). This scandal proceeds from the association between the material signifier and things, the vulgar matter of materialism, and therefore also the body. And, since the body is not an unmediated natural object, the system of signifiers articulated in language is necessarily connected to the articulation of signifiers by and on a body which structures language. "Discrete quantities of energy move through the body of the subject who is not yet constituted as such and, in the course of his development, they are arranged according to the various constraints imposed on this body—always already involved in a semiotic process—by family and social structures."[25] This articulation can be understood intersubjectively. It is worked out in the relation between parents and infants, in the labor of infancy, in the constant dialogue of call and response, need and care; language is material to each of us because we learned it in the material practices that inducted us into its structures.

We could see Jürgen Habermas's analytic reduction of language to proposition and illocution as an attempt—ultimately a failed attempt—to evade the implications of the materiality of language. Two elements of language interest Habermas: proposition and illocutionary force, the making of a claim and the opening of that claim to criticism and valida-

24. Roman Jakobson, "Closing Statement: Linguistics and Poetics," in *Style in Language,* ed. Thomas Sebeok (Cambridge: MIT Press, 1960), 350–77.
25. Kristeva, *Revolution in Poetic Language,* 25.

tion.[26] Such a dual analysis displaces the analytic singularity of classical philosophy, concerned with questions of truth and validity, and introduces the issue of intersubjective rightness to philosophical reflection.

Literary scholars, for whom the weaknesses of Habermas's theory are patent, need to understand what he also gains. An analysis of language that focuses on proposition and illocution need not be simpleminded or insensitive to the social relations of discourse. Issues of social context or of the relations among speakers remain open, since the claim of a proposition is not to be read off its face, and speech acts can encode propositions in quite diverse ways, including assertion, implication, and negation. The precise speech act chosen among propositionally synonymous forms can express, through its illocutionary force, both the normative relation between speaker and hearer that the utterance bids to establish and a range of other contiguous normed relationships. Further, such an analysis does not concede the propositional content of an utterance to positivism or to narrow disciplinary discussions. Propositional content is after all neither a trivial aspect of any of the discourses of modernity nor an issue that contemporary literary theory handles easily.[27] Proposi-

26. A cursory treatment of self-expression can also be found in *Theory of Communicative Action*, 2:66–67.

27. My argument here is directed against the content-neutral analytic mode of the early Foucault, especially in *The Order of Things: An Archeology of the Human Sciences* (New York: Random House, 1970). Although such a stance of neutrality can be a useful analytic device, relieving the reader of the task of evaluating claims in exotic or defunct disciplines, the brackets of neutrality also block a discourse's claim to efficacy, which is not a trivial aspect of its content. Specifically, such neutrality renders fictional discourse analytically identical to nonfictional discourse—a reduction which, among other things, makes it impossible to deconstruct or think through the claim to representation which is intrinsic to expository writing.

For similar reasons, I would hold that the analytic neutrality of sociologists of science, as in Bruno Latour and Steven Woolgar's *Laboratory Life: The Social Construction of Scientific Facts,* Sage Library of Social Research 80 (Beverly Hills: Sage, 1979), or G. Nigel Gilbert and Michael Mulkay's *Opening Pandora's Box: A Sociological Analysis of Scientists' Discourse* (Cambridge: Cambridge University Press, 1984), can only be useful as a temporary methodological reduction. To hold that neutrality toward the representational truth of content is a permanent condition for the analysis of scientific prose blocks the possibility of any reflexive, dialectic reading of the documents of science. We can only maintain content neutrality when we are surveying the works of a discipline, like molecular biophysics, in which we have no stake. Such a difference, I would hold, is not a failure of objectivity but simply part of our situation as readers who have direct interests in a discipline rather than as external analysts. This distinction would mark nothing but an interesting discontinuity in reading practices were it not for its implications for self-reflection in the analysis of scientific and expository prose. Such self-reflection, if it is performed

tional content forms a limit, a necessary limit, to expository discourse and to the rhetorical and literary criticism that responds to it.

If propositional content is, as Foucault has demonstrated, an instance of the text's claim to represent, and of its location within, the network of power, it is simultaneously an invitation to test the text. A propositional speech act is happily taken up by criticism and negation: such responses can be neither solicited nor forbidden with any assurance. Although nothing guarantees the truth of any referential discourse, and nothing ever will, all propositions can be tested, and contested. And so intersubjective relations emerge in the sphere of illocution: referential texts, by virtue of their openness to refutation, become collaborative, not because of the disposition of either reader or writer, but because of the constituting structure of the text. No writer is sufficiently authoritarian, no reader sufficiently passive, to bar the possibility of critique. The pope forbids birth control in an infallible text, and my neighbor invites him to "take a walk in the Vatican gardens—no disrespect to His Holiness intended."

There are many ways to produce the social effect of conviction: repression, manipulation of the sources of information, the spread of disinformation. None of them transforms subjectivity with the same effect as reason, the claims of which Habermas describes as "gentle but obstinate . . . never silenced although seldom redeemed."[28] In any discourse more complicated than pure totalitarian fiat, we can discern an intersubjective and textual (i.e., interpretable) claim to represent the world. This claim is located in the constant openness of each and any validity claim to whatever challenge the hearer deems appropriate. Such intersubjectivity is formal and procedural rather than a matter of

---

as it is likely to be, by rhetoricians and literary critics, will be a reading internal to the discipline. It will not, therefore, be content neutral; if content neutrality is a precondition of the analysis of expository prose, such analysis can never reflect on its own conditions of production and presupposition. It will never become fully mature.

The paradigmatic content-neutral study in the history of science is of course T. S. Kuhn's, *The Structure of Scientific Revolutions* (Chicago: University of Chicago Press, 1962). Another historically important study, Ludwig Fleck's *Genesis and Development of a Scientific Fact,* ed. T. Trenn and R. Merton, trans. F. Bradley and T. Trenn (Chicago: University of Chicago Press, 1979), reconstructs the logic of early serological experiments.

28. Jürgen Habermas, "Historical Materialism and the Development of Normative Structures," in *Communication and the Evolution of Society* (Boston: Beacon, 1979), 97.

sentiment and belief. Precisely because it is without positive content, precisely because it can coexist with the worst of intentions, the intersubjective tie implicit in referential discourse can be attended to theoretically, and even thematized politically.

Habermas's reduction of language to proposition and illocution, then, opens to reflection and critique the concrete processes of representation, and it allows us to differentiate among them. A rhetorical analysis can recognize multiple claims, complex relations between them, and contradictory modes of testing and validation.

But Habermas's reduction of language to proposition and illocution also obscures the materiality of the signifier, the multiplicity of interpretations, and the distinct practices of art and literature. These issues connect the formal analysis of proposition and illocution to the specific problems of the texts of modernity.

Language Is Indeterminate.

It is not easy or noncontroversial to determine the propositional content of a text. The propositional content of a text is not exhausted by its theme, the subject of discourse available on its face. From the infinity of possible propositions, we are not necessarily able to eliminate any by knowing that an utterance includes at least one. We know that the text asserts; we cannot know reliably what it asserts.

It is also very difficult to project a reliable way of classifying statements as claims of a certain kind, oriented to either natural, social, or subjective life.[29] We might assume that we could classify claims by looking at context: we seldom find it hard, in everyday life, to determine what kind of conversation is in train. People talk about the weather as a way of making conversation or as a way of deciding on plans without danger of aporia. But the set of cues that determines context in conversations frames proposition and intersubjectivity as mutually determinant. The propositional content of an utterance, the speaker's intention, and the uptake of proposition in conversation are seen as synonymous. But that synonymy was not necessarily imprinted in the initial speech act: at the time of utterance, more than one interpretive frame was intersubjec-

---

29. For a similar argument, see Richard Shweder, "Post-Nietzschian Anthropology: The Idea of Multiple Objective Worlds," in *New Essays on Human Development,* ed. Michael Krausz (Notre Dame: Notre Dame University Press, 1991).

tively available. Uptake is not a reliable index of intention; nor does intention necessarily determine propositional content.

Indeed, such a multiplicity of interpretive frames is already implied by Habermas's theory of the proposition as an assertion open to critique. If all constatives are open to discourse and critique, then so are interpretive statements, assertions about the meanings of utterances. Interpretations are subject to critique, correction, and possible replacement. If multiple interpretive frames and multiple interpretations were not possible, then, interpretive discourse would be exempted from critique, guaranteed.

This issue is not merely formal. Interpretive frames, the determination of propositional content, and their relations become, in Habermas's theory of the public sphere, deeply political. In the public sphere, Habermas holds, participants in discourse bracket status differences and deliberate about their common good as if they were social equals.[30] Such bracketings and restrictions are operational elaborations of the assumption that propositional content can be both determined and controlled. And as ways of understanding public discourse in modern conditions of differentiation, of multiple competing publics, they fail to take into account the propositional force of material practices of speaking and hearing. Nancy Fraser has worked out a convincing criticism of this position, which assumes the possibility of participation without the expression of one's own cultural identity, in an impossible public sphere with no culture of its own. But public spaces are not equally comfortable to all participants and not equally open to all possible forms of participation.[31]

Literature Is a Specific Practice of Reading and Writing, Not a Category of Texts.

For contemporary literary theory, pressing and salient issues concerning style, idiom, and the institutions of culture focus on the specificity of

30. Habermas, *Structural Transformation of the Public Sphere,* and *Theory of Communicative Action,* vol. 2.

31. Nancy Fraser, "Rethinking the Public Sphere," in *Habermas and the Public Sphere,* ed. Craig Calhoun (Cambridge: MIT Press, 1992), 126. See also Fraser's "What's Critical about Critical Theory? The Case of Habermas and Gender," in her *Unruly Practices: Power, Discourse, and Gender in Contemporary Social Theory* (Minneapolis: University of Minnesota Press and Polity Press, 1989).

literary discourse. Here, especially, Habermas's focus on proposition and illocution reduces our understanding of the specific signifying powers of language.

Habermas asserts that literature and literary criticism have a special status. In the chapter "On Levelling the Genre Distinction between Philosophy and Literature" in *The Philosophical Discourse of Modernity,* Habermas approaches the problem of the aesthetic, arguing for the special status of literary criticism and criticizing the "despecializing" of literary criticism. Habermas asserts that literary criticism should be limited to the explication of patently literary texts, defined by their fictional force. The distinction between fictional and nonfictional texts is seen as a precondition for stable linguistic community rather than an "arbitrary, logocentric" act.[32]

Habermas has here extended the theory of differentiation, a central category in his thought since *Knowledge and Human Interests,* to the specific practices of an academic discipline, literary criticism. For Habermas, differentiation distinguishes modernity from traditional societies. Discursive formations develop autonomous and self-regulated practices of reason, with distinct modes of proof and relations among participants. By *The Theory of Communicative Action,* Habermas had evolved a complex typology of communicative actions in their orientation to the transmission of cultural knowledge, the coordination of actions, and the formation of personal identity.[33] He had also placed these forms of communicative rationality within the context of a structurally differentiated society: institutions are uncoupled from lifeworlds; interpersonal relations are established contingently rather than through traditional structures; traditions themselves are subjected to critique and innovation. As the possible domains for inquiry expand, social relations become more reflexive.[34] According to the theory of differentiation, a communicative act can make claims in three dimensions: truth, rightness, and sincerity. An utterance can claim to represent the world as it is, to represent the relations between speaker and hearer, or to represent the intention of the speaker. Validity claims are open to separate justification and separate styles of agreement, taking up, and elaboration in institutionally distinct practices of rationality. Such elaborated texts may be opaque to

32. Habermas, *Philosophical Discourse,* 197.
33. Habermas, *Theory of Communicative Action,* 2:144.
34. Habermas, *Theory of Communicative Action,* 2:146.

public audiences, since they follow modes of argument and proof situated in professions and disciplines and are narrowly oriented to specific
dimensions of the communicative act. For Habermas, within this typology scientific discourse represents nature, whereas literary discourse
is organized by the project of forming values.[35]

But it is inconsistent with the admission of multiple and differentiated
truth claims to rule out a priori the poetic force of scientific or philosophical texts, a force that could be recovered through specific interpretive procedures. Given the multiple determinations of academic disciplines, including ideology and practical exigency, it seems prudent to
uncouple the fact of a study becoming a disciplinary formation from
its theoretical status as a practice of knowledge. Discourses can be characterized by their *predominant* truth claims, but they need not be
understood as making *singular* claims. Reading a scientific document
poetically is unusual, but if the theory of differentiation is applied consistently, such a reading would not be mistaken. Habermas's understanding of the special status of literature and literary criticism, then, is
inconsistent with his broader theory of differentiation. Although communicative action does distinguish fictional utterances from nonfictional utterances, such distinctions are always highly contextual, and
choice of interpretive frame is subject to reflexive critique, just as is the
intention of the speaker.

In fact, disputes over choice of interpretive framework are common,
bitter, and socially significant: legal disputes about whether someone
can be prosecuted as a criminal for symbolic speech; educational disputes about whether evolution is a scientific fact or a "theory" among
many others; the dispute about pornography within feminism. The reflexivity of language emerges, not only as a salient feature of poetic
discourse, but also as an ungovernable waywardness in propositional
discursive forms. Habermas has insisted correctly that there is no meta-
language, no discursive register standing over intersubjectivity that
guarantees the truth of a discourse. It follows that there is also no decision rule for interpretive frames and that problems of interpretive
method can always emerge. Literary criticism cannot be safely confined
to fictional texts, any more than scientific texts can be declared innocent
of aesthetic designs.

Such questions bear directly on our understanding of the discourses

---

35. Habermas, *Theory of Communicative Action,* 1:334.

of modernity, particularly those representing nature and social life. In traditional literary criticism, scientific or policy texts were consigned to the dubious category of "exposition." (Such a segregation reflects by reversal the mass culture's consignment of aesthetic texts to the category of "high art.") "Exposition" designates texts that literary critics would not ordinarily study, texts thereby given over to their propositional content; just as literary criticism renounces any claim to deciding issues of truth for expository writing, expository texts are denied the self-reflexive powers of art. Habermas's theory of literature reflects and ratifies these limits rather than calling them into question, although we can discern different positions at different points in Habermas's work. In *Theory of Communicative Action,* works of literature are the exemplary reflections of value standards and are categorized by Habermas as dramaturgical action, which can "embody a knowledge of the agent's own subjectivity. . . . Expressive knowledge can be explicated in terms of those values that underlie need interpretations, the interpretations of desires and emotional attitudes. Value standards are dependent in turn on innovations in the domain of evaluative expressions. These are reflected in an exemplary manner in works of art."[36] Here, the subjective (desires and emotions) is disjoined from the rational (underlying values); values are propositions, subjects move from deception to truth, and cultures make innovations in value. Would that all this were true.

Art is conflated, on the one hand, with all possible means of self-expression and, on the other, with literary criticism and interpretation. Dramaturgical action includes, and must include, such expressions of intersubjectivity as dreams, parapraxes, confessions, sonnet sequences, *Gone with the Wind,* and Derrida's *Of Grammatology.* But agency is problematic in all these texts: because the author is unconscious; because she is situated in a system of legal constraints; because she operates within a genre, lies, or plagiarizes; or because the author is a corporation or does not believe in agency. Insofar as we appreciate these forms aesthetically, their quality as innovations in the sphere of values, or as acts of self-expression, is precisely not at issue.

In the later *Philosophical Discourse of Modernity,* Habermas works at the limits of this problem. While continuing to categorize aesthetic texts as value assertions, he also speaks of them as "pure demonstration of the world-disclosing force of innovative linguistic expressions,"[37] a formu-

---

36. Habermas, *Theory of Communicative Action.*
37. Habermas, *Philosophical Discourse,* 205.

lation which at least does not require literary texts to teach morality. What the literary text discloses is not necessarily propositional but rather a demonstration of qualities and potentials of language. And it is precisely those qualities of language Habermas finds most problematic that we are most likely to encounter in contemporary literary texts: indeterminacy, exploitation of the material signifier, problematization of interpretation, play with the distinction between high and mass art, between art and other signifying practices. Those experiences of language are likely to infect or contaminate literary criticism, so that the scholar is unlikely to fulfill the task of "unleashing" the experiential content of a text by bringing it into "normal language."[38] Which literary critics can Habermas have been reading?

If we cannot use Habermas as a theorist of the indeterminacy of language, or of the particular reflexivity of literary reading practices, we can find in Lacan's narrative of the formation of the subject some guidance on these issues.

The Subject Is Formed in Language.

For Lacan, the theory of the formation of the subject in language is not a theory of infant development but a way of conceiving how the self is structured. Indeed, Lacan's most famous aphorism, "the unconscious is structured like a language," is, in one of its uses, situated in a narrative of self-formation: "The unconscious is constituted by the effects of speech on the subject, it is the dimension in which the subject is determined in the development of the effects of speech, consequently the unconscious is structured like a language."[39] It is in speech that desire is constituted; it is also by language that desire is balked, or contradicted, most particularly by Law, the language associated with the father. Language, as a relation between signified and signifier, realized in the acts of speech imputed to others, embodied or imagined, moves the subject through years of comic and tragic enactments of deferral and plentitude, the "common lot" of vicissitudes, a narrative that Lacan

38. Habermas, *Philosophical Discourse,* 205.
39. This use is to be found in *Four Fundamental Concepts,* 149. But see also *Encore,* 20, where the aphorism introduces a typology of discursive forms discussed in my section on reading.

never falsified with the title "maturation."[40] The relation between truth and the subject is rendered more complex by Lacan's relentless location of truth among relations of speaking subjects: he places the "register of truth" "entirely elsewhere [outside the domain of reference], strictly speaking at the very foundation of intersubjectivity."[41]

In that register of truth, we exact a tribute from the signified and deliver it to language, with its multiplicity and contradictions: the possibility that speech "constitutes truth."[42] No magical subject, no happy story of personal development, guarantees this possibility. The axis of reference, for Lacan, is moved from the relation between subject and referent to the relations among subjects: the truth of language is not to be sought in its representation of a world but in its power to produce the ground onto which representations will be summoned.

Lacan repeats many of his crucial arguments, returning to major themes and to textual details. And he tells the story of the formation of the subject in language twice. In his early work, Lacan posits a subject organized through a signifying process analogous to the signifying structures of language. The infant encounters language as a series of incitements for individual capabilities and weaknesses, encountering it as an external, even alien, system. Lacan later writes a second story of the individual's formation in language: the story of the subject's demand, its assignment to the Other, and the formation of an alienated ego from a discourse imputed to the Other. This baroque story unfolds the scandal of gender, of the division of speaking beings into sexes depending on the positions they take up in relation to signification, the Other, and the dilemmas of castration.[43] Such a doubled and redoubled narrative scheme—a story of individual growth, a story of induction into the scheme of desire which also determines gender—invites us to speculate on the gaps and missed encounters in Lacan's narrative. A

40. Lacan understood this story and its possibilities in different ways at different points in his own development; early on, he held that a "full speech," expressive of desire and freed from the illusions of the imaginary ego, was a realizable goal for analysis. See, for example, "Function and Field of Speech and Language," in *Écrits*, 46. Later, Lacanian analysts will speak of "the little bit of consistency and truth that is his" as the most that the subject can hope to piece together (Schneiderman, *Returning to Freud*, 157).

41. Lacan, "Seminar on 'The Purloined Letter,'" 35.

42. Lacan, *Écrits*, 43.

43. Lacan, "Love Letter," in *Feminine Sexuality*, 149–51.

doubled narrative frame invites choice, if only by requiring us to normalize the existence of two stories within a narrative of Lacan's own theoretical development.

The first of the Lacanian stories of the formation of the subject, the story of accession to language, has been ably summarized by Ellie Ragland-Sullivan, in *Jacques Lacan and the Philosophy of Psychoanalysis*.[44] The infant, born into the frustration of biological prematurity, lives a reality in which the body is organized as a set of localized signifiers, distinguished from each other like letters in an alphabet, so that the body is the initial site of symbol formation. These part objects fuse at the mirror stage, when the infant triumphantly recognizes her whole body. The self is now separate from the part objects previously available to desire: breast, excrement, the imagined phallus, urinary flow, phoneme, gaze, and voice, objects which are now introjected as unconscious representations. The baby's identification with the mother prefigures the formation of one aspect of the self, the *je*, the deferred and identificatory speaking subject. Simultaneously, the *moi* forms, in a necessarily narcissistic and paranoid process. The *moi* imputes its discourse to an Other represented by a series of partial and imperfect others, subjects of identification and projection, in the domain of the real. Lacan uses *Other* to refer to a constructed location of significance outside the subject; *other* to refer to the individuals who may be assigned that role.

At about eighteen months, the unconscious subject, identified with the mother, divides from the conscious subject alienated into language. From this division the superego emerges; the dilemma of castration is posed. The subject, formed by language as an arbitrary structure, necessarily suffers absence and separation from meaning. The subject comes to being through a series of illusory identifications and divisions, or "scissions," effected by events associated with the accession to language. Lacan's terministic screen here is linguistic. He speaks of the initial constitution of the body in "letters" and of the mediation of the self through language as a series of imputed "demands." And the final scission of the self, at the Oedipal moment, is effected, not by the father, but "in the name of the Father." Language, then, is both the incitement for the formation of the self and a repository of metaphors for that process.

44. See chap. 1, "What Is 'I'? Lacan's Theory of the Human Subject," 1–67.

Lacan's second, more complicated story of the accession to language and the formation of the self is less rich in episode. It is told diagrammatically, in a sketch Lacan refers to as schema L. Schema L is narrative in both its structure and its agency; it puts into play for the subject a question, "What am I there?" which is itself an incitement to narrative. Like the "register of truth," it is a foundation which is both structure and event. Schema L appears in its simplest form thus:[45]

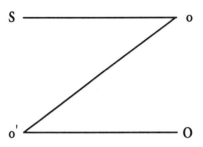

The scheme shows the subject (S) supported by the imaginary Other (O), whose imputed discourse arrives at the subject only through the mediation of identificatory objects o and o'. The ego is constituted by relations among those objects. It is this imputed discourse, passing from O to S, that constitutes a subject, who is necessarily split and arrayed, as we see in schema L, at the four corners of the field. The subject is formed in relations of language, having no unmediated access to objects, least of all to that Object whose discourse constitutes us. We are brought to being in a discourse that is always in error: "Human language constitutes a communication in which the emitter receives from the receiver his own message in an inverted form."[46] And it is a discourse that is implicated in the material and bodily: "a subtle body, but body it is."[47] Here, the propositional content of an utterance is available, to be sure—but only in inverted form, subject to negation and denial. Discourse is seen as an intersubjective play in which proposition is contingent but figure is obligatory, in the form of metaphor, metonymy, and their unconscious analogues, condensation and displacement. Proposition supports the subject, its identifications, and the

45. Lacan, *Écrits*, 193.
46. Lacan, *Écrits*, 329.
47. Lacan, *Écrits*, 87.

project of delay and repetition: the associations and resonances of its phonemes are as significant for the subject as its truth content.[48]

The narrative of schema L duplicates itself, investing with analogical significance the subject's choices of imaginary objects, dispersing the subject temporally into imagined and allegorical presents and futures: "The subject enters the game as the dummy [*mort*], but it is as a living being that he plays it; it is in his life that he must take up the suit [*couleur*] that he may bid. He will do so by means of a set of imaginary figures, selected from among the innumerable forms of animic relations, the choice of which involves a certain arbitrariness."[49] There is no end to the story of division. The subject does not enter analysis and escape into a utopian tale of integration and authenticity. Rather, psychoanalysis provides the subject with a new entrance into her story, a language that constitutes her as a player with a chance to win or lose, contesting on the constrained ground of the quadratic structure the outcome of her story and her fortunes within it.

In the narrative of schema L, no relationship of signification can be studied in isolation from the others. The subject chooses a "set of imaginary figures" from which to form representations, necessarily erroneous, of her engagements with various manifestations of the Other. Language, in this story, is the framework that permits and limits such signifying choices, reducing the range of available relations to a discrete terrain on which the subject passes, through division and error, from death to life.

We face similar signifying choices as we confront the alternate stories that Lacan has provided us. Do we understand the subject of language as the divided hero, struggling into language, or as the perplexed and comic player in a card game? In neither story is language guaranteed by anything outside itself; in neither does the subject know himself. If knowledge is a contagious division, we can read in Lacan's doubled representation of the genesis of the subject an image of how that contagion can be complicated and infected by choice. We can see the subject either as determined by personal history and intersubjectivity or as free to bid,

48. Nicholas Abraham and Maria Torok, *The Wolf Man's Magic Word: A Cryptonomy* (Minneapolis: University of Minnesota Press, 1986); but see also Lila Kalinich, "Some Reflections on the Wolf-Man," in *Lacan and the Subject of Language,* ed. Ellie Ragland-Sullivan and M. Bracher (New York: Routledge, 1991).
49. Lacan, *Écrits,* 196.

to pass from death to life. The rooted subject, the subject coming to language, is divided; his history, one of triumph enclosed by loss, is inaccessible to him. And the subject arrayed on the quadrature of desire is equally divided: he can know the fact of division, can take it into account without entertaining a hope of recovery. Each scheme reveals; each elides. In moving between these two accounts, we encounter ourselves as readers. The accession to language is not simply an event in our past; as we struggle with the Lacanian text, we recover a sense of its difficulty, and of the singular status of reading.

Reading Displays the Work of Language in Time.

For Lacan, many of these possibilities culminate in the theme of reading, itself organized as a story. The ideal Lacanian reading practice is understood by analogy with psychoanalysis as an act of interpretation concerned with metaphors. Regularly and insistently, beginning with the early seminar on the "Purloined Letter," Lacan compared the work of reading to the work of the analyst. The sagacious reader, like the astute analyst, listens to the text unfold and hears within it the resonances of unconscious discourse. Reading calls out for the adequate listener, who does not approach the text at its own valuation or accept its sense of what is important. The relations posited by reading, necessarily intersubjective, are not limited to the communicative intent with which one social subject proffers a text to another. They also include unconscious identificatory relations, unspoken acts of aggression, movements of paranoia, and the creation of supports for fantasy and specular identification. We can even include in this list the possibility of decoding, deciphering, and rendering intelligible some portion of the relations between reader and writer, not through introspection, but through a detached, unacquisitive attention to the surface of the signifier.

Such a reading generates interpretation and performance: Lacan delighted in literal inscription of schemata, in verbal performances that turn on inscription: "You can see that in this case we have to use writing, which even gives *jamais j'amais.*" [50] His habitual punning can be seen as a debt paid to the materiality of the signifier, a way of smuggling morphemic distinctions into spoken discourse. Lacan's reading practice

50. Lacan, "Love Letter," in *Feminine Sexuality,* 155.

anticipates the second term in this rhetoric of modernity—narrative. For Lacan, to read is to translate proposition into episode. Narrative, the insistence of the signifying chain, implies the repetition of the homologously arranged signifiers, responding to such vicissitudes as repression, denial, and foreclosure. Narrative also implies the displacement of symbolic meaning into a series of signifiers whose fulfillment, whose meaning and stability, is always anticipatory. Reading demonstrates exactly such an insistence: the events of the story can be seen as repetitions and rearrangements of similar materials, displacing the reading subject. If, in the process of reading, the narrative cohesion of the story is disturbed—and what theorist has engendered more distrust of narrative closure than Lacan?—that disruption itself becomes a narrative event, analogous to disrupted analytic speech: "That the subject should come to recognize and to name his desire, that is the efficacious action of analysis. But it isn't a question of recognizing something which would be entirely given, ready to be coapted. In naming it, the subject creates, brings forth, a new presence in the world."[51] The fable, says Lacan in opening the seminar on "The Purloined Letter," demonstrates how the subject organizes the travels of the signifier, but if we attend to that route, we may well lose the thread of the fable's coherence.[52] Reading, then, is a practice generative of truth when it disrupts the machine of repetition that is the text's coherence. What Lacan suggests is neither a hermeneutic of belief nor a hermeneutic of suspicion. It is a hermeneutic of subversion, in which fidelity to the text, or to the intention of the writer, implicates the reader in a deceptively coherent narrative chain.

For Lacan, as for Habermas, reading practices are differentiated. In his eighth seminar, Lacan constructed a typology of the discursive forms, distinguishing four forms of discourse according to their relation to the signifier, the signifying chain, the divided subject, and the object of desire. In identifying the discourses of the master, of the university, of the hysteric, and of the analyst,[53] Lacan's interest was not to categorize discourses by genre but to defend his own practice, to define the field the investigation of language in its relation to the unconscious. Language opens into the relations of intersubjectivity, relations characterized by

51. Lacan, *Écrits,* 228–29.

52. Lacan, "Seminar on 'The Purloined Letter,' " 27.

53. Lacan, *Encore,* 21; Steven Melville, "Psychoanalysis and the Place of Jouissance," in *The Trial(s) of Psychoanalysis,* ed. Françoise Meltzer (Chicago: University of Chicago Press, 1987).

elision, forgetting, and illusion: *"Qu'on dise rest oublié derrière ce qui se dit dans ce qui s'entend"* (What one might say remains forgotten behind what is spoken in the one who listens).[54]

Lacan's typology draws our attention to structures of speaking and listening, of delayed and forgotten speech, of the material signifier. But all these discourses, the subject of knowledge is available only in the form of fantasy. In all of them, one of the key terms—object of desire, signifying claim, signifier, or knowledge—is inaccessible. Specifically, language can be elided and rendered transparent, as in the discourse of the university, articulated as symptom, as in hysteria, or subtended to the known subject, as in the discourse of the analyst. Language becomes an object of knowledge only in the discourse of the master, which excludes fantasy.

Lacan insists on the discontinuity between language and the object of knowledge, on the saturation of all discursive formations with desire. Discursive forms contradict and combat one another; they change into each other, entail and assume one another. *"Je ne dis pas autre chose en disant que l'amour, c'est le signe qu'on change de discours"* (I meant nothing else in saying that love was a sign that one was changing discourses).[55] Further, no discursive formation has a privileged relation to the real or to truth: even though Lacan scorned academic hierarchy, he credits the discourse of the university with the production of a form of knowledge.

The texts that strayed into the path of Lacan's attention—dreams, translations of Freud, Poe's story, case studies, symbolist poems—all received the same dislocated and subversive reading. All become, sooner or later, objects of interpretive violence. As with the multiple redreamings and misreadings of the dream of the burning child or with the repeated analysis of the *Meno,* Lacan's interpretations, changes of evaluative frame, and redirections refuse to stabilize the intersubjective relations between reader and writer: those relations vary, bringing different aspects of the text to light. The weapon of such heroic misreading cuts across distinctions of genre to generate multiple, novel category systems. It is bad enough that, in Lacan's typology of the real, the imaginary, and the symbolic, virtually all referential discourse would occupy the register of the imaginary. Worse, Lacan's reading practice refuses to

54. Lacan, *Encore,* 20.
55. Lacan, *Encore,* 21.

admit the primacy of the initiating text, instead relocating writer and reader in shifting discursive frames.

This strength of Lacan's reading practice also establishes its rhetorical limit. Psychoanalysis implies a radical bracketing of the truth claims enacted by the analysand, as the analyst practices instead a form of listening in which all the analysand's discourse is so significant that its truth is irrelevant. The analysand demands that the referential content of his or her discourse be recognized; this demand is taken by the analyst as an illocutionary act, an episode in a story of desire and substitution, just as Dora's objections represented to Freud the plausible and embarrassing thought, the "sound and incontestable train of argument," that is used "for purposes of cloaking others which are anxious to escape from criticism and from consciousness." [56]

Lacan acknowledges the corollary of Freud's framing move: if the correctness of the analysand's argument is not the point, then neither is its error. Both are equally irrelevant to the processes of analytic discourse. Although a traditional goal of psychoanalysis is the removal of anamnesis, the restored memory "reconstructs" the past in an action that is "less a remembering" than a "rewriting history." [57]

The discourses of modernity can be read with indifference to their truth claims. But such a reading cannot reconstruct those discourses as they seek to persuade, cannot analyze their efficacy as texts organizing action. When we bracket the truth claim of an expository text, we translate it to an alternative register of reading, as when we look at Chaucer's *Treatise on the Astrolabe* as a poetic text. We bring to the discourses of modernity analytic tools for distinguishing true propositions from false ones and for evaluating those distinctions as they are made within disciplines, schools, and professions. If, in one mode, we agree with Lacan that error is obligatory in all texts—that it is the defile through which the subject passes to knowledge, the moment when the discourse in its

56. Sigmund Freud, *Dora: An Analysis of a Case of Hysteria,* trans. Douglas Bryan, ed. Phillip Rieff (New York: Macmillan, 1963), 51.

57. Lacan, *Freud's Papers on Technique,* 20, quoted in Dews, *Logics of Disintegration,* 63. But consider also this example: "The symptom initial appears to us as a trace, which will only ever be a trace, one which will continue not to be understood until the analysis has got quite a long way, and until we have discovered its meaning. . . . What we see in the return of the repressed is the effaced signal of something which only takes on its value in the future, through its symbolic realization, its integration into the history of the subject. Literally, it will only ever be a thing which, at the given moment of its occurrence, *will have been*" (Lacan, *Seminar II,* 159).

heterogeneity wanders from the writer's intention or the reader's direct understanding—in another moment, we will want to securely separate it from something we will treat as truth. Some discursive practices of modernity—scientific writing, administrative writing—exclude error from their accepted signifying practices and organize the production of texts to guarantee accuracy of reference and the containment of error. Other practices—psychoanalysis and fiction—locate error at the heart of their productive practice and are oriented to coherence or theoretical and formal rigor rather than to accuracy of reference. A rhetorical reading of all these discourses will take none of them at their word but instead will note, observe, and make use of their diverse orientations to error and to language.

But to continue our examination of these issues, we will need to turn to the second of our rhetorical terms, narrative—the structure of "fiction," and therefore synonymous with error and falsification, but also the organizing vehicle of disclosure, the privileged figure accounting for origins.

Narration

In traditional rhetorical systems, narrative is a mobile topic. In the grand plot of the oration, *narratio* is itself an episode; in Roman technical rhetoric, it was both a pedagogical exercise and, reduced to the lapidary *exemplum*, a particularly telling figure.[58] Fable, dream, and fictional narrative all figure in the Renaissance arsenal of *copia*.[59] Narrative is both an assertion of facts that support a claim and also the most easily confected of ornaments. Aristotle takes for granted both the resemblance of the invented fable to the historical example and the multiplicity of possible interpretations of historical examples:

58. See Quintilian, *The Institutio oratoria of Quintilian,* 4 vols., trans. H. E. Butler (Cambridge: Loeb Classical Library, 1921), 2:iv, for exercises in narrative; for narrative as a figure, see, for example, the influential *Ad C. Herennium de ratione dicendi (Rhetorica ad Herennium),* trans. Harry Caplan, Loeb Classical Library (Cambridge: Harvard University Press, 1954), 4:xlix–lii.

59. See, for example, Desiderius Erasmus, *Collected Works of Erasmus,* ed. Craig R. Thompson, vol. 24, *Literary and Educational Writings,* bk. 2, *De Copia: De Ratione Studii,* trans. Betty Knott (Toronto: University of Toronto Press, 1978). For *copia* in literary theory, see Terence Cave, *The Cornucopian Text: Problems of Writing in the French Renaissance* (Oxford: Oxford University Press, 1979).

Fables are suitable in deliberative oratory and have this advantage, that while it is difficult to find similar historical incidents
that have actually happened, it is rather easy with fables. They
should be made in the same way as comparisons, provided one
can see the likenesses, which is rather easy from philosophical
studies. (Aristotle, *Rhetoric,* 2, 20, 7–8)

Humanist rhetoric would manage these resemblances through the techniques of the commonplace book:

Some material can serve not only diverse but contrary uses, and
for that reason must be recorded in different places. For example, if you are describing the incurable greed of a miser, you
may properly bring in the tale of Charybdis; but if you are talking of insatiable gluttony or woman's inexhaustible lust Charybdis will fit again." (Erasmus, *De Copia,* 4, method 11)

In the antirhetorical tradition, this prodigality is a reason to mistrust
narrative: Socrates drily dismisses both the fable of Boreas's rape and the
rationalizing explanation of a violent north wind as exercises of "simple
minded erudition"—going on, of course, to tell the compelling fable of
the chariot of the soul.[60]

Modernity inherits both the mobility of narrative and a distrust of its
charms. In both the tradition of classical German philosophy and current literary theory, narrative is seen as limited, conservative, and unre-
liable in its purchase on knowledge. In traditional philosophical accounts, the luminous transparency of narrative's account of the world
pales before the candor of more analytic discourses which offer their
operating assumptions and rules of evidence on their face: philosophical
reflection, the political treatise, the scientific monograph. Narratives
conserve and transmit social relations; only critical discourse can open
those relations to reflection or emancipate subjects from their unacknowledged dependence on them. Lyotard, no traditionalist, distinguishes
between a metanarrative of progress and critical knowledge.[61] Derrida
proposes an "excessive" reading over and against the straightforward
performance of the narrative text.[62] The questions therefore arise: What
is the nature of the knowledge (if any) that narrative constructs? Can

60. Plato, *Phaedrus,* trans. W. C. Helmbold and W. G. Rabinowitz (Indianapolis:
Bobbs-Merrill, 1956), 256.
61. Lyotard, *Postmodern Condition,* 37.
62. Jacques Derrida, *Dissemination,* trans. Barbara Johnson (Chicago: University
of Chicago Press, 1981), 103–4.

narrative disrupt the ideological frame in which it is organized and trans-mitted? As the second term in a rhetoric of modernity, narrative does not resolve these questions but keeps them in play.

Narrative Characterizes the Lifeworld.

Habermas discusses narrative as a form of reference and a way of orga-nizing knowledge in the second volume of *The Theory of Communica-tive Action.* For Habermas, narrative maintains the lifeworld's "cul-turally transmitted and linguistically organized stock of interpretive patterns."[63] Those interpretive patterns shape everyday life, familial re-lations, and the repertoire of face-to-face interactions in the lifeworld, a domain of customary relations. While the lifeworld regulates itself through narratives and conversations, it coexists with system, where re-lations are regulated outside language, by money and power. Since ev-eryday communicative practices cannot be transcended—language, in Habermas's expression, is always at the backs of speakers—the forms of customary discourse do not open directly into reflection without media-tion. It follows that no reflection will bring to light everything latent within the discourse of the lifeworld.

The lifeworld is constitutive of both mutual understanding and its objects. It is through the lifeworld, for example, that we know how chil-dren ought to be raised and that there are children who need a kind of care called raising. Narrative mediates the intersubjective relations of the lifeworld and places the objects of understanding within the context of received ideas: "*Narration* is a specialized form of constative speech that serves to describe sociocultural events and objects. Actors base their narrative presentations on a lay concept of the 'world,' in the sense of an everyday world or lifeworld, which defines the totality of states of affairs that can be reported in true stories."[64] Narratives coordinate tasks—consider such narrative schemes as "we get ready to open for business" or "the family celebrates the holidays." They locate speakers and hearers in personal identities, securing them roles in the narratable stories of their communities. Insofar as narratives become consensual, they maintain collective identities and can be invoked in highly com-pressed speech acts. Habermas gives the example of a new construction

63. Habermas, *Theory of Communicative Action,* 2:124.
64. Habermas, *Theory of Communicative Action,* 2:136.

worker getting beer for the morning break: the errand presumes a whole set of stories about customary morning snacks, about seniority, about the articulation of the working day.[65] Habermas's theory, then, coheres with traditional understandings of narrative as conservative, prereflective, and socially integrating.

Habermas proposes that the structure of the lifeworld is explicated in narrative fiction. Criticism illuminates the lifeworld by making explicit what is latent in narrative texts. As a kind of "theoretical presentation," criticism opens the structures of the lifeworld to reflection, especially as the lifeworld reproduces itself and its subjects. Such a critical analysis, Habermas further claims, can give us access to what is problematic in the lifeworld more directly than the narrative texts themselves. Narratives are concerned with events in the lifeworld, rather than its structures: "The everyday concept of the lifeworld that we bring to narrative presentation as a reference system has to be worked up for theoretical purposes in such a way as to make possible statements about the reproduction or self-maintenance of communicatively structured lifeworlds."[66] Analysis is a "working up" of the raw material of narration, just as language, earlier in *The Theory of Communicative Action*, was the working up of propositional content. But just as Habermas's theory of language overlooked the work of interpretation, so his treatment of narrative divorces narration from reflection, as if readers and writers were unable to reflect as they read, as if the structures of narrative were spontaneously generated in a natural outpouring of language.

Reading Narrative Is a Reflective Practice.

The limits of such an approach might be clarified by considering a specific text, say Charles Dickens's *Little Dorrit*.[67] Following Habermas, we would find in the text's presentation of the events of the text's lifeworld a critique of imprisonment for debt. That would not be a striking discovery. Imprisonment for debt, as every English major knows, was already dead letter when *Little Dorrit* was written. We can only read the novel sympathetically by seeing imprisonment for debt as a metaphor for a series of what Habermas calls "higher level reproduction pro-

---

65. Habermas, *Theory of Communicative Action*, 2 : 120–26.
66. Habermas, *Theory of Communicative Action*, 2 : 137.
67. Charles Dickens, *Little Dorrit* (Oxford: Oxford University Press, 1987).

cesses,"[68] such as education or the transmission of culture, in which social "debts" are repaid. In order to read the novel, we must undertake the kind of reflection that Habermas segregates into critical analysis, moving beyond the level of inchoate affective response he associates with reading. Since we perform this abstraction in the act of entering the narrative, we cannot confine it to the text (as theme) or to our reading (as the most economical covering term available to a contemporary reader). Nothing in the text forbids a relocation of its analysis to our intersubjective sphere; in fact, readers have always been required to make some presentist translation of the theme of debt. To read *Little Dorrit* as a meditation on social reproduction is simply to extend its thematics to a somewhat higher level of generality.

A formal analysis of the novel might uncover propositions distinct from those that the narrative presents to the reader. Consider the narrative figure of coincidence, which has a long and respectable role in the history of the novel, and which is understandably associated with Dickens. An analytic working up of the theme of coincidence might see it as a means of representing society as a totality, as a narrative figure for that transparency of structure and history which is represented philosophically in Hegel. The analysis might then consider the impossibility of understanding difference and separation in a world where everything is obsessively related to everything else, questioning the limits of the narrator who represents social totality. What are the implications of such a reduction to transparency of the opaque and resistant forms of social connection? Who is it who presents us with knowledge as illumination rather than construction?

These remarks, however, simply translate into critical propositions ideas that are freely available within the narrative: there are no secure boundaries among the territories of the text, response, and critical analysis. When Dickens sets his protagonist, Clenham, in search of a narrative connection with Little Dorrit, the girl born and raised in a debtor's prison, we are invited to see his quest ironically, as a symptomatic and unreflective displacement of his inability to find a place in the bleak milieu of the text. The very arc of the narrative supports this irony, bringing Clenham all too inevitably into prison himself, and finally linking his history to Little Dorrit's. That link, slender and improbable, is withheld from Clenham, since he unknowingly burns the sole record of

68. Habermas, *Theory of Communicative Action*, 2:137.

it on the day of his wedding to Little Dorrit, an act that can be read as a figure of an irreducible difference between them. All of the material that might be "worked up" in an examination of the form of the narrative is available on its face. We could not locate this labor in either the author's intention, the structures of the text, or the interpretive habits of the reader; in all three of these locations, something has already been worked up, abstracted, if the text is to be read at all. No general rule can allocate all the propositions suggested by a text among the various agents who interpret it; criticism traces specific propositions in specific ways, rendering us conscious of the relations between our readings and other forms of interpretive labor. My reading of *Little Dorrit*, for example, would have been different if it were not provoked by a text of Habermas that raises the issue of social reproduction, or if Lacan had not written so persuasively about hidden and patent inscriptions.

Habermas's reduction of narrative content to the representation of the events of the lifeworld consigns narrative to the role of transmitting an available referential content in an emotionally acceptable way, as a particular mixture of proposition and illocution. Narrative only appears, in this theory, as a sequence of normalized episodes, divorced from the context of reading and writing and from the story's complex articulation of events in time.

Narrative Is Concerned with Time.

Such a theory is especially problematic because it obscures the relation of narrative to time. Time, like narrative, distinguishes the lifeworld from system. Since the lifeworld is populated by mortal beings, all of its discourses are open to the operation of time: narrative represents that openness. Narrative, as a discourse of the lifeworld, does not offer the structures of temporality as abstractions but represents them as preconditions of experience "at our backs," which can be opened to reflection but not transcended.

System deploys time as a resource like any other. The operation of the system (of the multinational money economy and of advanced techniques for state administration) is rationalized and increasingly differentiated; it operates through the delinguistified media of money and power. System supports no narrative tempo, tells no story. Such an ignorance of time is also, paradoxically, the mark of disciplinary knowledge. Scientific experiments are replicable—they can be done again and again; the good historian ruptures the conventional structure of memory; philosophical reflection locates itself outside time, as a reflection on it. In *Capital,* for example, Marx poses again and again the problem of analytically capturing the passage of time, formulating under the tropes of value, of labor power, and of variable capital expressions for the entry of human lives into the rationalized relations of the market economy, for their articulation, not into seasons or stages of life, but into the hours and minutes of the working day. But *Capital,* however persuasive and emancipatory, does not itself convey the lived experience of capital's transformation of time. Time is told in narrative; narrative permits the complex subjective and objective structuring of time to be laid onto the structures of language, which, as Lacan has shown, can itself be understood narratively.

Habermas understood narrative as a necessary body of knowledge and error at the back of analytic thought, as a set of assumptions that can never be brought whole to consciousness. Narrative therefore functions as a limit, guaranteeing that no analysis of society will achieve foundationalist status. Narrative also prompts reflection on the structures of the lifeworld, particularly on structures of temporality. But if we accept narrative as the discourse of the lifeworld, and there are good reasons to do so,[69] we must ask why we ever leave narrative to take up analysis at all? If the material "worked up" in analysis is already available in the narrative text, why do we ever need to present it analytically?

Perhaps the provocation to analysis does not proceed from either the excellence of analytic discourse or from the poverty of narrative, but from the ambiguous relation of narrative to system. As lifeworld and system differentiate in modern societies, the lifeworld becomes available for colonization by system. Its structures are instrumentalized and silently put at the service of the system. Such processes set the canonic themes of the Frankfurt School: the commodification of leisure time and the subordination of education to the training needs of a market economy. The colonization of the lifeworld, like any effect of system, is not intuitively available to subjects in society:

> The subjective inconspicuousness of systemic constraints that *instrumentalize* a communicatively structured lifeworld takes

69. For narrative as a conversational structure, see William Labov, "The Transformation of Experience in Narrative Syntax," in *Language in the Inner City* (Philadelphia: University of Pennsylvania Press, 1972), 354–96, and the work of Harry Sacks.

on the character of deception, of objectively false consciousness. The effects of the system on the lifeworld, which change
the structure of contexts of action in socially integrated groups,
have to remain hidden. . . . This gives rise to a *structural violence* that, without becoming manifest as such, takes hold of the
forms of intersubjectivity of possible understanding. Structural
violence is exercised by way of systematic restrictions on communication; distortion is anchored in the formal conditions of
communicative action in such a way that the interrelation of the
objective, social, and subjective worlds gets prejudged for participants in a typical fashion.[70]

Structural violence is not a dramatic act of abuse or a local degeneration
of communicative practices but a ubiquitous, pervasive distortion of
communicative rationality. It subjects consensual relationships to extra-
linguistic power, so that the interchange of ideas becomes a ritual whose
predetermined outcome reproduces unequal social relations. Colonized
and distorted interactions undoubtedly form the majority of our written
and spoken acts.

The notion of structural violence, however, assumes a prior uncolo-
nized state of the lifeworld, in which communication produces truth
directly. Just as Habermas understood propositions as preexistent to
their expression in language, so he projects the discourse of the lifeworld
as preexistent to the structuring division of society into lifeworld and
system. If we elide this narrative of fallen innocence, the lifeworld can
be specified in opposition to system as a repertoire of communicative
acts not integrated into delinguistified steering media. Although such
a definition focuses on precise distinguishing characteristics of modernity—the multiplicity of discursive forms, the differentiation of
modes of social organization—it should not be taken as a way of identifying uncontaminated texts of a pristine lifeworld. Lifeworld and system are not descriptive or historical categories but mutually defining
analytic terms. Criticism is not a uniquely reflective discursive form but
a means of tracing out the exchanges between system and lifeworld,
of making available to communicative rationality ideas formulated in
narrative.

The colonization of the lifeworld by system is, for us, permanent and
unavoidable. Confronted by such discursive violence, the communicative relations of the lifeworld reveal gaps and disjunctures, narrative dis-

70. Habermas, *Theory of Communicative Action*, 2:187.

continuities that solicit rectification by other practices of language. Narrative may be a relatively easy target for the operations of system, an absorbent discursive practice, permeable to the structural violence of colonization. But that same heterogeneity permits narrative to sustain multiple voices and locations, ironic inflections, and formalized representations of absence. Such gestures are alternative forms of critique, forms which can be explicitly realized, as when the prejudged outcome of debate is shown to be a reproduction of unequal social relations, or the aura of nature and custom is removed from the unequal distribution of roles in discussion. A discursive realization of narrative assumptions also can be answered, criticized, or affirmed. It is rhetorically available for exchange.

Over against the violence of the colonized lifeworld, then, we place the discursive violence of critique. It interrupts the narrative of a discourse unrolling to its prejudged conclusion, disrupts the seamless connection among ideologically segmented episodes, proposes alternative connections, and calls into question the narrative structures that underwrite them. Above all, it requests an answering discourse. None of these operations of critique represents a distinct form of mental labor or a discursive practice at odds with narrative. It is not the implicit and allusive nature of narrative discourse that demands critique but the distorted and monologic structures of system, its resistance to relations of exchange, and the dialogic preconditions of language. Since the structures of system are delinguistified, to translate them into language is to open them to transformation.

We can find a cognate theory of the relation of narrative structures and analytic reflection, according to Claudia Brodsky's bold and imaginative reading, in Kant.[71] Brodsky's reading of Kant establishes him as a

71. Claudia Brodsky, *The Imposition of Form: Studies in Narrative Representation and Knowledge* (Princeton: Princeton University Press, 1987). Undertaking the unlikely task of deriving a narrative theory from Kant, Brodsky begins by insisting that, for Kant, the representational quality of knowledge connects it (although how accurately we cannot reliably say) to the world of sensory experience to which it refers. Critical philosophy, which creates its concepts rather than constructing them from experience, is therefore a heterogeneous discourse without referential power but with considerable self-critical force. Both knowledge and philosophy are to be understood as practices within language and therefore as linked to literature.

Brodsky develops readings of the three critiques into a device for critical analysis. What is relevant to our purposes is her discussion of the relation of narrative to analysis in Kant as it bears on Habermas in particular and on the problem of time and narration in general.

critical, rather than a transcendental, philosopher, and thus suggests a new basis for linking him with Habermas.[72] If we follow Brodsky, then Habermas and Kant are both engaged in a project of critique. Both acknowledge, via different strategies, the heterogeneity of discursive forms, and both understand knowledge and critique discursively. For Kant, this discourse is monologic; for Habermas, it is intersubjectively dialogic. But for both Habermas and Kant, the relation between critique and narration turns on an abstraction of discourse from either history or rhetoric, an abstraction we need not make.

The resistance of the experience of time to critical reflection makes such an abstraction untenable. Paul Ricoeur has shown that time apprehended through reflection—as it is in Kant—deprives reflection of phenomenological descriptive power, while remaining mortgaged to the unanalyzed assumptions of experience. Ricoeur distinguishes two senses of time: time as context for motion, for change in the world, and time as the context within which the soul lives, perceives, and remembers. These two perspectives occlude each other in philosophic speculation, a disjunction which is mediated and joined in narrative.[73] A narrative poetics represents the text's mediation of these "distensions of the soul."[74] The impossibility of thinking time simultaneously as both subjective experience and arena for the operation of force can only be mediated in narrative, whether fictional or historical: "The mimetic activity of narrative may be schematically characterized as the invention of a third time constructed over the very fracture whose trace our aporetics has brought to sight."[75] Narrative uniquely raises to consciousness what is assumed and undergone in the experience of time.

Narration is an act situated in time, a punctuation of the experience of intersubjectivity. The story takes time to tell, and reading and under-

72. Readers of Habermas have often connected him to Kant because of his use of universals and because of his formal understanding of rationality. But Habermas has always refused categorization as a neo-Kantian (Dews, *Habermas: Interviews,* 184). The basis for this refusal has been dual: Habermas's critique of Kant's strict separation between theoretical and practical reason (Rüdiger Bubner, "Habermas' Concept of Critical Theory," in *Habermas: Critical Debates,* ed. John Thompson and David Held [Cambridge: MIT Press, 1982], 48) and his critique of the isolated, socially unsituated subject as the origin of meaning (McCarthy, *Critical Theory,* 325–27).

73. Paul Ricoeur, *Time and Narrative,* 3 vols., trans. Kathleen Blamey and David Pellauer (Chicago: University of Chicago Press, 1984–88), 3:22.

74. Ricoeur, *Time and Narrative,* 3:21.

75. Ricoeur, *Time and Narrative,* 3:245.

standing it also require time.[76] Socially sanctioned relations of power are enacted when the tale is requested and performed, but they are also suspended and subverted by the audience's dependence on the storyteller, who continually chooses how, and how much, to challenge their preconceptions about good and bad stories. The story itself also articulates temporal connections among episodes as their order is rearranged, their seamless connection punctured with discontinuities which we may or may not be invited to notice, and their tempo accelerated or retarded.

There is, of course, a body of texts that reflects on precisely these temporal relations—history.[77] Like rhetoric, history is a textual practice inherited from antiquity; its continuity as a school subject has been broken by its emergence, first, as a specialized literary practice and, later, as a fully developed academic discipline. History is therefore exemplary of the movement from a discourse rooted in the lifeworld, pedagogical and moral in its impulses, narrative in its organization, and disseminated throughout society, to a social science, mortgaged to the truth of its

76. The relation between narrative and temporality is a central question in contemporary narrative theory. For the relations between narrator and narratee, see Gerald Prince, *Narrative as Theme: Studies in French Fiction* (Lincoln: University of Nebraska Press, 1992). For a general treatment of narrative temporality, see Seymour Chatman, *Story and Discourse: Narrative Structure in Fiction and Film* (Ithaca: Cornell University Press, 1978), and his more recent *Coming to Terms: The Rhetoric of Narrative in Fiction and Film* (Ithaca: Cornell University Press, 1990). Influential treatments of narrative temporality include Gerard Gennette's *Narrative Discourse: An Essay in Method* (Ithaca: Cornell University Press, 1983) and his *Narrative Discourse Revisited* (Ithaca: Cornell University Press, 1990) and Tzvetan Todorov's *The Poetics of Prose* (Ithaca: Cornell University Press, 1977). For psychoanalytic theories of narrative, see Peter Brooks, *Reading for the Plot: Design and Intention in Narrative* (Cambridge: Harvard Univ Press, 1991), and the more Lacanian collection edited by Robert Con Davis, *Lacan and Narration: The Psychoanalytic Difference in Narrative Theory* (Baltimore: Johns Hopkins University Press, 1984). A political analysis of narrative can be found in Fredric Jameson's *The Political Unconscious* (Ithaca: Cornell University Press, 1982). Useful summaries and collections include James Phelan, ed., *Reading Narrative: Form, Ethics, Ideology* (Columbus: Ohio State University Press, 1989); Thomas Leitch, *What Stories Are: Narrative Theory and Interpretation* (College Station: Penn State University Press, 1986); and Shlomin Rimmon-Kenan, *Narrative Fiction: Contemporary Poetics* (London: Routledge and Kegan Paul, 1983).

77. See Hayden White, *Metahistory: The Historical Imagination in Nineteenth-Century Europe* (Baltimore: Johns Hopkins University Press, 1973); Hayden White, *Tropics of Discourse: Essays in Cultural Criticism* (Baltimore: Johns Hopkins University Press, 1978); Linda Hutcheon, *A Poetics of Postmodernism: History, Theory, Fiction* (New York: Routledge, 1988); Renato Rosaldo, *Culture and Truth: The Remaking of Social Analysis* (Boston: Beacon, 1989).

representations, oriented to the modes of persuasion and proof developed in a professional community. Disciplinary differentiation is a renunciation of narrative history in favor of empirical investigation or of a
broader cultural history. Such renunciations inevitably provoke rehabilitations, in quite different forms, of both narrative and a broad educational mission for history.[78]

In the slightest syncopation with these developments, we can trace
the emergence of a body of reflections by historians and cultural critics
on the precise structures of historical narrative, on its ideological assumptions and persuasive force, a body of reflections that is very quickly
taken up by literary critics and historians of science. The practice of narrative in the nineteenth century has been painstakingly analyzed as it
emerged in the writing of history and in the nascent disciplines of natural history, geology, and evolutionary biology. Those studies cannot be
recapitulated here. I want to recover instead the uneven relations among
narrative's constitution of the lifeworld, narrative as originary moment
in a differentiated discipline, and narrative as a submerged and rejected
trace within a developed discipline. From those disjunctions, we may
recover a sense of narrative as a critical or oppositional practice.

Narratives Form Disciplines; Disciplines Reject Narratives.

In the nineteenth- and early-twentieth-century demarcation of disciplines, a series of discursive practices emerged, homologous with one
another and with the narrative forms of modernity. This trajectory did
not characterize every science (chemistry, for example, emerged outside
narrative forms).[79] But it marked many of the new disciplines and invested them with ideological power. Stories of the formation of the
planet and the evolution of species opened new dimensions and senses
of time to readers who had already learned, through generations of
novel reading, to take in radical distensions and compressions of the
temporal, to shift focus from a momentary crisis to the broad expanses
of the quotidian, and to consider the possibilities of multiplied counter-

78. As an example of the growing body of work concerning history addressed to
popular audiences, see Simon Schama's *Dead Certainties (Unwarranted Speculations)* (New York: Vintage, 1991). For the rehabilitation of narrative, see Lawrence
Stone, *The Past and the Present* (London: Routledge, 1988).

79. But see the account of experimental narratives in Steven Shapin and Simon
Schaffer, *Leviathan and the Air-Pump: Hobbes, Boyle, and the Experimental Life*
(Princeton: Princeton University Press, 1985).

factual pasts. The development of a disciplinary discourse in both geology and evolutionary biology required the resolution of a grand narrative into manageable episodes, episodes that could organize the work of an individual scientist and that could become objects of coherent controversy.[80] Scientific disciplines also formulated extended narratives of their own emergence, telling a story of origins and vicissitudes, up to the present of readers (now distinguished as either "lay" or "professional"), and indicating a broad arc of the future. Similar narrative arcs marked inaugural moments in the social sciences: Tönnies's treatment of the transition from *Gemeinschaft* to *Gesellschaft*,[81] Weber's general narrative of the iron cage of rationality or his historical account of the Protestant ethic,[82] the stories of primitive tribes offered by early anthropologists as metaphors for the origins of civilization or as elegiac evocations of doomed survivors.[83] The discipline is established as an organized framework for gathering stories, deciding on their relations to one another, and adjudicating among their competing versions.

But neither the natural sciences nor the social sciences rested with such narratives. As disciplines matured, explicit narrative was rejected. Saussure's rejection of diachronic historical linguistics in favor of the synchronic adumbration of the structures of language[84] foreshadows the reorientation of biology from the narrative of speciation to the analytic story of alleles in their combinations, the movement of sociology from classic narrative theories to studies of social structures, and—returning to our initial example—the rejection of narrative history.

But of course the resources of narrative were still at the service of institutionalized disciplines. That institutionalization is often called "professionalization," although professions, organized by an ideology of service to clients, intersect unevenly with disciplines. Disciplines and professions both share sites of research and publication, both reproduce

---

80. Misia Landau, *Narratives of Human Evolution* (New Haven: Yale University Press, 1991); and Gillian Beer, *Darwin's Plots: Evolutionary Narrative in Darwin, George Eliot, and Nineteenth Century Fiction* (London: Routledge, 1983).

81. Ferdinand Tönnies, *Community and Society* (New York: Harper Torchbooks, 1957).

82. For practices of rationality, see Weber, "Science as a Vocation." For the Protestant ethic, see his *The Protestant Ethic and the Spirit of Capitalism*, trans. Talcott Parsons (New York: Scribners, 1958).

83. James Clifford, "On Ethnographic Allegory," in *Writing Culture: The Poetics and Politics of Ethnography*, ed. James Clifford and George E. Marcus (Berkeley and Los Angeles: University of California Press, 1986).

84. Ferdinand de Saussure, *Course in General Linguistics*, ed. C. Bally and A. Sechehaye, trans. Wade Baskin (New York: Philosophical Library, 1959).

themselves in universities, but they differ in their legal status and their relation to the production of knowledge.[85] For professions, narration continues as a critical local figure in the case history and as an organizing principle in the profession's story of its own growth and development. Neither professions nor academic disciplines do without stories: the development of discrete episodes for investigation; the elaboration, outside the formal discourse of the profession, of exemplary narratives of good and bad practice; the slow consolidation of narrative problems into central issues demanding elucidation, such as grand unified theories of the physical forces in the universe, broad issues of periodization, and complex local narratives like those that describe the mysteries of the immune system. These narratives coexist with disciplinary distrust of narrative—they are sometimes ironically tolerated, sometimes seen as "theory" rather than "story," sometimes opened to critique as "nice stories."[86] It is not accidental that these movements of irony, disguise, and critique occur simultaneously with the cultural rejection of narrative in such diverse forms as Godard's early films, critical histories of the sciences,[87] and Lyotard's critique of the narratives of modernity.

Given these uneven, suspiciously synchronic appropriations and rejections of narrative, given the signal power of narrative in the representation of time, why do disciplines avail themselves of, or reject, this power?

Narrative Is Concerned with Multiple Times.

Narrative, even conventional realistic narrative, operates in multiple times. The time of telling opens out temporality by establishing an uneven relation between reading a story and the time of the represented action. This relationship is necessarily figural; the time of reading matches, accelerates, or retards the time of the narrated action, just as the tone of the telling places the narrated action as, for example, nostal-

85. Magali Sarfatti Larson, *The Rise of Professionalism: A Sociological Analysis* (Berkeley and Los Angeles: University of California Press, 1977).

86. See, for example, S. J. Gould and R. C. Lewontin, "The Spandrels of San Marco and the Panglossian Paradigm: A Critique of the Adaptationist Programme," *Proceedings of the Royal Society of London,* 1979, and the essays on this text in *Understanding Scientific Prose,* ed. J. Selzer (Madison: University of Wisconsin Press, 1993).

87. Kuhn, *Structure of Scientific Revolutions.*

gic memory, recollection of superseded past, shameful episode, or glorious story of origins. Further, narration can carry the episode as factual account or counterfactual, telling both an asserted story and alternative, more or less discounted, versions.[88]

This impossible conjunction of the new, of truth, and of the unreal emerges from the text's shaping of time, from its articulation of tense and mood, from the relation between assertion and quotation. As Lacan put it, "Every act of speech which is formulated as such brings into the world the novelty of the emergence of meaning." Or, in more somber tones:

> In each obsessional case, there necessarily is a certain number of temporal scansions, and even numerical signs. . . . The subject thinking the thought of the other, sees in the other the image and sketch of his own movements. Now, each time the other is exactly the same as the subject, there is no other master than the absolute master, death. But the slave requires a certain time to see that. All because, like everyone else, he is much too happy being a slave.[89]

Lacan's dimension of truth is constructed by the artful and complex orchestration of the act of telling, inviting the reader to inhabit counterfactual and contradictory positions. The reader who experiences that truth within the real of reading is rhetorically situated in a time of narration, placed at a bias to his or her own ideology. The time of narration can also consider alternative historical paths, alternative futures of the reader's historical past. In narrative, the reader enters the domain of the master and discovers the master as "exactly the same as the subject." The price for this demystification is identification with the narrator, a speaker with transcendent powers, able to make even the dead talk. The narrative construction of temporality therefore also articulates a social space; the reader is invited to stand with the narrator on the narrow ledge that overlooks the quoted and elided prior narratives, received versions of the story, commonplaces of ideology. On the narrow ledge of the narrative is constructed the text's dimension of truth. Within academic disciplines, this dimension is articulated in specific disciplinary practices: reviews of literature, critiques of previous scholarship, the obbligato of footnotes, with or without their diegetic glosses. Narrative

88. Lacan, *Seminar I*, 263.
89. Lacan, *Seminar I*, 287.

space, already impossibly folded, is doubled: at the top of the page, we read of events; at the bottom, homologously, of texts in dispute. The author's power to invoke the upper story of history is guaranteed by his magisterial control over the lower story of previous writers.[90] The reader is invited to read in the documentation a disciplinary narrative of progress, in which the current text is inscribed as climactic. Such disciplinary documentation differs from the traditional critical forays we read in the footnotes of Marx's *Capital,* a specifically critical practice noted by Jameson.[91] Derrida's "Double Session" parodies and dismantles both traditional critical dialogue and disciplinary documentation.[92] The doubled narrative of documentation asserts the inauguration of a discipline, a profession, an intellectual practice: it demonstrates, under the foundation of the text, that the story is not available to anyone for the telling, that it is a discourse that requires initiation. In the doubled narrative of scholarship, a new discipline claims a discourse that refers to truth.

The time of narrative discourse, particularly in academic disciplines, then, is not seamless and whole but punctuated, folded, and torn. It incites the mutual misidentification of narrator and reader, which we call here rhetoric. In homage to Hayden White, I will trace out these relations in a short passage from Gibbon's *Decline and Fall of the Roman Empire.*[93] Gibbon is discussing the destruction of the pagan temples under the Christian emperors. He outlines an alternative policy: moderate secularization of the temples, converting them to "magazines, manufactures, or places of public assembly." That, however, did not happen; instead:

> So long as they [the temples] subsisted, the Pagans fondly cherished the secret hope that an auspicious revolution, a second Julian, might again restore the altars of the gods: and the earnestness with which they addressed their unavailing prayers to the throne increased the zeal of the Christian reformers to extirpate, without mercy, the root of superstition. The laws of the emperors exhibit some symptoms of a milder disposition: but

90. Ben Agger, *Socio(Onto)Logy: A Disciplinary Reading* (Champaign: University of Illinois Press, 1989).

91. Fredric Jameson, *Marxism and Form: Twentieth Century Dialectical Theories of Literature* (Princeton: Princeton University Press, 1971), 9.

92. Derrida, *Dissemination,* 173–286.

93. Edward Gibbon, *The Decline and Fall of the Roman Empire,* 3 vols. (London: J. M. Dent, 1910), 3:128.

their cold and languid efforts were insufficient to stem the tor-
rent of enthusiasm and rapine, which was conducted, or rather
impelled, by the spiritual rulers of the church.

Gibbon goes on to describe Martin of Tours destroying idols and
temples; "the prudent reader will judge" whether Martin was supported
by carnal or spiritual powers.

Gibbon treats the rise of Christianity as an inevitable process of
nature, embodied in the reformers' zeal. The Christian reformers inau-
gurate a lineage extending from antiquity to the present of Gibbon's
readers: the last lines of *The Decline and Fall* mention the Plantage-
nets and thus initiate something that could have been called "modern
history."

The text also elaborates a different temporal structure in its counterfactual moderate positions: the ineffectual hope of the pagans for restoration, the failed "milder disposition" of the emperors, and the rationalism of the reader whose "prudence" ascribes Martin's success to
"carnal powers." All three of these positions describe distensions of the
soul, in the form of failed or impossible narratives. The speculation that
Gibbon's readers would have been skeptical of Martin opens the perspective of an alternative history, the especially impossible story of a rationalized Christianity that would have preserved the valuable elements
of antiquity. All these counterfactuals are located in a time that is entirely reversible, flexible, and subject to change, placed in a narrative
future that is also the real present of the reader, who "will judge." The
terrain of probabilities, the privileged domain of rhetoric, stands over
against the time of what came to be and what had to be done, the time
of history and obligation. Although their ideological assumptions contradict each other, all these counterfactual positions—including, of
course, the reader's—are folded together in analogous temporal sta-
tions, heteromorphous to the time of the Christian zealot.

The doubled temporality of the text brings the prudent reader into
conjunction with pagans and emperors in a counterfactual space where
desire, memory, and hope mark the passage of time and where time,
including even past time, is open to other possibilities. The text's temporal structure locates the reader in a deferred desire, organized as an
impossible identification. The reader is invited to negotiate the gap between the irreversible, impersonal time of the zealot and the subjective
time of the text's counterfactuals. Gibbon grants primacy to the irre-

versible force of external time: the fall of Rome, after all, is a byword for
the inevitable. But everything in the text's libidinal economy leads the
reader to distrust and regret that process, to seek refuge in the text's
multiple invocations of alternative times. The gap between the time that
might have been future and the time that was indeed past, then, is one
that the text makes negotiable, not in its overall syntagmatic force, but
repeatedly, in the time and work of reading.

The mediation of the text's temporal gaps is effected by desire, which
implicates the reading subject in a system of identification and deferral.
In Gibbon, these relations are doubly complicated because the other of
the passage, the Christian zealot, is ideologically the same as the reader,
is her ideological forebear, whereas the objects of identification—pagans
and emperors—are historically other. The text thus operates through
the reader's desire. Lacan dramatized such relations of simultude and
difference in his first seminar. Early in the seminar, Lacan had counseled
his students that "to think is to substitute the word *elephant* for elephants, and a ring for the sun." [94] Thought works out of the similarities
and differences of language as a system of substitutes which are neither
identical with material objects nor secondary to them. The elephant
reappears at the last session of the year, when Lacan, immediately after
his invocation of the happy slave, "has figurines representing elephants
handed out." [95] The figurine is not an inscription of the word "elephant" but a different kind of representation: iconic, cheap and available, but pleasant to look at and handle. A token. It is one thing to
represent thinking; it is another to give an acceptable gift, to invoke
efficaciously Freud's distribution of rings to his inner circle. The gift of
figurines claims successors and also establishes a different kind of *mag-
isterium,* public, open to contest, militantly lay. The gift of figurines is a
double negation: they are not elephants, and so they represent thinking.
They are also not rings—not representations of the sun—and so they
pay homage to Freud while tacitly claiming to found a new lineage of
psychoanalytic thinkers. The figure disrupts and extends a narrative
chain that reaches through the work of the year and, in another line,
back to Freud.

The narrative, an act that takes place in time, is a verbal gift to the
reader; like other gifts, it represents alliances and obligations. Narrative

94. Lacan, *Seminar I,* 225.
95. Lacan, *Seminar I,* 287.

presents the reader with objects of identification which punctuate narrated time; they create sites and structures outside the lived time of the presumed reader; they enable counterfactuality; they raise the possibility of time having worked out otherwise, even in that most constrained of its tenses, the future.

Narrative is central to the discourses of modernity because of its heterogeneity, its complex articulation of time, and its construction of the narrator's fluid subject position. These texts are marked by deep diversity of styles, forms of argument, and rhetorical relations. Precisely this multivoiced heterogeneity has been associated with the development of vernacular prose in general[96] and fictional prose in particular.[97] Within all narrative texts, the narrator offers herself as analogue to the "subject supposed to know" who authorizes the disciplinary discourses of modernity, or who is dismantled in their critical moment. Finally, modernity is distinguished by its reflexive self-consciousness; the foregrounding of temporality in narrative contains and sponsors this self-reflection, offering multiple temporal perspectives which organize separate trajectories of knowledge and reflection.

The discourses of modernity employ narrative both locally and generically. On a small scale, narrative articulates causal links, accounting for different states of a system, connecting actants, and eliding awkward voids in the evidence. Such connections can be quotidian, as in a student report in a technical writing class suggesting a new method of balancing submarine turbines. The student, James Mariani, tells a small story: "The system is also relatively large (over 200 pounds), which becomes a problem. We have to use a crane to raise and lower equipment through the hatch."[98] We read here about an action (balancing turbines), an episode (moving the equipment on board), retarding action (too big), actants (system, programmers, crane), and a crisis (movement through the hatch).

Narrative also shapes the discourses of modernity in broad generic terms, orienting texts to coordinated action. Writing that orchestrates a common project is often organized as a story about what needs to be

96. Jeffrey Kittay and Wlad Godzich, *The Emergence of Prose: An Essay in Prosaics* (Minneapolis: University of Minnesota Press, 1987).

97. M. M. Bakhtin, "Discourse in the Novel," in *The Dialogic Imagination*, trans. C. Emerson and M. Holquist (Austin: University of Texas Press, 1981).

98. James Mariani, "The New SSTG Microbalance System" (Dec. 1990, typescript), 1.

done. Writers of government documents are advised to present procedures as narratives in which the reader is the primary character.[99] For the
discourses of modernity, an argument is often a story. In Mariani's report, the argument for a new microbalance system is essentially a narrative of rescue: "This report explains why the inconveniences of the G.E.
system are problems and how the new microbalance system corrects
these problems."[100] These remarks return us to the question of narration's relation to reason. For literary criticism, for normal rhetorical
theory, and still more for the pedagogical discipline of composition,
what counts as good reason is a quality of expository texts understood
intersubjectively.[101] This meditation on language and narration, however, incites a skeptical and provisional treatment of all claims of "good
reason." If more is going on in an utterance than its propositional content, then ordinary statements can be quite wild and contingent in their
force. If all propositions emerge only in language, then they must also
be understood as material objects, shaped by a specific labor or practice,
a *techne* with its own specificity. The representational force of a proposition exists heteronomously with demands of language for cohesion,
for generic decorum, and for bodily satisfactions specific to reading
and writing. Language inscribes its own narrative of missed encounters
with meaning, the story of the self-creating action of the speaking self
through deflections, mistaken identities, and all the good and bad fortunes of desire.

Many of the discourses of modernity present themselves as located in
a transparent world, controlled by a simple intention to represent it. To
see such discourse as work of language, a narrative located in history and
responsive to a number of orientations, allows us to think about scientific or administrative discourse with something like the flexibility that
classical rhetorics enjoyed for analysis of a repertoire of socially credited
public speech forms. Even this is not enough. Our discourses are not
simply or transparently rational; they are marked by all the sources of
error, misprision, and deflected understanding that accompany our own
entries into language as speaking subjects. A rhetoric of intersubjectiv-

99. Linda Flower, John Hayes, and Heidi Swarts, "Revising Functional Documents: The Scenario Principle," in *New Essays in Technical and Scientific Communication: Research, Theory, Practice,* ed. Paul V. Anderson, R. John Brockmann,
Carolyn R. Miller, Baywood Series in Technical and Scientific Communication
(Farmingdale, N.Y.: Baywood Publishing, 1983).
100. Mariani, "The New SSTG Microbalance System," i.
101. Perelman and Olbrechts-Tyteca, *The New Rhetoric.*

ity, then, recognizes the pressure of drive, aggression, and symptom and takes into account the torsion of the institutional settings of discourse and the consequent unequal relations among speakers. Rather than reading the happy story of society as a good student, rhetorical analysis finds in the structures of communicative action the discontinuous and unedifying story of domination and resistance.

Reading so many stories and finding teleologies of intention, subject formation, and power erupting thematically at the corners of every text, a rhetoric of intersubjectivity calls into question the stories texts tell about themselves. Here reason sweetly redeems the intersubjective promise made at the entry of the speaking subject into language: every attempt to analyze or to step outside narrative entangles discourse in narrative structures, which are both the sign and the means for the location of discourse in time. Temporal location enacts and renegotiates the positions of reader and writer. Telling a story enables the writer to invent or take up a position relative to the past, to trace its articulation into the present: what is coherent and unproblematic in the ideology of the assumed reader can be put into crisis by relocating it to a contradictory—and counterfactual—temporal location. If understanding and knowledge, deriving their temporal structure from experience, are inevitably compromised by error, inevitably located at our backs, the discourses of modernity transform the time of experience and make available to us the distensions of the soul that shape it. Narrative presents itself unproblematically as representation and refuses to acknowledge itself as a negotiation between author and reader, as a complex resituation of all the parties to the discourse in a fictional, impossible time. It is useful, fruitful, and necessarily in error.

But it is precisely this counterfactual and fictional quality of narrative time that supports our reflection on time, narrative, and discourse. The gaps and syncopations of narrative time and the demands that its contradictions make on readers bring to light what would otherwise be obscure: the discontinuity between time as a domain of subjective experience and time as the arena of force and motion. By performing this discontinuity in a text, narrative discourse permits us to see and understand what is unacknowledged in the representation of time as mechanical, uniform duration. If such reflections are only exceptionally sponsored by the narrative text itself, they are for the rhetorically astute reader always an available piece of freedom.

Narrative prompts the creation of a supplement, a translation, an

analysis that runs along the thread of the story, articulating its own relation to time and performing in a different register its transformative
and revelatory possibilities. This critical discourse, the discourse of rhetorical analysis, is not scandalized by error: rhetoric has never known
anything but probability, approximation, opinion, words seen only as
words. Rhetoric does not add to or substitute for the text's articulation
of time but transposes its work with time into a different register, one in
which a different sort of critical exchange is possible.

CHAPTER TWO   •   •   •   •

Reading Science
Rhetorically

•   •   •   •   Among the texts of modernity, none are more forbidding than those of the natural sciences. Bristling with equations, studded with graphs and charts, these texts are everything the culturally valued literary text is not: inaccessible, arid, barely language at all. Indeed, the professional study of English literature was founded in a doubled relation to science: first, the attempt to imitate science, largely through textual study, and then by constituting literature, particularly poetry, as a body of works to be read differently from the scientific text.[1] Science offered knowledge of the world; poetry, an experience of language. New criticism colluded with the scientific myth, current since Sprat's *History of the Royal Society,* that the transparent discourse of science, concerned with things rather than words, is innocent of rhetorical seductions. The scientific text, for new criticism, could not be read because it simply presented sterile facts. When the first works presenting alternative, more complicated, notions of scientific writing became popular—and I am thinking here of Kuhn's *Structure of Scientific Revolutions*—the weakening new critical framework conceded that science was rhetorical, but that concession was dismissive, debunking: if the physical sciences proceed through paradigm shifts, then science's claim to represent the world is compromised. The scientific text is no longer one that *cannot* be read; now, it *need not* be

1. Hugh Grady, *The Modernist Shakespeare: Critical Texts in a Material World* (Oxford: Clarendon, 1991).

read: it has already been placed, its claims refuted, its self-understanding ruled out a priori.

Meanwhile, the texts of science are written, read, cited. They organize vast domains of production; an initiation into them forms a scientific cadre entrusted with crucial elements of social reproduction. Scientific texts interpret the natural world, from the cosmos to the immune system; those interpretations emerge both in material practices (building a supercollider, timing AZT treatment) and in the multiple discursive practices that place us in relation to nature, modulating our understandings of gender, perception, growth, of what can be hoped for and feared in the material world. The texts of science are central to such diverse cultural forms as *Star Trek,* the debate on abortion, intelligence testing, computer bulletin boards, the development of grand unified theories, and the uneven appropriation of those theories in popular culture.

The texts of science proliferate, and a practice of reading them rhetorically has developed in relation to the academic disciplines of the history of science, sociology of science, and the teaching of technical writing.[2] The rhetoric of science has begun to read scientific texts, to

2. For a demonstration of the range of methods available in the rhetoric of science, see Jack Selzer, ed., *Understanding Scientific Prose* (Madison: University of Wisconsin Press, 1993), for which Selzer commissioned fourteen essays analyzing a text by S. J. Gould and M. Lewontin. The most significant recent works in the rhetoric of science include Charles Bazerman, *Shaping Written Knowledge: The Genre and Activity of the Experimental Article in Science* (Madison: University of Wisconsin Press, 1988); Alan Gross, *The Rhetoric of Science* (Cambridge: Harvard University Press, 1990); Lawrence Prelli, *A Rhetoric of Science: Inventing Scientific Discourse* (Columbia: University of South Carolina Press, 1989); Greg Myers, *Writing Biology: Texts in the Social Construction of Scientific Knowledge* (Madison: University of Wisconsin Press, 1990); and Peter Dear, ed., *The Literary Structure of Scientific Argument* (Philadelphia: University of Pennsylvania Press, 1991), all of which include very full bibliographies. Dilip Gaonkar critiqued the project of rhetoric of science in an important article, "The Idea of Rhetoric in the Rhetoric of Science," *Southern Communication Journal* 58 (1993): 258–95; the same issue of the *Southern Communication Journal* includes replies by Leff, Gross, Fuller, Campbell, and Prelli. Michael Halloran's "The Birth of Molecular Biology: An Essay in the Rhetorical Criticism of Scientific Discourse," *Rhetoric Review* 3 (1984): 70–83, a study of Crick and Watson's writing about DNA, was one of the first sustained readings of a scientific article; another such reading is John Lyne and Henry Howe, "'Punctuated Equilibria': Rhetorical Dynamics of a Scientific Controversy," *Quarterly Journal of Speech* 72 (1986): 132–47. Collections of essays in the rhetoric of science include Charles Bazerman and James Paradis, eds., *Textual Dynamics of the Professions* (Madison: University of Wisconsin Press, 1991); and Herbert W. Si-

provide ways of understanding them as labors of language, constructions of our natural world. This chapter extends recent work in the rhetoric of science, offering an analysis of scientific texts as practices of rationality suffused with desire. But it is offered first of all as an act of reading, as a lay and secular labor of understanding some scientific texts, of opening to reflection some forms of scientific thought. I want to see how the scientific text works if we read it, attending to its offerings of time, syntagm, narrative entrainment, doubling, wandering, and error, seeing it as a material object and a discursive practice.

Like the other discourses of modernity, those of science are marked by differentiation and organized by desire. They do not announce themselves as texts; neither their narrative structure nor their production of reading and writing subjects is available on their face. They do not entitle themselves, as it were, to the desires that they organize. Rather, the discourses of modernity appear within disciplinary boundaries, often patrolling those borders and enforcing their integrity. I will follow those contours and discuss a group of scientific texts within the disciplinary territories they inhabit, so that they can be understood as an ensemble of social and textual practices.

The discourses of the natural sciences are paradigmatic of modernity, differentiation, and rationality. Nowhere else is the claim to rational representation of the natural world more universally assumed. The scientific text provides us, for better or worse, with the model of the authoritative writer, the subject supposed to know. Emerging disciplinary discourses will either appropriate that model, as Lacan did in the early seminars,[3] or argue for an alternative model of rationality. And it is no idle envy that leads writers to emulate the authority of science: scientific discourse is powerful, fighting free of institutional ideological control. Its institu-

---

mons, ed., *The Rhetorical Turn: Invention and Persuasion in the Conduct of Inquiry* (Chicago: University of Chicago Press, 1990). Joseph Margolis's *Texts without Referents: Reconciling Science and Narrative* (Oxford: Blackwell, 1989), has important implications for the rhetoric of science. Recent specialized works include Londa Schiebinger's *Nature's Body: Gender in the Making of Modern Science* (Boston: Beacon, 1993); Henry H. Bauer, *Scientific Literacy and the Myth of the Scientific Method* (Urbana: University of Illinois Press, 1992); and M. A. K. Halliday and J. R. Martin, *Writing Science: Literacy and Discursive Power* (Pittsburgh: University of Pittsburgh Press, 1993). Essays treating the relations of rhetoric, philosophy of science, and history of science appear regularly in *Configurations*, a journal published by the Johns Hopkins University Press.

3. See, for example, Lacan, *Seminar II,* 17.

tions are invested with enormous authority; they dispose of vast social resources for research, education, and dissemination of scientific knowledge. Advanced capitalist society, agreeing on very little, agrees that it needs science. And scientific texts represent values held in high esteem: emancipation, maturity, responsibility to the social, and solidarity among intellectuals.

In the last ten years, this chorus of praise has heard some dissenting voices. Scientific texts have come to be seen as the vehicles for the domination of nature and for practices which we have come to see as deeply dangerous and problematic.[4] The scientific text reductively segments nature into connected objects of knowledge, open to manipulation in time and capable of being transformed without affecting the knowing subject. Although this critique is currently associated with feminism, it was formulated most globally by Max Horkheimer and T. W. Adorno in *The Dialectic of Enlightenment*.[5] For Horkheimer and Adorno, the practices of language most closely associated with the physical sciences were those which, transferred to the social, rationalized domination and the Holocaust: Enlightenment, in its moment of triumph, emerged as chaos and terror. Both the feminist critique and that of the Frankfurt School can be understood as reflexive to the social valuation of scientific writing's authority and efficacy.

Scientific writing is palpably, materially, differentiated. No other discursive formation is so relentlessly inaccessible to a public, so exclusively addressed to practitioners of scientific disciplines. Studies of the reading practices of natural scientists demonstrate that even professionals very seldom venture far from their own narrowly defined disciplines.[6] Serious scientific writing never addresses an audience outside the scientific community: a broad audience is one that includes readers outside the immediate research program of a discipline. Exercises in high popularization, such as articles for *Scientific American,* are seen as promotions for specific research programs—and, in any case, reach limited audiences.[7]

Scientific writing demonstrates what Habermas means by differen-

4. Evelyn Fox Keller, *Reflections on Gender and Science* (New Haven: Yale University Press, 1985); Donna Haraway, *Simians, Cyborgs, and Women: The Reinvention of Nature* (New York: Routledge, 1991).

5. Max Horkheimer and T. W. Adorno, *The Dialectic of Enlightenment* (New York: Seabury, 1969).

6. Charles Bazerman, "Physicists Reading Physics: Schema-Laden Purposes and Purpose-Laden Schema," *Written Communication* 2 (1985): 3–23.

7. Myers, *Writing Biology*, chap. 5.

tiation. It is addressed to a body of readers qualified by extensive training and disseminated through channels normally used only by those readers, who are expected to evaluate its arguments according to the distinct criteria of the discipline. Only astrophysicists will read and judge a given research report as "good astrophysics" or "bad astrophysics." No public intervention in this debate among specialists is possible; it is extremely unlikely that the debate can even be made publicly intelligible. The social practices organized by texts in the scientific disciplines are sometimes subjected to the steering and control of political bodies, but debates within the disciplines are, by and large, independent of direct intervention from them.

Scientific writing is organized by instrumental reason, a relentless focus which obscures concrete objects: "The multitudinous affinities between existents are suppressed by the single relation between the subject who bestows meaning and the meaningless object, between rational significance and the chance vehicle of significance."[8] Science, and the scientific text, aim at mastery and become homologous to hegemonic social domination.

Scientific texts assume an author who is particularly and paradigmatically modern. Horkheimer and Adorno refer to Sade's Juliette, who "believes in science," and for whom "nature remains only as a material mass."[9] The disenchantment of nature is irreversible: Habermas speaks of a nature which cannot be "re-enchanted."[10] Scientific writing is differentiated, instrumental, and attributed to a powerful speaking subject; it is the writing of modernism, as surely as *Ulysses,* and therefore, as it becomes conscious of itself, it is also postmodern.

Lacan's typology of four discursive forms, already discussed in chapter 1, relates the scientific discourse to its objects and its subjects. Lacan speaks of a "discourse of the university," which we may take as representative of scientific writing.[11] Such a discourse generates a specific set of subject positions as organizations of desires which confront other, similarly partial and divided, forms of the subject. In the equation Lacan composes for the discourse of the university, material signifiers are subordinated to the signifying chain of the discourse constituted as knowledge, so that knowledge is seen as an object of desire, detached

8. Horkheimer and Adorno, *Dialectic of Enlightenment,* 10–11.
9. Horkheimer and Adorno, *Dialectic of Enlightenment,* 96, 99.
10. Habermas, "Reply to My Critics," 238.
11. Jacques Lacan, *Le seminaire XVII,* 1969–70 (Paris: Seuil, 1991).

from the necessarily divided subject.[12] Scientific discourse elides both its speaker and its object; it privileges its own signifying system and divides the subject irrevocably from both the knowledge it produces and the object it initially sought.

For Lacan, Horkheimer and Adorno, and Habermas, the subject of science is an emblem of modernity, sign and symptom of its division. To extend this analysis rhetorically, I will read scientific texts using the initial analytic terms, "language" and "narration," to attend to the relations among subjects that they organize and effect, including the representations of the writer they imply.

To read the scientific text as a narrative coheres with recent work in the rhetoric of science, beginning with G. Nigel Gilbert and Michael Mulkay's *Opening Pandora's Box*. In Greg Myers's *Writing Biology,* in Charles Bazerman's *Shaping Written Knowledge,* and in Alan Gross's *The Rhetoric of Science,* narrative is a central issue.[13] Narrative tells the story of a natural process (the origin of the universe, the process of smooth muscle contraction), of an experimental procedure (how I discovered strange properties of light using a prism), or, finally, of the continued encounter between science and nature (spectroscopy develops in tandem with theoretical physics). For these rhetoricians, and for sociologists who have studied scientific discourse closely, scientific writing appears less as a global practice of objectification than as an unevenly successful labor to construct arguments from resistant and refractory materials.[14] For Lacan, the discourse of the university constitutes knowledge as an object of desire; for Latour, after three years in a molecular biology lab, that desire appears uncertain, risky, barely supported by the structure of investments and narratives with which it is sustained.

The scientific narrative's construction of intersubjective relations among tellers of stories and their listeners is therefore rhetorically significant. These relations are mediated by social institutions such as journals and foundations and marked in the text by evidence of its stationing in a social context, such as acknowledgments, ordered lists of authors, and notes of thanks. A scientific text, unlike a government report, as-

12. See the treatment of this equation by Juliet Mitchell and Jacqueline Rose in the volume they edited: Jacques Lacan, *Feminine Sexuality: Jacques Lacan and the École Freudienne* (New York: Norton, 1982), 161.

13. See also n. 2 above.

14. See Latour and Woolgar, *Laboratory Life;* and Michael Lynch, *Art and Artifact in Laboratory Science: A Study of Shop Work and Shop Talk in a Research Laboratory* (London: Routledge and Kegan Paul, 1985).

sumes an audience of peers: the readers of a scientific document are the potential writers of other documents. Reading and writing are structured, however counterfactually, by values of falsifiability and universal access: the reader of a scientific text is assumed to be skeptical and is invited to test the claims of the text, to replicate its experiences.

The "story" of the scientific text, whether it is the story of an experiment performed, a hypothesis tested, or an observation confirmed, is assumed in principle to be replicable: it is a story which becomes true only if it can be repeated. But simple replication is a story too simple to warrant the telling. The form of mastery represented by scientific narrative, then, is paradoxical: the teller of the story claims to hear the speech of nature and to report that speech to readers who are invited to falsify it. By the same token, the scientific writer's claim to mastery is always at risk, is assumed to be temporary: even if the text earns and survives replication, its truth is provisional and will be discarded in its turn. The speaker of the scientific story is doubled: he asserts the truth of what he utters, and he is indifferent to it; he discloses, in the discourse of science, what he truly believes, and he is not at all concerned with the truth of what he utters.

The reader and writer of the scientific text, then, are entrained in an agonistic and interdependent narrative whose general structure supports and ironizes each of the particular experimental and observational narratives recounted in individual scientific texts.

These relations are supported and punctuated by a quite distinct form of temporality. Scientific texts are themselves uneven and contradictory in their markings and reportings of time. Michael Lynch, one of the most astute and patient observers of scientific work, gives a fascinating account of the difference between the protracted, uncertain, and provisional temporality of experimental procedures and the crisp reporting of temporal locations and constraints in experimental reports.[15] The temporalization of an experiment in a scientific report lifts the story of the experiment from the other work that goes on simultaneously with it, elides false starts, blind alleys, and mistakes, and gives closure to a process that is likely to have ended in exhaustion and frustration rather than in triumph. The experimental narrative normalizes the time of scientific work. It even normalizes its object, the time of the natural process.

The idealization of experimental time is an astonishingly fluid repre-

15. See especially section 1.3, "Projects and Temporalization of Lab Inquiry," in Lynch, *Art and Artifact;* and Latour and Woolgar, *Laboratory Life,* 53–81.

sentation of the time of nature. The experiment is intended, often, to reveal something that happens too quickly or too slowly to be seen: retarding the action of instantaneous chemical reactions, or running the movie of the origin of the universe at wildly divergent speeds, so that the reactions that took a hundredth of a second are unfolded in slow complexity, and those of the succeeding millennium are summarized in a second. Finally, a significant temporal dimension of the narrative is indicated only implicitly: the text replies to previous stories, progressing beyond them or contradicting them. Each text is an episode in the narrative of progress and development that a discipline or research program tells about itself ("we used to think . . . but now we know"). That narrative is usually available only as a chain of citation dates in the text's review of the literature, constructing an anomalous temporality in which time's arrow moves backward, wavering at the uneven dates of citation, which are, for the reader, simultaneous. Paradoxically, this sophisticated temporal structure suggests a conventional narrative of progress, culminating in the text it supports.

All three of these temporal structures—the times of the experiment, of the natural process, and of the development of science—present themselves as transparent records of a natural and uniform temporality. The experiment takes its course; the natural process proceeds in stages; science progresses; and each normalized temporality supports the other, whether by collocation (bold experiment reveals startling complexity) or by contrast (patient experiment demonstrates unforeseen discontinuity).

It is not a scandal to literary critics that narrative temporality is a disruption of the lived succession of events; it is not a scandal to rhetoricians that temporality, like any other textual feature, can be used persuasively. Both literary critics and rhetoricians, however, have an interest in tracing out the particularities of these structures in scientific writing. I read the texts of science as an academic eavesdropper, a more or less imperfectly informed observer who is not, at least in this role, a sanctioned member of the scientific discourse community, which takes membership very seriously. My position is both privileged and precarious. Overhearing a discourse not addressed to me, unable to speak directly with its readers and writers, unable to understand much of what is being said or all of what is being meant, I face the perennial embarrassment of eavesdroppers: how can I report, publicly, what I was not meant to hear?

The figure of the eavesdropper, however, might be refunctioned to the equally complex figure of the electronic listener, trolling the airwaves for something interesting, inhabiting an isolated and compromised territory, always in danger of losing the transmission or of becoming implicated in a talk that is none of his business. We would think of Coppola's *The Conversation,* where an idle itch to understand becomes dangerous, or of the comic aliens who, in science fiction films, confuse television with human social life. These images suggest dangers of implication and misprision rather than of shame and exposure, possibilities of comic surprise and enlightenment rather than of strategic advantage. If the subject of language is always divided, then any reader whatever of a scientific text will encounter division in its multiple codes of text, equation, and graph. If those divisions are not silently negotiated but opened and made explicit, the scientific text is a shocking document: it speaks from several locations at once and demands a similarly plural reader. The rhetorician's position as alien listener therefore represents the shock of any observer, even one closely integrated into scientific communities, at the prospect of objectifying scientific discourse, itself a central mode of objectification.

The materiality of the signifier is especially pressing in scientific writing, which claims to represent objects directly, to present within the text, by pictures, measurements, or tracings, not one story among many but direct and veridical evidence of the path of the object through time. To this claim, the rhetorician advances a doubled rejoinder: first, a recognition of the material (rather than transcendent) nature of all linguistic representation, so that a sentence is continuous with a graph rather than its imperfect corruption; second, an assertion that the material practices of scientific investigation are themselves deeply mediated by and constituted within language,[16] so that relations among scientific texts and the objects of scientific experimentation are relations among signifiers—there is no direct access, either in scientific work or in the scientific text, to the signified. The scientific text carries within it syntactic representations of its claim to transparency and of the limits of that claim, representations of the reader and writer as masters of knowledge and as limited agonists, representations of the work of science as temporal, and, finally, representations of the claim of science as transcendent. A rhetoric of intersubjectivity traces out such representations in the figures of thought and language sponsored by the disciplines—authorship claims, acknowledgments, disturbances in tense structure,

16. Latour and Woolgar, *Laboratory Life.*

relations between graphic elements and the text. Prominent among those figures is the unintended foregrounding of language produced by error: a breach in the norms of the discourse community, a parapraxis, a failure to supply the evidence that sustains a truth claim, a contradiction within the program of scientific discourse. Error demonstrates both what is unstable or radically mixed within the practice of scientific discourse and the centrality of falsifiability and counterfactuality in scientific argument.

Reading the Scientific Text: Narration

In order to look closely at narrative and language in scientific writing, I will examine a series of articles and letters that appeared in *Nature* in 1984. These texts treat the issues that were then central in cosmology: the origin and end of the universe, the nature of dark matter, and the identification of very light subatomic particles. The texts are, in order of their publication:

> M. Demianski, "Large Anisotropy in the Universe Does Not Prevent Inflation" (letter), *Nature* 307 (Jan. 12, 1984): 140–41.
>
> S. A. Bludman, "Thermodynamics and the End of a Closed Universe," *Nature* 308 (Mar. 22, 1984): 319–22.
>
> Ramesh Narayan, Roger Blandford, and Rajaram Nityananda, "Multiple Imaging of Quasars by Galaxies and Clusters," *Nature* 310 (July 12, 1984): 112–15.
>
> Lawrence M. Krauss, Sheldon L. Glashow, and David N. Schramm, "Antineutrino Astronomy and Geophysics" (review article), *Nature* 310 (July 19, 1984): 191–98.
>
> Piet Hut and Simon D. M. White, "Can a Neutrino-Dominated Universe Be Rejected?" (review article), *Nature* 310 (Aug. 23, 1984): 637–40.
>
> A. C. Fabian, P. E. J. Nulsen, and C. R. Canizares, "Cooling Flows in Clusters of Galaxies" (review article), *Nature* 310 (Aug. 30, 1984): 733–40.
>
> C. J. Hogan and M. J. Rees, "Gravitational Interactions of Cosmic Strings," *Nature* 311 (Sept. 13, 1984): 109–14.
>
> George R. Blumenthal, S. M. Faber, Joel R. Primack, and Martin J. Rees, "Formation of Galaxies and Large-Scale Structure with Cold Dark Matter" (review article), *Nature* 311 (Oct. 11, 1984): 517–25.

These articles are located at a particularly fruitful juncture in cosmology: they begin to flesh out an emerging picture of the universe now and at its moment of origin. Writing to scientific peers, if not exclusively to cosmologists, the authors portray a universe at critical density—constituted of just enough matter to keep expanding indefinitely—a universe that expanded exponentially in its first moments, in a dramatic "inflation," a universe constituted by a symmetrical, but exotic, array of particles. Cosmology, in the mid-eighties, faced a challenging research program: cosmologists were generally optimistic about explaining the origin and nature of the universe through conjectures about a specific kind of dark matter, "cold dark matter." Their research focused on identifying cold dark matter by sifting through a series of candidates: particles, gases, matter in various mundane and exotic forms. Currently, although cosmologists generally agree that cold dark matter exists, and there is growing consensus on its composition, it is much less central in the cosmological scenario. Cosmologists in the mid-eighties also thought that "cosmic strings," one-dimensional structures within the vacuum of space, could have played an important role in the formation of galaxies and clusters of galaxies. As with cold dark matter, cosmic strings are still objects of investigation, although less central to the evolving picture of the early universe.

The cosmology of 1984, then, had embarked on the projects that generate current excitement—the elaboration of grand unified theories (or GUTs), the mapping of large-scale structures of the cosmos, the search for ever more subtle subatomic particles—but those projects had not entered their current triumphal phase. As a discipline, cosmology had become symbiotic with physics: what happens in accelerators, where particles collide at high speeds, was taken by cosmologists as a direct representation of the behavior of the very early universe, while the distribution of particles in the current universe was taken by physicists as a representation of how particles behaved in the irreproducible heat and energy of the big bang. The particle accelerator and the big bang became interchangeable metaphors for one another, uniting physics and cosmology. The authors represented in this sample demonstrate the collaboration between the disciplines: Demianski, Bludman, Krauss, Glashow, Schramm, Primack, and Rees are physicists; Nityananda, Blumenthal, Faber, Hut, White, Fabian, Nulsen, Canizares, and Rees are astronomers; and Narayan and Hogan are members of departments of astrophysics. (Although in folk science an astronomer is an observer of the heavens, in this group only Nityananda, Blumenthal, and Faber are affiliated with observatories.) In a popular text written several years after these articles, David Schramm, an important cosmologist, proclaimed that cosmology had become an experimental science. These articles demonstrate the fruits, and perhaps the tensions, of that transformation.[17]

Within this sample, a number of interlocking stories are told, stories of experiments, of natural processes, and of the development of the discipline. The vicissitudes of the universe are often organized as alternative "scenarios," which become, at their most general level, heroic representations of the origin and end of the universe. All of these stories, and particularly the heroic scenarios, are quite complex in their episodic and temporal structure; all of them require quite singular agents.

Narratives of experimentation can serve as a demonstration of the difficulties of telling stories about invisible—and possibly unseeable—objects, separated from us by staggering times and distances. They are, in a sense, ghost stories.[18] The experiment can be seen, has been seen since Bacon, as a forced speech by nature. In cosmology, the experiment makes visible what would otherwise be unseen: the experimenter concentrates a dispersed substance by collecting rare particles or models reactions that would have taken place in the very early universe in an accelerator or takes advantage of distance and space by deploying a range of collectors, putting a telescope in orbit, or sampling molecules collected on the moon.

The cosmological articles in this sample include one proposal for an experiment, which repays close analysis. In "Antineutrino Astronomy and Geophysics," Krauss, Glashow, and Schramm project the construction of a collector that would measure and analyze the antineutrino flux from the center of the earth. Since antineutrinos, as antimatter counterparts of neutrinos, have no charge and a mass too light ever to have been measured, they are not easy to find. The procedure suggested by Krauss and his co-writers is modeled on an experiment to detect solar neutrinos: a tank filled with four thousand liters of perchloroethylene, a common household cleaner, was buried deep in the Homestake Gold Mine. As neutrinos from the sun penetrated the earth and struck the tank, they transformed very small quantities of chlorine into argon. One argon atom was formed about every two days. Those atoms were isolated and separated from the chlorine and from the argon produced by back-

17. Michael Riordan and David N. Schramm, *The Shadows of Creation: Dark Matter and the Structure of the Universe* (New York: Freeman, 1991), 225.
18. I am indebted to Arabella Lyon for this telling characterization.

ground radiation; they served as evidence of a flow of otherwise unde-tectable neutrinos from the sun.

Krauss and his colleagues, adapting the neutrino procedure to anti-neutrinos, search for a well-formed story: they comb the lists of possible reactions looking for suitable materials, for something cheap, some-thing that can be subjected to very efficient separation techniques, something that produces an isotope long-lived enough to be detected but unstable enough to decay within the frame of the experiment. These technical problems generate narrative perplexities; the authors must tell a convincing story about a series of extremely challenging procedures, to be done in the future, requiring technology which is not yet devel-oped. And that story must persuade the reader that the procedure is worth doing. The story of the experiment sets in train another narrative, that of the growth of the discipline: eventually antineutrino detectors will become "more useful for astrophysical purposes" than neutrino detectors.[19]

The authors rely on two analogical supports for these narratives: the development of antineutrino detectors is compared to the development of neutrino detectors; the detection of terrestrial antineutrinos is com-pared to the detection of antineutrinos from space. As with neutrinos, so with antineutrinos; as below, so above. The comparisons locate a projected experimental procedure in the actual: neutrinos have been measured indirectly, using detection devices such as those the authors project; physicists had agreed on the existence of terrestrial antineutri-nos for fifteen years at the time the Krauss article was written. These two instances of the real anchor the experiments that the authors propose: "The experimental situation with regard to terrestrial antineutrino de-tection today is similar to that at the time when the first experiments for solar neutrinos were designed" (195). Aristotelian rhetoric would iden-tify here a skillful deployment of the available means of persuasion, drawing upon the normalizing power of the formal scientific text. An experimental procedure that cannot be performed with the current lev-els of technology is confidently projected as a series of soluble problems: the antineutrino detector will be built, even though several generations of technological development will be required for its construction, be-cause we have already built the neutrino detector, a much simpler de-vice. In fact, the antineutrino detector will be easier:

19. Krauss, Glashow, and Schramm, "Antineutrino Astronomy and Geophysics," 196. Subsequent references to this article are given parenthetically in the text.

Other aspects of the experimental situation are encouraging. First, such detectors will be able to be calibrated using nuclear reactor antineutrinos: this was not possible for solar neutrino detectors. Such calibration is important both for terrestrial antineutrino measurement and for checking cross-sections of low-energy antineutrinos on complex nuclei which have never been directly measured. (195)

What is technically difficult is presented as easier than what was technically simple; such an improbable argument is buttressed by the narrative of an advancing discipline, capable of meeting ever more difficult challenges. Latour and Lynch, among others, have convincingly described similar normalizations of difficult experimental procedures that were subject to repetitions, multiple errors, and approximations but are written up as well-formed stories, one episode leading to the next with only minor perturbations.[20]

"Antineutrino Astronomy and Geophysics" draws logical force from an extended comparison of the earth with the cosmos, projecting the center of the earth as an unknown territory. That space is associated with the neutrino and the antineutrino, objects that, since they are known only through weak interactions, cannot be directly perceived and never will be. The experiment is an exchange, moving weak interactions into the domain of the knowable and familiar, establishing that the center of the earth is a strange and inaccessible analogue to the remote reaches of the heavens. If the analogy between neutrinos and antineutrinos worked metaphorically, the analogy between the earth and the cosmos is a chiasmus: what was familiar becomes strange; what was strange becomes familiar. Such a strategy is especially appropriate for the multidisciplinary audience of *Nature*.

Repeatedly, the earth is presented as an unknown, and perhaps unknowable, object. The authors speak of "the inaccessibility of much of the Earth's surface" (191), an ironic concession for people who are planning to bury several thousand tons of matter (to be determined at a later date) deep in an abandoned mine in order to detect an atom every few days. The authors conclude that measures of antineutrinos will provide "the first fundamental empirical data on the Earth's interior structure and dynamics" (197).

This text establishes invisible objects as knowable. The projected experiment would demonstrate the benefits of working with weak inter-

20. See, for example, Lynch, *Art and Artifact*, 150–55.

actions to discern objects which are in principle invisible: they do not appear on the electromagnetic spectrum. This paradox—invisible objects as tools of demonstration—presents the authors with a rhetorical problem, one they address with measured pathos:

> If there are more things in heaven and Earth than are dreamt of in our natural philosophy, it is partly because electromagnetic detection alone is inadequate. For sources which are visually obscured or which emit most of their energy in a form other than photons, new methods of detection must be developed. . . . Although the usefulness of the weak interactions in probing astrophysical sources has been recognized, the potential of antineutrino detection has not been widely explored. That is our objective. (191)

The allusion to Hamlet places us at the borders of modernity: like the Shakespearean audience, we are about to find that both the earth and the sky are not what they appear. In this case, what is invisible is displaced from the voids of space and relocated below our feet, in the most material and indisputably real of places, the center of the earth.

The article draws on, and reenacts, the emergent relation between physics and astronomy; just as particle accelerators model the early universe, the study of terrestrial antineutrinos will support the study of those produced in space. The narrative of the experiment supports the narrative of a developing discipline. Just as antineutrino detectors are bound to succeed neutrino detectors, the study of weak interactions is bound to succeed the study of electromagnetic effects. These comparisons can be read as tropes for the management of anxiety through displacement and the creation of supporting objects: the swerve of a discipline's development is assimilated into a story of technical mastery; an invisible object is associated with a very local, reassuringly material structure. In a parodic reversal of the usual vectors of sublimation, what is unknown and threatening is displaced from the "out there" of space to the "down there" of the earth.

The experiment is a temporal trope: it will make a slow process (the production of argon atoms as a by-product of neutrino collisions) detectable by concentrating the materials for this process. Space substitutes for time; quantities of argon-generating substances, for years of antineutrino bombardment. What will be built is represented by what has been built. This narrative structure supports a scientific practice that forms falsifiable propositions about the extremely complex structures of the cosmological narrative. For that practice, past, present, and future states of the universe become reversible representations of one another.

S. A. Bludman's "Thermodynamics and the End of a Closed Universe," one of the most remarkable texts in the sample, demonstrates similar temporal complexity. Bludman's article composes a scenario for the origin and end of the universe from the most "conservative" of materials. The title announces the author's project: to theorize the end of the universe without recourse to particle physics, let alone such exotic theories as quantum gravity or black hole formation. Instead, Bludman will rely only on the classic foundational relations of thermodynamics. As a disciplinary intervention, the article argues that past conceptual frameworks are sufficient for the current work of cosmology. Bludman literally reinscribes the past of cosmology in its present: "Following Einstein, we assume that classical thermodynamics 'is the only physical theory of universal content concerning which I am convinced that within the framework of applicability of its basic concepts, it will never be overthrown.'"[21]

Such direct quotations are rare in scientific texts. As Greg Myers notes: "When a review uses quotations, it offers them the way that natural history narratives offer facts, as bits of the world that speak for themselves. But the purpose is seldom just to say what those words say; the mere fact of quotation indicates that the writer thinks these words are particularly apt or, more often, particularly and obviously vulnerable."[22] Myers is correct in seeing direct quotation as a complex figure. Bludman's quotation, representing what has already been said, asserts what will be the case in the future. This central argument also asserts that the future is known by looking at the past, that traditional disciplinary forms can resolve emerging problems. Bludman also effects a particularly complex identification between the speaker of the article and Einstein. Einstein's words are framed as a speech of a fictional "we" who follow Einstein, but their force is identified as his. Bludman has created a speaker of the article who is not "Bludman" but "we," not Einstein but someone who makes Einstein speak again.

"Thermodynamics and the End of a Closed Universe" examines a future that is final and therefore ultimately significant. That future is

---

21. Bludman, "Thermodynamics and the End of a Closed Universe," 319. Subsequent references to this article are given parenthetically in the text.
22. Myers, *Writing Biology*, 215.

inscribed in the relations among four parameters, terms of art that express basic relations among the quantity of matter in the universe, its motion, speed, direction, and shape. A new story of the future of the universe will be phrased as a new equation using the four parameters, which, as descriptions of the current state of the universe, function as direct quotations. They represent the past state of the universe as it is carried into the present. They suggest alternative possibilities for the future of the universe, scenarios that, finally, shape a theoretical argument about its origin. The past predicts the future; the future determines the past.

This beautifully complex structure also presents Bludman with some rhetorical difficulties, which we can appreciate by reading his first paragraph:

> Two most important conceptual (and ultimately practical) questions in cosmology are whether space is closed (positive curvature $k = +1$) or open (negative curvature $k = -1$ or flat $k = 0$) and whether the present expansion will continue monotonically or reverse itself some time in the future. In a universe with vanishing cosmological constant (Friedman universe), which may be the case in our Universe now, an open universe will expand monotonically and a closed universe will be ultimately reversing. Here, we begin by reviewing significant recent limits on the cosmological parameters λ_0, q_0, ω_0, H_0, assuming only global homogeneity and isotropy, but not λ_0 or flatness. We will show that, so far as present observations are concerned, the Universe may be open or closed, monotonically expanding or reversing. We then show (in agreement with Guth and Sher but not with Petrosian) that even if the present expansion were to reverse, the Universe cannot bounce in the future, but must end in a "final crunch." Our proof does not depend on particle physics, but follows directly from conventional thermodynamic stability requirements in any gravitational theory incorporating the newtonian limit and the equivalence and Birkhoff principles. Finally, we show that if space is closed and the Universe began with low entropy, then it had to begin, not with a big bang, but with a non-singular tepid little bang. (319)

The initial question in this article concerns the "shape" of the universe, although what is in question is more precisely the precondition for there being any shapes in the universe. In current cosmology, the destiny of the universe is directly entailed in its shape, which expresses the configuration of matter in the universe. Different quantities of matter react differently to gravitation and undergo different vicissitudes. Three scenarios were (and are) generally accepted as possibilities. If the universe is dense, then it is closed. It is visualized as the three-dimensional surface of a four-dimensional sphere. Space in such a universe is finite, and the universe will eventually contract in a "final crunch." If the universe is less dense, then it is hyperbolic, infinite, and indefinitely extended. It will continue to expand until it exhausts its fuel. At a certain critical value, the universe is flat; in this universe alone, Euclidean geometry accurately represents space. The flat universe will remain in balance, containing enough matter to expand relatively slowly but not enough to cause gravitational contraction. These three alternative states of the universe are expressed as ratios of curvature, or values of k, and as values of "omega," ω, the parameter expressing the density of the universe.

Cosmologists have strong investments in these configurations and their associated outcomes. It would be surprising, given how high, if remote, the stakes are in this game, if they did not. Such investments double the narrative force of any theory of the shape and density of the universe. On the one hand, we have a parameter like any other, expressed as a ratio that hovers near 1. On the other hand, that ratio is given the foreboding name "omega" and associated with various teleologies. We read for example, in Hut and White's article, about a density of visible matter "sufficient to close the Universe," as if there would be something wrong with a universe that failed to close. Similarly, Bludman speaks parenthetically of an "ultimately practical" implication of cosmology, as if there were something we could *do* about a universe that gaped open.

There is a deep separation, however, between our situation as readers and the ultimate time when any of these questions become practical; in that time, for readers of "Thermodynamics and the End of a Closed Universe," the future fans out as a series of mutually exclusive scenarios. Bludman begins by specifying the three canonic scenarios—open, closed, and flat—and then specifying the assumptions about cosmic structure that would support his reflections on them: an expanding but homogeneous universe in which conventional thermodynamics obtains. Within this space, Bludman uses four parameters to study the configuration of the universe: measures of vacuum density, deceleration, the density of matter in the universe, and the Hubble constant, a measure of the rate at which the universe expands. Calculating values of the

Hubble constant for current measurements of the other variables, Bludman recombines various configurations of space with various densities of matter and suggests an array of universes beyond the conventional three. Bludman considers the possibility that the universe may be closed but continue to expand, that it may expand independently of its shape, or that it may contract independently of its shape. Narrative openness and closure is differentiated and uncoupled from topographical openness and closure. The narrative paths in the story of the universe are multiplied; its story is complicated.

The array of possible scenarios that Bludman redundantly presents in a graph and in a series of equations (320) can be read as a series of family romances, reconfiguring a limited cast of characters: given a range of values and relations, how can we expand the possibilities of their arrangement? All of these parameters are deeply entailed in one another, so that we know the Hubble constant, for example, only through deceleration. All the parameters define and constrain one another like characters in a novel. As they are reconfigured, temporality becomes the most elastic of containers. Bludman uses $H_0 t_0$, the current rate of the universe's expansion, to delineate a domain of possible futures for the universe. This expression concentrates a temporal paradox: located in the present, it speaks about the universe as it was, because what we now see happened in the past, when the light of distant objects emerged. We see those objects only within a limited horizon that speaks of origins: our vision cannot exceed the distance that light could have traversed since the beginning of the universe.

"Thermodynamics and the End of a Closed Universe," then, creates multiple futures from multiple pasts, all seen as parameters operating in the present. These relations can also be reversed, so that multiple pasts can be created from multiple futures: "Thus, if the Universe is open or began with significant entropy ($\alpha > 1$), it started in a big bang and later expanded into the unstable de Sitter phase. If the Universe is closed and (as seems reasonable) began with low entropy, it started non-singularly, but already in the unstable de Sitter phase" (322). The present shape of the universe determines its future; that future determines its past. It is not surprising that English verb tenses do not carry these temporal relations very easily:

> Just because the energy density of empty space (cosmological constant) is observed to be small or zero at present, it must have been huge in the very early and very late Universes, when its

gravitational effects can be most important. In any particle theory in which symmetry is restored in the high-temperature phase, there must be a huge cosmological constant induced in the very early Universe and, if the expansion reverses, in the very late Universe. (321)

The very early and very late universes become equivalent to each other, so that both of them are covered in "must have been huge." And because the gravitational effects of high initial energy density are still with us—and, indeed, will determine the end of the universe—the hovering historical present of "can be most important" is a syntactic representation of the complex time that the text manages. What also wavers before us, and is expressed in the next sentence, is the text's consciousness of the constructed nature of the linear time on which it is arrayed. Although the beginning of the universe, the present, and the end of the universe are three distinct domains within cosmology, it is also the force of cosmological work to undermine the simplicity of such an articulation. In Bludman's article, time is simply a parameter, like density or deceleration or entropy. The universe is not a film that can be unrolled or reversed but is a series of dioramas, connected by multiple and intersecting pathways called scenarios. Within such a structure, it is strange to read of a cosmological constant being *induced:* although no conceivable agent is capacious enough to effect this participle, it is credited to "particle theory," so that cosmology posits itself—quite rightly—as the agent responsible for the future and the past. At the beginning of this section, I mentioned Bludman's choice of "conservative" working assumptions, including his abstention from particle theories closely associated with those he invokes here to "induce" a high cosmological constant. That "conservative" is always laudatory but sometimes ironic. Bludman uses audacious and complex narrative structures to advance a narrative argument, which could also be called "conservative":

Closed Friedman universes were once called oscillatory universes. We now appreciate that, because of the huge entropy generated in our Universe, far from oscillating, a closed universe can only go through one cycle of expansion or contraction. Whether closed or open, reversing or monotonically expanding, the severely irreversible phase transitions transpiring give the Universe a definite beginning, middle and end. (322)

Having opened up the cosmological narrative and introduced a number of variations on what had been common knowledge in his field, Bludman here associates his argument with the most conventional plot structure in narrative theory, a tripartite narrative in "natural" temporal order, moving from clear initiation through complication to final closure. This conservative structure leads in Bludman's final paragraph to an invocation of Einstein:

> Until the present expansion does or does not approach reversal, it will be practically impossible to distinguish between open big bang and closed tepid little bang universes. Until then, however, for those who prefer to maintain conventional gravitational and thermodynamic concepts, the tepid little bang enjoys the theoretical advantage of avoiding the initial singularity which would otherwise signal the incompleteness of Einstein's theory. (322)

The text withdraws from its dizzying opening of representations of the universe, asserting closure and the sufficiency of normal theory, Einstein's theory. Einstein's theory, like thermodynamics, is immune from the effects of time, since it "will never be overthrown." The incompleteness of Einstein's theory, like the universe's failure to close, becomes a problem we can solve.

"Thermodynamics and the End of a Closed Universe," then, couples narrative audacity, marked by radical freedom in the arrangement and multiplication of alternative temporalities, to a normalized temporality, used to tell a well-formed story. Cosmological narratives are seen as credible, not only if they are potentially falsifiable, but if they meet criteria of economy and theoretical consistency that are virtually aesthetic, or matters of personal choice. Such narratives are also invested with agency: at certain crucial points in the argument, it is the narrative which causes the universe to change, rather than vice versa.

Just as readers of novels make sense of their relation to the lifeworld, readers of cosmology must make sense of the text's narrative tensions and perturbations of agency. To unfold the temporality of the cosmological text, to render explicit the work of reading, requires analytic tools as sophisticated as those used to analyze fictional temporality. The temporal structures in Bludman's text are not at all contained in the Aristotelian framework of beginning and middle and end. The time of the text recalls Lacan's description of the return of the repressed: "How then should one explain the return of the repressed? As paradoxical as it may seem, there is only one way to do it—it doesn't come from the past, but from the future." Lacan goes on to borrow an image from cybernetics, of two beings whose temporal dimensions move in opposite dimensions. If one sends a message to the other, the message will be initially received at the moment when it vanishes. Lacan says:

> That is what we see as well. The symptom initially appears to us as a trace, which will only ever be a trace, one which will continue not to be understood until the analysis has got quite a long way, and until we have discovered its meaning. . . . What we see in the return of the repressed is the effaced signal of something which only takes on its value in the future, through its symbolic realization, its integration into the history of the subject. Literally, it will only ever be a thing which, at the given moment of its occurrence, *will have been*.[23]

Similarly, events like the initial inflationary growth or the final contraction of the universe, events at the borders of time and space, cannot be described in any coherent sense as "happening"; no context ties such an event to others, and no framework of time supports them all. Exactly that context and framework are in question in Bludman's text. We can only know such events by telling stories about them, stories necessarily organized as sequences of episodes so that they are transformed into things that "will have been," or in Bludman's terms, as future events that "must have been huge."

In raising such issues, I have already embarked on the second term in our analysis: the analysis of language in scientific texts.

Reading the Scientific Text: Language

Astronomers studying objects at the edges of galaxies noted that they moved in ways that could only be explained by large nearby masses exerting huge gravitational forces. But no such masses were visible on the electromagnetic spectrum: no light, no radio waves, no microwaves. The invisible matter surrounding galaxies was designated "dark matter," and astronomers began the work—still unfinished—of specifying its constituents and structures. Dark matter had two important functions in the narrative of the universe. Dark matter, uninfluenced by the vicissitudes of the very early universe, would have been available to "seed" the first objects and so suggested a possible solution to the puzzle of why matter had formed into objects, into galaxies and clusters, rather than simply distributing itself uniformly after the big bang. And

23. Lacan, *Seminar I*, 158–59.

dark matter, since it seems to constitute some 90 percent of the matter in the universe, raises the value of the omega constant to something near 1, closing the universe.

Although dark matter had taken on such a central narrative role, it was itself virtually unknown—nobody knew what it was, where it came from, or why it was dark. In terms of the normal procedures of astronomy, dark matter is in principle unknowable. Unlike extremely small or distant objects that emit light, unlike quasars and pulsars, which emit other forms of radiation, dark matter is not something that we don't happen to see; it is rather something that can never be seen at all and could only be known through weak interactions and particularly heroic experiments. (One article in this sample, that by Narayan, Blandford, and Nityananda, describes such an experiment, the use of enormous masses as a kind of gravitational lens to produce a doubled image of a quasar.) Cold dark matter is an object created by the language of cosmology.

Dark matter has, at this writing, still not been identified. Candidates include undetected accumulations of protons and neutrons, such as large planets or rocks; black holes, which might concentrate large masses of undetected matter; neutrinos in various flavors; and exotic particles, such as positrons or axions, which have not yet been identified anywhere. Dark matter is specified as either "hot" or "cold," depending on whether it moved quickly (hot matter) or slowly (cold matter) at the time of galaxy formation. Dark matter has many of the attributes of a conventional narrative character: it is an agent; it links episodes in a narrative; it gathers together traits that vary independently. Like the omega constant, cold dark matter has a double status. It is, on the one hand, simply another variety of matter. On the other hand, it is invested with pathos, mystery, and a strong disciplinary significance: it announces the end of astronomy as a science that "looks at" the heavens.

Dark matter, then, is both a central object of investigation and a story that displaces previous stories of the cosmology. In principle invisible, it can be assigned agency for the beginning and end of the universe. Cold dark matter is, in the narrative of cosmology, a character without traits, invested with tremendous agency. It is central to the structure of the universe because there is a lot of it, and because of its crucial role in the formation of objects. But the narrative of cold dark matter must exfoliate these critical actions while remaining agnostic about its qualities, and indeed its identity. The two articles from this sample that focus on dark matter are Hut and White's "Can a Neutrino-Dominated Universe Be Rejected?" and Blumenthal, Faber, Primack, and Rees's "Formation of Galaxies and Large-Scale Structure with Cold Dark Matter." In both cases, cold dark matter appears as the central agent in the cosmological story, even though it can only be identified by projecting a series of alternative candidates, situating them within competing scenarios, and judging the plausibility of the cosmological story that each generates.

One of cold dark matter's central functions is to organize within the text a displaced representation of the material practices and relations of science, of astronomy as a practice of "seeing," the practices, precisely, that cold dark matter calls into question. Cold dark matter is invested with elegiac pathos that floats free of any specific qualities: astronomical texts "see" cold dark matter, although cold dark matter establishes astronomy as blind; scientific texts ascribe their material practices to cold dark matter, representing it as a kind of ideal subjectivity, a displacement of the subjectivity elided from their own discourse. These texts work out a language for seeing what is in principle invisible and decouple agency from quality, assigning narrative power to a character that is not only unspecified but that is specified in contradictory ways.

At the opening of both the articles in our sample, the cosmological question to which cold dark matter is the answer is posed in nontechnical terms. The difficulties of determining the constitution of cold dark matter are conceded, and the candidates are reviewed. Hut and White then move to a comprehensive review of the implications of identifying various species of neutrinos as cold dark matter, searching for one whose mass and rate of decay are coherent with big-bang cosmology. Blumenthal and the other authors of "Formation of Galaxies and Large-Scale Structure" construct a series of alternative scenarios, or "pictures," of the formation of galaxies corresponding to the various candidates for cold dark matter and argue for the predominance of cold dark matter in the universe. This argument was widely accepted and is still current in cosmology.

Let us turn to the opening paragraphs of each text, beginning with Hut and White:

> The masses of large astronomical systems, such as groups and clusters of galaxies, can be determined from the requirement that gravitational forces be sufficient to induce the observed random motions of their constituent galaxies. This procedure is directly analogous to determining the mass of the Sun from

its distance from the Earth and from the orbital velocity of the Earth. Masses found in this way exceed by more than an order of magnitude the total mass of the stars in the visible parts of the galaxies. A similar discrepancy shows up when the motion of stars and gas in the outer parts of the disks of spiral galaxies is used to analyze the distribution of mass within them. Most of the mass seems to be located far from the centre, well outside the regions which contain most of the light. This difficulty has been dubbed the "missing mass problem" although, in fact, it is the light which seems to be missing—the mass is certainly there. It seems that at least 90% of the mass of the Universe is in some form which is dark and has so far remained undetected except by its gravitational effects.[24]

The authors bring cold dark matter before us by recapitulating its initial discovery as a "discrepancy" in the mass of galaxies, a discrepancy that creates a problem. Nothing positive is said about cold dark matter; instead, the authors refunction the problem to which it is a solution. Cold dark matter is not a "missing mass." It is, not a substance, but light that is nonexistent. Since light (and by analogy all electromagnetic radiation) makes matter deep in space apparent to us, the authors reassign the difficulty in perceiving cold dark matter from what is being studied to the perceiving subject—we cannot see it because, limited creatures that we are, we need light or something like it. Dark matter is understood, not as something which is not, but as an absence, and particularly as an absence in relation to *us;* the force of the article is to specify what it is an absence of.

Blumenthal and his co-authors use quite a different strategy. They begin:

> Why are there galaxies, and why do they have the sizes and shapes that we observe? Why are galaxies clustered hierarchically in clusters and superclusters, separated by enormous voids in which bright galaxies are almost absent? And what is the nature of the invisible mass, or dark matter, that we detect gravitationally roundabout galaxies and clusters but cannot see directly in any wavelength of electromagnetic radiation? Of the great mysteries of modern cosmology, these three may now be among the ripest for solution.
>
> Because there is evidence that the mass of dark matter in the Universe exceeds that of the visible matter by at least an order

---

24. Hut and White, "Can a Neutrino-Dominated Universe Be Rejected?" 637.

of magnitude, the third question may hold the key to the first two. We now consider the hypothesis that the dark matter is cold, that is, that its thermal velocity is cosmologically negligible in the early Universe.[25]

This text is relentlessly presentational and visual. We are given an initial spectacle: the visual array of galaxies, clusters and superclusters, designated not only by their arrangement but also by brightness. The stars are bright, the voids are dark, and some mysterious form of matter lurks around them both. The bright stars and defined voids collocate with the action of science: science solves mysteries, creates enlightenment. Science can even use dark matter to adumbrate the structure of the bright.

Cold dark matter is created, specified, and attains agency within the structures of language. The language of cosmology, knitting together the objects in the universe in a web of gravitational influences, hollows out the vacuity that cold dark matter must fill. The language of cosmology specifies that vacuity as missing matter or missing light, as mysterious shape or as ground for understanding why there are shapes at all. Although cold dark matter is itself invisible, it is defined discursively as the location where doubt is resolved. If we cannot see it "directly in any wavelength," we can use its existence as evidence for the largest structures of the universe. In both texts, although cold dark matter is itself unknown, it is a source of knowledge, capable of reorienting the discipline.

For Blumenthal et al., that reorientation is emancipatory: if matter is no longer necessarily associated with light, then light is uncoupled from matter, available as an investigative tool. But for Hut and White, cold dark matter presents an aesthetic problem, so that their text speaks eloquently about what counts as an error in the cosmological narrative and about how such narratives are understood as well formed or badly formed. Cold dark matter was essential to preserve the coherence of cosmology, but nearly all the candidates for cold dark matter, when identified and entrained in that narrative, violated the shape of the cosmological story as its outlines were then known. Cold dark matter had to be, but it was very hard to discern just what it could be:

> Although the amount of mass inferred from observations of galaxy clustering and of the outer parts of spiral galaxies is just

25. Blumenthal et al., "Formation of Galaxies and Large-Scale Structure," 517.

marginally consistent with the hidden matter being made of baryons, the observed element abundances are not consistent with a present baryon density sufficient to close the Universe and to ensure that its expansion will one day be arrested. However, inflationary models for the early Universe and general philosophical considerations suggest that the present total density should be extremely close to that required for closure, otherwise the fact that it does not differ from this value by many orders of magnitude would need to be ascribed to some improbable cosmic coincidence. Retention of a flat Universe and of standard cosmology requires that the dark matter cannot be baryonic; the only such candidates known to exist are the three types of neutrino (tau neutrinos, mu neutrinos, and beta neutrinos).[26]

The issue is urgent: there must be "enough" dark matter to close the universe. The narrative of cosmology becomes an agent in the cosmological story, as if a satisfying scientific text would not only achieve its own narrative closure but also close the universe. Hut and White specify satisfaction as a connection between the basic assumptions of contemporaneous cosmology and "general philosophical considerations." Those unspecified considerations might be named more properly as aesthetic constraints.

Hut and White are reasoning from the consensus within their discipline that the value of the omega constant is either 1 or some number very close to 1. This consensus is based, not only on observations, but also on extrapolations from the standard scenario for the very early universe, the inflationary scenario. Inflation describes a universe that grew extremely rapidly in a fraction of its first second and then slowed its expansion as matter was created. The inflationary scenario requires that the value of omega not be much smaller or greater than 1, or the universe would not have continued its expansion for 15 billion years. The inflationary scenario is a well-formed story, moving from an early inciting event through slow development; cold dark matter, a minor character at the beginning (like Uriah Heep?), looms large as the narrative develops. So far so good.

Hut and White's "general philosophical considerations," however, warrant their belief that if the density of the universe is close to that "required for closure," then it must be at least 1, since a value very close

26. Hut and White, "Can a Neutrino-Dominated Universe Be Rejected?" 637.

to 1 but not sufficient for closure would be coincidental—too close, as it were, for comfort. Their "improbable" does not seem to have technical force: there are reasons why omega should be close to 1, but not why it could not vary from 1 only slightly. It is a question, rather, of narrative improbability, the same aesthetic judgment that led the authors to observe that the range of possible candidates for cold dark matter was "embarrassingly large." Cold dark matter endangers the cosmological narrative, not only because it renders observations difficult, but also because it is a scandal, an error, a disturbance in the story. It is a character that refuses to remain stable, that forbids the stabilization of the cosmological scenario. To define or "characterize" cold dark matter is to preserve the consistency and order of the cosmological story; it is a labor of language.

We have seen something that could be called desire inhabiting the scientific text, combing a huge tank of chemicals for a single argon atom, searching the universe for sufficient matter to close it, seeking to preserve the consistency of Einstein's theory. Hut and White's article demonstrates one of the ways that, in accordance with Lacan's equation for the language of the university, desire is invested in a practice of scientific language and incites the writer to represent the natural world. What exists and is named as cold dark matter is indicated by multiple signifying chains—or, better, by their relations. Its coming to be elides the subject of discourse, the gazing astronomer, whose desire is nonetheless fixed on the signifying chain which promises to transform itself into knowledge, rather than on any of those objects it presents itself as seeking to know. I am not at all arguing here that Hut and White are "misled"; there is no evidence that their desire for narrative coherence generates representations of the universe that are more or less accurate reflections than representations sponsored by a different narrative logic. (How could such evidence be gathered? What observer could be located outside language to make such a judgment?)

Desire is an attribute of subjects, not of texts or lines of argument, so that one way to refute a position is to say that it is based on "wishful thinking." But as Lacan's equation for the discourse of the university suggests, scientific texts hold together, in fact compress, the desiring subject, the chain of signifiers ordering his or her thought, and discourse as an object of desire.

The text that demonstrates wishful thinking is also an instance of the wish to think. In chapter 1, I described the Lacanian theory of desire as a narrative, in which the distance of the desiring subject from the object in which he or she is constituted incites a swerve toward the object of desire, a motion which never culminates in triumphant arrival. Desire has to do with the unconscious, with what is radically beyond direct knowledge, manifesting itself instead in the perturbations of daily activity, in unguarded and accidental performances, and in dreams. In scientific writing, the object of desire is not nature or the universe but scientific discourse itself. For Lacan, such a perverse desire is scandalous, especially compared with the more erotically saturated discourses of the hysteric or the analyst. But we need not share his squeamishness. Rather, we read here desire effecting a delayed and displaced construction of the self, so that the Other is designated as the source of the subject's identity and significance. It calls, interpellates, the subject into being. It was Lacan's signal contribution to show that such a self, so constructed, is the only one available to us.

In such a reading, cold dark matter stands in a place analogous to that of the unconscious. It is not only unseen but unseeable; its organization and constitution are obscure. It is huge; it surrounds known and visible structures. Just as the discovery of the unconscious marked an epoch in the understanding of the psyche, the discovery of cold dark matter transforms astronomical practice. Like the unconscious, cold dark matter appears as a limit to knowledge but also as a ground of explanation; the unconscious emerges simultaneously with the ego and remains as a reservoir of both libido and death instinct; cold dark matter seeds the galaxies and closes the universe. It therefore represents within the discourse of cosmology agencies of the subject that cannot be directly narrated.

If, as rhetoricians of science or feminist critics of scientific agency, we understand the subject of science as irrevocably divided from its objects, we find in such analogies that our understanding has been anticipated and inscribed in the scientific text. We arrive at it after the fact, after the feast, and can read in it an injunction to complementary self-consciousness about the presuppositions of agency in our own work. The material practices of language emerge as the ground of all disciplinary investigations, whether rhetorical or scientific. It is within the strange class of objects that are formed by language that all other objects are formed.

My last reading from the sample investigates this paradox. In Hogan and Rees's "Gravitational Interactions of Cosmic Strings," strings, structural "defects" within vacuum, are constructed as objects of investigation by predicating a series of their traits: size, density, and topography.[27] Strings, like cold dark matter, are invested with narrative agency. We read that the network of strings "strives to reduce its length by ironing out small scale wrinkles at close to the speed of light and allowing strings, when they cross, to intercommute or change partners."[28]

The central argument of this text turns on the levels of energy at which string loops could condense matter, a condensation that would be detectable as gravitational radiation. Hogan and Rees also discuss "relic" strings: strings formed during the very earliest stages of the universe and assumed to be detectable in some form today:

> Gravitational waves redshift in exactly the same way as electromagnetic ones, so loops which formed and decayed during the radiation-dominated era produce a background with [certain characteristics]. This flat specimen extends down to waves emitted by loops which formed near the time of the phase transition itself, at temperature $\simeq \varepsilon^{1/2} m_p$. . . . Therefore, the waves in this scenario are relics of the early stages of the expansion, emitted by loops which formed shortly after nucleosynthesis. (110)

It is difficult to keep alive our sense of how *constructed* the time of this passage is. It concerns structures of the universe that nobody has identified, objects existing in and characterizing a vacuum that are impossible to visualize or to conceptualize in any ordinary way. Some of these structures, distinguished from others by their frequency of gravitational radiation, function as signs of the initial differentiation of matter in the universe and therefore as possible central agents in the formation of all the objects that we do see. Such relic strings may still exist, or they may have disintegrated long ago. What is being discerned—or, more properly, proposed as an object for discernment—is not the string but a radiation emitted by it, a radiation so subtle that it will require considerable development in pulsar technology to measure it reliably. The radiation of the primordial relic string presents the temporal border of the universe as a palpable fact; the radiation continues, independently of the

27. This structure is similar to that specified by Gross in his discussion of the constitution of species in evolutionary biology, *The Rhetoric of Science*, 32–53.

28. Hogan and Rees, "Gravitational Interactions of Cosmic Strings," 109. Subsequent references to this article are given parenthetically in the text.

object that produced it. Just as this radiation, if detected, would bring the ultimate *then* of nucleosynthesis directly before us, it establishes the singularity of that event, marking it and signing it as the discrete origin. The cosmic narrative is interrupted—then is now—and, simultaneously, its teleology is guaranteed. Temporality is not, for this discourse, a groundwork holding objects in a well-formed series. It is rather a predicate of objects.

Such relics are very similar, in their narrative status, to those Darwin studied, and like Darwin's fossils and geological strata, they strain the borders of available narrative temporality. Hogan and Rees display wavering verb tenses that recall Bludman's: "It is possible that loops would establish 'seeds' of some kind (meaning astrophysical sources of energy) even if ε were too small to have a direct influence on galaxy clustering. The energy sources could then be used to generate clustering by some secondary process" (113). Here, an event in the deep past of the universe is given future force with "would" and "could then be used," tenses which, although they are marked as past, can also have future force. Darwin faced similar rhetorical difficulties. Consider this passage from *The Origin of Species:*

> It may metaphorically be said that natural selection is daily and hourly scrutinising, throughout the world, the slightest variations; rejecting those that are bad, preserving and adding up all that are good; silently and insensibly working, *whenever and wherever opportunity offers,* at the improvement of each organic being in relation to its organic and inorganic conditions of life. We see nothing of these slow changes in progress, until the hand of time has marked the lapse of ages, and then so imperfect is our view into long-past geological ages, that we see only that the forms of life are now different from what they formerly were.[29]

There is a well-developed literature in the rhetoric of science analyzing Darwin's narratives.[30] I might note here that Victorian fiction taught readers to imagine precisely the accumulated effects of slight variations, repeated over time, and that, however imperfect the view of such readers,

29. Charles Darwin, *The Origin of Species,* ed. Philip Appleman (New York: Norton, 1979), 53. A similar passage can be found on p. 125.

30. See, for example, Landau, *Narratives of Human Evolution;* Beer, *Darwin's Plots;* and John A. Campbell, "The Polemical Mr. Darwin," *Quarterly Journal of Speech* 61 (1975): 375–90.

they had considerable practice conjecturing about the influences of fore-bears long dead upon the living. Victorian readers had learned to trust precisely the sensibility that scrutinizes and judges slight variations, the unwavering eye of the omniscient narrator. Darwin shared with our cos-mologists the problem of representing what seemed to be an intractable temporality. For him, that time was a continuous open terrain where causality operated, much larger than the reaches of history; for cos-mology, it is a discontinuous time, uncertain in many of its elements, a time that is a quality of objects and relations rather than the precondi-tion for their formation. Both Darwin and our authors use specific ob-jects, made present in the text, as signifiers to resolve their problem of narration. Such objects speak for nature. Gravitational lenses and cosmic strings, objects which may or may not exist, which may or may not have the qualities ascribed to them in alternative scenarios, become rhetori-cally present and serve as loci for arguments. Darwin described his own signifying objects in loving detail—the projecting point in the folds of the ear, structures of the embryo, Lyell's cliffs. Like cold dark matter, cosmic strings in the vacuum, and the proposed antineutrino collector within cosmological texts, these objects are taken up within the discur-sive space of *The Origin of Species* and redeemed from their unremarked habitation in daily life. They are specified, rendered present by the text, and used as evidence of an invisible and disputed past.

Latent within these passages from Darwin is a second strategy for nor-malizing anomalous times. Scientific texts reflect a practice: the scientist represents a discourse community that is assumed to understand, collec-tively, the language it deploys, with all its dislocated times and translated places. Science, as a discursive formation, guarantees the unorthodox temporalities of its texts.

Science as a Discursive Formation

In the cosmological texts in this sample, a disciplinary narrative and a cosmological narrative mutually support one another: we can know about what happened deep in the past because science has developed tremendously in the last twenty years. We will know more soon (includ-ing, perhaps, the truth of the present text) because science is developing apace. Darwin used the same narrative vectors, albeit in a more melan-choly key: just as natural selection and geological change worked un-abated, silently and slowly, to differentiate species, so science patiently collects myriad examples and illustrations, finally producing the striking and irrefutable theory. Such disciplinary narratives have been well studied by Gilbert and Mulkay and given the name "Truth Will Out Device."[31] Gilbert and Mulkay claim that scientists' work is haunted by the ideology of scientific progress, which holds that any proposition in science is likely to be found wrong and replaced by a better one. All the daily work of science is born in error and subject to replacement. The Truth Will Out Device normalizes this vexing situation: even if a scientist is wrong, even if his work is replaced, it is all for the best, because the new proposition will be closer to the truth than the old.

The Truth Will Out Device, along with other rhetorical figures of scientific progress, such as "the shoulders of giants," constitutes the discipline itself as a fictional knowing subject, repository and guarantee of arguments, capable of transcending and comprehending the temporal dislocations of the discourse.[32] Such a fictional subject defends the discourse against the inevitable shocks of a practice that proceeds through negation and falsification.[33]

Shock and dislocation are well documented in the anthropology of science. Lynch noted that, while the "methods" section of papers in neurobiology portray experimental procedures as well ordered and nicely articulated sequences, "the fact of the achievement of a displayed-reported correspondence occurred as a locally managed social production."[34] Experiments are not sequential or uninterrupted; projects are more often abandoned than closed; repeated actions are subject to local variations, failures, and improvisations. Latour and Woolgar analyzed how such problems are interpreted or managed in informal conversations which construct and dismantle facts, "microprocessing" them as a series of claims about the reliability of researchers, institutions, and procedures.[35] No anthropological study of scientific practice is complete without the scene of a frustrated and hostile technician who curses and manhandles the experimental apparatus (usually an animal), trying in vain to make it come out right.[36] Scientific work is inhabited by error and the shock of its discovery, which are not contained within the mo-

31. Gilbert and Mulkay, *Opening Pandora's Box*, 90–112.
32. For the "shoulders of giants," see Stephen J. Gould, *Hen's Teeth and Horse's Toes* (New York: Norton, 1983), chap. 1.
33. Karl Popper, *The Logic of Scientific Discovery* (New York: Harper and Row, 1934; reprint, 1968).
34. Lynch, *Art and Artifact*, 58.
35. Latour and Woolgar, *Laboratory Life*, 158.
36. See Lynch, *Art and Artifact*, 70–79; Latour and Woolgar, *Laboratory Life*, 150.

ment of the experiment. Scientific fact rapidly becomes error: landmarks in the history of science evolve into records of mistakes. Thus, Fleck speaks of Wassermann's identification of blood serum:

> His basic assumptions were untenable, and his initial experiments irreproducible, yet both were of enormous heuristic value. This is the case with all really valuable experiments. They are all of them uncertain, incomplete, and unique. And when experiments become certain, precise, and reproducible at any time, they are no longer necessary for research purposes but function only for demonstration or *ad hoc* determinations.[37]

Over against the individual scientist's practice, a practice of error and uncertainty, scientific discourse posits a potentially omniscient subject only available in the future. Whenever an error in the body of scientific knowledge is identified, the future intervenes in the present. Omniscience is not imputed to individual contemporary scientists. On the contrary, one of the consistent figures in scientific writing is the unease that accompanies any overt reference to an observer. Rather, the impossible, future, omniscient subject motivates the discipline's story of its own forward motion. Scientists can tell that story ebulliently—"This is a golden age. We have the basic framework. We just need to fill in the gaps."—or soberly—"The go-go junk bond days of cosmology are over."[38] In either case, the discipline is constituted as a knowing subject, moving toward greater knowledge.

In popularization, the formal constraint against reference to an observing subject conflicts with the imputed need of a lay audience for personal involvement. The future subject who knows becomes embarrassingly present in the text. For example, in Stephen Hawking's treatment of the expanding universe in *A Brief History of Time:*

> There is a fundamental paradox in the search for such a complete unified theory. The ideas about scientific theories outlined above assume we are rational beings who are free to observe the universe as we want and to draw logical deductions from what we see. . . . Yet if there really is a complete unified theory, it would also presumably determine our actions. And so

---

37. Fleck, *Genesis and Development of a Scientific Fact*, 85.

38. Quotations are from David Schramm and Michael Turner, respectively, in "Universal Truths," *Scientific American* 263, no. 4 (Oct. 1990): 111, 117.

the theory itself would determine the outcome of our search for it! [39]

Later, Hawking explicitly dramatizes the disjunction between the limited, individual observer and a perfected future observation. At the very end of his book, Hawking laments the current disjunction of philosophy from physics and concludes hopefully:

> However, if we do discover a complete theory, it should in time be understandable in broad principle by everyone, not just a few scientists. Then we shall all, philosophers, scientists, and just ordinary people, be able to take part in the discussion of the question of why it is that we and the universe exist. If we find the answer to that, it would be the ultimate triumph of human reason—for then we would know the mind of God. [40]

In this projected future for scientific communication, the differentiation of the discourses dissolves, modernity unravels, and everyone speaks a common language. Just as the cosmological story unrolls time backward, cosmological talk simplifies and broadens itself, figuring its own transparency as divine. The observer extends metaphorically outside time, so that, in Hawking's account, to know the full range of temporality is to know "why" observers and objects exist, to take up the position traditionally ascribed to God. We have moved from Darwin's omniscient narrator of details to a sublime, temporally dislocated spectator.

We can see this kind of language as a long-overdue turn of scientific self-reflection back to ultimate issues, as Stephen Toulmin does in *The Return to Cosmology: Postmodern Science and the Theology of Nature*, which argues for a reunification of natural science and natural theology. [41] In Toulmin's less popular text, the future subject is less catholic than Hawking's "we all." Toulmin imagines scientists, philosophers, and theologians coming together, but there will be no ventures into the vernacular. There is something very powerful, under conditions of differentiation and fragmentation of knowledge, in even this limited image of philosophers and scientists conferring about the fascinating and pro-

---

39. Stephen Hawking, *A Brief History of Time: From the Big Bang to Black Holes* (New York: Bantam, 1988), 12.

40. Hawking, *A Brief History of Time*, 175.

41. Stephen Toulmin, *The Return to Cosmology: Postmodern Science and the Theology of Nature* (Berkeley and Los Angeles: University of California Press, 1982), 254.

vocative materials of cosmology. Somehow, we hope, they will wring meaning from science, meaning that we can use. This hope is not idle: it would be good if scientists and philosophers—and rhetoricians and "just ordinary people"—conducted sustained discussions. The difficulty of staging or locating that talk is not simply an invidious social implication of academic specialization but an effect, as we shall see chapter 4, of the erosion of the public sphere.

We could respond to this situation more modestly and more secularly, following Habermas, who holds that modernity is an "incomplete project."[42] Invocations of the mind of God and calls for a natural theology are evidences of that incompleteness, as are disruptions of the limited and differentiated rationality of science by contradictory and fragmentary invocations of "feeling" or undifferentiated "thought." Habermas might see here a program for an impossible reenchantment of the world; in any case, such invocations elide the deep feeling and careful thought that inform cosmological discourses. A call for the subsumption of scientific discourse into a renovated theology evades the central project of modernity: to develop the autonomy of differentiated discourse forms, elaborate their specialized content, and then place that content at the service of a secular lifeworld. As Habermas admits:

> The 20th century has shattered this optimism [the Enlightenment belief that knowledge would promote progress, justice, and happiness]. The differentiation of science, morality and art has come to mean the autonomy of the segments treated by the specialist and their separation from the hermeneutics of everyday communication. This splitting off is the problem that has given rise to efforts to "negate" the culture of expertise. But the problem won't go away: should we try to hold on to the *intentions* of the Enlightenment, feeble as they may be, or should we declare the entire project of modernity a lost cause?[43]

These issues are intractable; they are not to be resolved by taking a poll (modernity: yes or no?), as if we could choose to become either happily postmodern or permanently modern. In the face of intractable problems, rhetoric proposes a series of partial solutions, deployments of such topics as the better and the worse, the prudent and the reckless—prosaic tactics for containing the sublime.

42. Jürgen Habermas, "Modernity—an Incomplete Project," in *The Anti-aesthetic: Essays in Postmodern Culture,* ed. Hal Foster (Seattle: Bay Press, 1983).
43. Habermas, "Modernity," 9.

The omniscient future subject of cosmology, perhaps, should be read as the effect, rather than the cause, of its temporal location, for it is precisely the dislocation, difference, and discontinuity of time that scandalize cosmological discourse. For that disease, traditional humanism proposes a remedy: continuity, the affirmation of history, the denial of historical difference. Against *that* disease, rhetoric proposes its own remedy: critique, analysis, a labor of reading to match the labor of writing.

Toward a Critical Rhetoric of Science

If neither Hawking's dream nor Toulmin's aspiration materializes and disciplinary discourses do not resolve into mutual intelligibility, we may have to learn how to read them. A critical rhetoric of science could attend especially to intersubjectivity as it is discussed by Habermas. Ever since writing *Knowledge and Human Interests*, Habermas has located the central dilemma of the physical sciences in their contradictory self-understanding. Because the specific rationality of scientific discourse is syllogistic, it is "in principle monologic," because "it is possible to think in syllogisms, but not to construct a dialogue in them."[44] Monologism is a structure of discourse, not a disposition of writers, who are generally acutely aware of their readers. Still less is monologism a quality of scientific practice, which requires the dialogic microprocessing of facts. The scientific text seems to give only one speaker voice; it elides the babble of voices that support it. Its rationality is marked by temporal dislocation: although every statement about nature is subject to refutation, it is in principle possible to describe nature correctly. Both the refutation of false statements and the production of truer ones depend on dialogue: they take place in a community of investigators, through organized and sustained public debate constrained by evidence.[45] Scientific discourse does not know its own intersubjectivity. Its monologic, syllogistic, arguments, however, are only intelligible in a dialogic context. There, behind its back, the text is refuted or confirmed, and its validation is imputed to a future knowing subject. That subject is a metaphorical parking place for the contradiction between scientific dis-

44. Habermas, *Knowledge and Human Interests*, 137.
45. For the early history of such debates, see Shapin and Schaffer, *Leviathan and the Air-Pump;* and Dear, *The Literary Structure of Scientific Argument.*

course's dialogic structure and its monologic self-understanding. No scientist thinks that such a subject will exist; the unease with which scientific discourse treats material subjects shows that it does not operate under a myth of a superman. Rather, the future subject who knows represents the completed and perfected discipline. That future knowing subject gestures toward what cannot be acknowledged: science is a practice undertaken among subjects, dialogically. Science's self-understanding as monologic is both correct (scientific texts are necessarily monologic and syllogistic) and erroneous (the body of scientific discourse is not monologic). Since reasoning never appears outside discourse, and since all scientific discourses present themselves as rational, both the "correct" understanding of scientific reasoning as monologic and the "erroneous" assumption that scientific discourse is monologic refer to exactly the same body of texts. The contradictory self-understanding of science is not a mistake, in the sense of a bad idea that can be corrected. It is embedded in the nature of scientific discourse, which performs intersubjectivity as individual agonism. This contradiction cannot be resolved but can only be contained, and that by modernity's most powerful normalizing devices—an image of the subject, a narrative of history.

Rhetoric does not debunk this contradiction. Rhetoric can claim no direct access to truth, over against the self-delusion of science, without contradicting its own commitment to the probable, the partial, the contextual. The rhetorician continues to overhear, reporting back in another voice a discontinuous overheard conversation in which participants unaccountably understand themselves as speaking alone. Our report becomes, not another voice in that conversation, but a supplement or translation of it.

Rhetorical critique is not the only conversation supplementary to science. Social movements have sought to redirect the disposition of scientific research and resources, to change the relation between producers and consumers of science, to respond to the centrality of scientific discourse. Such groups and movements as Engineers for Social Responsibility, Science for the People, and, most recently, ACT-UP, have raised issues about the deployment of scientific resources and the control of scientific work.

But since some of the essential work of science goes on at the level of the sentence, around questions like the choice of verb tense, we also need an approach to scientific practice tuned to those frequencies. We need a critical practice that explains how science creates its objects, rather than arguing for their redeployment. The central models for such a critical theory are the analysis of instrumental reason associated with the Frankfurt School, particularly Max Horkheimer and Theodor Adorno in *The Dialectic of Enlightenment,* and the feminist critique of scientific practice in works such as Evelyn Fox Keller's *Reflections on Gender and Science,* Sandra Harding's *The Science Question in Feminism,* Kathleen Woodward's *The Myths of Information: Technology and Post-industrial Culture,* and Donna Haraway's *Simians, Cyborgs, and Women: The Reinvention of Nature.*[46]

Horkheimer and Adorno do not argue for a reenchantment of the world but find in the scientific practices sponsored by the Enlightenment a reduction to the general categories of instrumental abstraction and the corresponding neglect of reflective and critical forms of thought in favor of calculation and the search for advantage. On this level, Horkheimer and Adorno's position is not so much a "critique of science" as a critique of a positivist overvaluation and exclusive reliance on science. Although they separated themselves from the traditional Marxist hagiography of science, Horkheimer and Adorno were not antiscientific.[47]

Horkheimer and Adorno also took issue with science as a practice of representation. They compared science to magic, since both substitute groups for individuals (sacrificial animals for the god) and both try to control nature. Scientific discourse, however, abandons representation: whereas in magic, one material object substitutes for another, in science all objects are equally subordinated to the empirical gaze; each can potentially be substituted for any other as an object of study. Whereas magic demonstrates its power in an attempt to change nature, science

46. Keller, *Reflections on Gender and Science;* Sandra Harding, *The Science Question in Feminism* (Ithaca: Cornell University Press, 1988); Kathleen Woodward, ed., *The Myths of Information: Technology and Post-industrial Culture* (London: Routledge and Kegan Paul, 1980); Haraway, *Simians, Cyborgs, and Women.* See also Helen Longino, *Science as Social Knowledge* (Princeton: Princeton University Press, 1990); Schliebinger, *Nature's Body;* and the special issue of *Configurations* on intersections between cultural, gender, and science studies (vol. 2, no. 1, winter 1994).

47. See, for example, Max Horkheimer, "Notes on Science and the Crisis," in *Critical Theory: Selected Essays* (New York: Seabury, 1972), 3–10; and T. W. Adorno, "Constellation in Science," in *Negative Dialectics,* trans. E. B. Ashton (New York: Seabury Press, 1973), 164–65.

demonstrates its power in reproducing nature. Our readings in cosmology have shown powerful tendencies to normalize divergent narratives, to elide the particularity of both scientific work and its objects.

But what is problematic in Horkheimer and Adorno is their understanding of scientific work as contagion or contamination, as if the scientist, operating *as* scientist, was himself "automated" by the mental
processes he deployed. In *The Dialectic of Enlightenment,* the subject of
science, known as the "scientific mind," is reduced by its own project of
dominating nature to an "eternally same *I think.*"[48] "Science" has been
reduced to a unitary activity, as if scientists could use only scientific representations in thinking about the world, or as if all scientific reflections
would necessarily degenerate into instrumental deployments of means
and ends.

Critical theory, here, has become entangled in scientific discourse's
self-understanding as monologic and unitary. A dialogic, rhetorically sophisticated response to the specificity of scientific practices would work
from other structures within the texts, recognizing them as complex,
resistant, and reluctantly self-conscious.

Feminism, the movement of thought most profoundly committed to
difference, has come closest to fulfilling that aim. In considering feminist analyses and critiques of scientific discourse, I will focus on the
deeply interesting work of Donna Haraway, concentrating on two chapters in *Simians, Cyborgs, and Women:* "The Contest for Primate Nature:
Daughters of Man-the-Hunter in the Field, 1960–80," originally published in 1983, and "Situated Knowledges: The Science Question in
Feminism and the Privilege of Partial Perspective," originally published
in *Feminist Studies* (1988) as a response to Sandra Harding's *The Science
Question in Feminism.* The first of Haraway's essays, "The Contest for
Primate Nature," concerns a group of female anthropologists who studied infanticide among langurs, a species of social primates. Haraway's is
a normal social constructivist account of scientific controversy.[49] The

48. Horkheimer and Adorno, *Dialectic of Enlightenment,* 26.
49. See Harry Collins and Trevor Pinch, *Frames of Meaning: The Social Construction of Extraordinary Science* (London: Routledge and Kegan Paul, 1982); Steven
Shapin, "The Politics of Observation: Cerebral Anatomy and Social Interests in the
Edinburgh Phrenology Disputes," in *On the Margins of Science: The Social Construction of Rejected Knowledge,* Sociological Review Monograph 27, ed. Roy Wallis
(Keele: University of Keele, 1979), 139–78; and Bazerman, *Writing Biology,*
101–40.

object of controversy is shown to have been constructed by the terms of the controversy, which is propositionally embedded in a narrative of disciplinary evolution and rivalry. Finally, the evolution of the discipline is related, very loosely, to a broader social and historical context. In the case of Haraway's data, the controversy concerns the interpretation of langur infanticide. Successive generations of anthropologists saw it, first, as a peripheral event and then, in series, as a "rational" strategy for maximizing a male's reproductive chances, as an equally "rational" strategy for female reproductive success, and, finally, as an artifact of the artificial stress of observation. These interpretations might be correlated with the politics of, respectively, first-wave feminism (critique of irrational patriarchy), early radical feminism (critique of patriarchal domination), liberal feminism (integrating women in the market economy), and a poststructuralist, critically informed feminism (embrace of situated knowledge, rejection of totality).

Haraway accounts for the evolution of her discipline from its early interest in man the hunter, based on studies of male baboons and their dominance struggles, to its current interest in broad social groupings, based on female primatologists' work with langurs, obligate generalist primates, distinguished by varied female activity and decision making. Here Haraway's story differs from the usual social constructivist account of scientific controversy. It is not agonistic, and it has no winner. Haraway describes the line of research she is tracing as a "revolt of the daughters" against primatologist Sherwood Washburn, but it is a revolt without battles, effected through abandonment rather than confrontation. Further, Haraway's account inverts the usual constructivist relation to propositional truth. Although constructivists normally remain methodologically indifferent to the positions they are describing, their narrative arc is necessarily triumphant, since the best side wins. We can assume that Shapin believes that there is such a thing as a vacuum, and even that Feyerabend thinks that the earth revolves around the sun.[50] But Haraway's account does not concede even a temporary victory of scientific reason. We leave her analysis with no firm ideas about langur infanticide. As Haraway puts it, "I cannot tell a story about who is weaving the best langur tales, though I have my favorites." Rather, the com-

---

50. Paul Feyerabend, *Realism, Rationalism and the Scientific Method: Philosophical Papers* (Cambridge: Cambridge University Press, 1981), 1:195–201.

peting stories are analyzed as myths: all of the langur stories can be translated into "public scientific meanings." Because these stories are "crucial to tales about human nature and human possibility," our choice of story is crucial.[51]

This is precisely the issue that Haraway confronts in "Situated Knowledges." "Situated Knowledges" takes up the problem of objectivity, specifically the desire to locate feminist and scientific knowledges on some ground more secure than belief and preference. The essay explores the consequences of successful social constructivist readings of science, including Haraway's own exemplary work.[52] It asks how antifoundationalism can avoid relativism and how political investments can be justified without a repressively totalized theory of rationality. If all of the objects of science are constructed, then what distinguishes cosmological from creationist constructions? Why not construct a Rapture of the just? How could we argue with a theorist who admitted that gender and racial differences in intelligence were constructed but claimed that they were politically useful.

Haraway confronts this issue by advocating a limited standpoint theory, in which all forms of subjectivity are seen as potentially revelatory of a "real" of nature and society to which no speaker has privileged access.

> I am arguing for politics and epistemologies of location, positioning, and situating, where partiality and not universality is the condition of being heard to make rational knowledge claims. These are claims on people's lives; the view from a body, always a complex, contradictory, structuring and structured body, versus the view from above, from nowhere, from simplicity. Only the god-trick [the claim of unmediated and disinterested vision] is forbidden. Here is a criterion for deciding the science question in militarism, that dream science/technology of perfect language, perfect communication, final order.[53]

There is much to admire in this passage: its confrontation of the difficulty of justifying political choice, its recognition that all knowledge is socially situated, and its attempt to find on that vexed terrain points

51. Haraway, *Simians, Cyborgs, and Women*, 105, 82.
52. See, for example, her "Teddy Bear Patriarchy: Taxidermy in the Garden of Eden, New York City, 1908–36," *Social Text* 11 (1984–85): 20–64; and *Primate Visions: Gender, Race, and Nature in the World of Modern Science* (New York: Routledge, 1989).
53. Haraway, *Simians, Cyborgs, and Women*, 195.

of reference that will not be totalizing or universal—the body, rationality, the rhetorical situation of "being heard." But how can this feminism, which celebrates partial forms of subjectivity, assert a theory of knowledge that corresponds to traditional subject-centered epistemologies? Here, myth—the self-interested representation of nature—has battled with enlightenment, won, and been declared reason. However often "Situated Knowledges" refers to the socially constructed quality of subjectivity, the subject is still the location of knowledge. Partiality and construction are two heavy mortgages that the subject pays off—but back in the "go-go junk bond" eighties, such debts may not have seemed unmanageable. There are many standpoints, but they do not contradict each other: the dialogue of the subject is with nature, which is reenchanted, capable of speech: "Perhaps our hopes for accountability, for politics, for ecofeminism, turn on revisioning the world as coding trickster with whom we must learn to converse."[54] We have returned to Bacon, to the scientist's interrogation of nature, now transmuted into a much politer conversation and entertainingly remythologized.

Haraway's terms of value—"rational," "the body"—are not accidental. These are the central terms of insurgent feminism. But there is no way for a constructed body to distinguish its interiority from the colonizing messages of advertising and ideology. And within the parameters of limited standpoint theory, nothing distinguishes rational arguments from irrational ones: fundamentalist Baptists arguing for the Rapture do not conveniently announce their irrationality by failing to distribute their middle terms. In the "Cyborg Manifesto," Haraway remarks acidly and appropriately that teaching children creationism "should be fought as a form of child abuse." Spoken by a true daughter of the Enlightenment. But without a formal notion of rationality, such positions are reduced to maneuvers of choice, as in "cyborg politics insist on noise"—even though "choice grounds a liberal politics and epistemology that imagines the reproduction of individuals before the wider replications of 'texts.'"[55] What constrains the speaker, textual or personal, cyborg or human, to be accountable to rationality?

We have at this point recapitulated the central argument of Habermas's *Theory of Communicative Action*. There is no authority outside

54. Haraway, *Simians, Cyborgs, and Women*, 201.
55. Donna Haraway, "A Cyborg Manifesto: Science, Technology, and Socialist-Feminism in the Late Twentieth Century," in *Simians, Cyborgs, and Women*, 152, 176.

discourse, and particularly no authority within subjects, which can enforce a preference for rationality, but there is also no discourse that does not depend, however counterfactually, on a preference for reason rather than force or whim. A standpoint theory, however astutely postmodern, which sees discourse as essentially monologic, cannot generate such a constraint and therefore cannot invoke without contradiction a preference for rationality. However, within the plural discursive structures of Haraway's political terrain, there is implicit a recognition that social stories are formed discursively and that such discourses must be tested, not only by their mythic power, but also by their accountability to norms of rational discourse: access of all speakers to all discursive roles, openness of the discourse to any relevant proposition, accountability to evidence rather than custom and authority. Such norms are not totalized. They are, sadly for a theorist of the postmodern, entirely universal, since they are formal constraints of discourse, not propositions. They are recognized within the analytic structures of Haraway's argument; her analysis of the relation of science and feminism would have been less contradictory if she had acknowledged them.

We can understand scientific discourse rhetorically as an intersubjective practice of differentiated rationality, as work with language, including work with objects situated in texts and with texts that create them. This work is not at all individual but demands, normally, a group of writers who have learned to collaborate, to join their individual disciplinary strengths, and to formulate arguments that will be seen as cooperative and informative within highly specialized discursive situations. We have seen, in the analysis of cosmology articles, that such rhetorical work requires complex figurative language—figures of temporality, of agency, of narrative—a figurative language that represents and projects a broader social practice in which the conversation among scientists is orchestrated through, and punctuated by, heroic labors of experiment.

Such writing and such work do not come naturally. They are situated in the social space of the academy; scientists are taught to produce them. Since rhetoric is traditionally a pedagogical as well as an analytic discipline, and since one of the crucial sites for instructing scientists in the norms of scientific discourse is technical writing, our investigation of these dynamics, and of the vicissitudes of rationality, can be grounded in a consideration of how scientific discourse is taught and how teachers of scientific and technical writing understand their work.

CHAPTER THREE　　　　•　　•　　　•　　　•

Teaching Technical Writing

　　　•　　•　　　•　　•　　B elow and around prestige forms of scientific writing, like articles in *Nature,* are a range of discursive practices, mundane and undervalued, which inscribe, record, and make available to production the natural world. People spend hours and hours writing and reading these texts: our best information suggests that entry-level technicians spend about eight hours a week writing and will spend more time as they are promoted.[1]

Such work demands the support of an educational practice. Hence the growth of technical writing. In 1969, some 25,000 technical writing textbooks were sold in the United States; by 1981, the number was 250,000.[2] University programs training students for diverse professions, from nursing to engineering, are required by professional organizations to include a technical writing course. Emerging professions determine that writing instruction will support their research practice and hope to prepare students for the demands of the workplace. Pedagogy for technical writing courses is concerned with helping students write their way into complex organizations; it is aware of the difference between "academic writing," oriented toward knowledge and its development, and "professional writing," oriented toward the solution of problems and

---

　　1. Lester Faigley and Thomas Miller, "What We Learn from Writing on the Job," *College English* 44 (Oct. 1982): 557-69.
　　2. Thomas E. Pearsall, "The State of Technical Writing," paper presented at the annual meeting of the Midwest Regional Conference on English in the Two-Year College, Minneapolis, Minn., Feb. 1981, 1.

the maintenance of organizations.[3] Instruction transmits organizational lore: how to write under pressure, how to write for a supervisor.[4] It also deals with the logic of expert arguments, the nature of evidence, and its deployment in documents. Here, technical writing becomes continuous with scientific writing: "From the perspective of rhetoric, the important distinctions [between science and technology] have to do not with any differences between activities in sciences and in technologies but with differences among the various contexts of these activities."[5] Technical writing instruction, then, is concerned with both professional and disciplinary discourses.

The issue for us, however, is to define the relation between scientific writing's organization of desire and reason and the pedagogical induction of students into those relations in a writing class. Our own professional lore is not much help to us here, dismissing technical writing as "not academic," or as "service teaching." In any advanced society, all teaching is service teaching; courses like technical writing are simply the first to get the bad news. For writers with critical and insurgent interests to dismiss such work, often performed by badly paid casual academic labor, is to obscure the relation between the current pedagogy of service and a possible pedagogy of subversion.

A body of scholarship supports teaching in technical writing. Published in journals such as the *Journal of Technical Writing and Communications, The Technical Writing Teacher, Technical Communication,* and *The Journal of Business Communication,* such scholarship can also be found in general composition and rhetoric journals such as *Rhetoric Review, JAC,* and *Written Communication.* It is a remarkable body of writing: ideas that would be hotly contested within more mainstream academic discourses are taken for granted. Writers routinely refer to power relations that shape discourse; they often reflect on the relation between their work and the reproduction of the professions. As teachers

3. See especially Barbara Couture, ed., *Professional Writing: Toward a College Curriculum* (n.p.: Association of Teachers of Technical Writing, 1987).

4. For lore within composition programs, see Stephen M. North, *The Making of Knowledge in Composition: Portrait of an Emerging Field* (Portsmouth: Boynton/Cook, 1987).

5. James Zappen, "A Rhetoric for Research in Sciences and Technologies," in *New Essays in Technical and Scientific Communication: Research, Theory, Practice,* ed. Paul V. Anderson, R. John Brockmann, and Carolyn R. Miller, Baywood Series in Technical and Scientific Communication (Farmingdale, N.Y.: Baywood Publishing, 1983), 123.

in programs that often include a very high population of international students, they understand English as a world language, modulating international movements of capital and skilled labor. Technical writing pedagogy handles such issues, to be sure, quite differently from literary or cultural theory: they are posed as problems to be solved, as anecdotal illustrations, or as simple facts of life to be taken into account in the classroom. And such a representation of the basic relations of discourse is not entirely an instrumental failure to reflect: it is in everyone's interest that technical language do its work efficiently. It is certainly important to understand how failures in engineering communication contributed to the *Challenger* and Three Mile Island disasters.[6]

In technical writing pedagogy, however, the central relations of our society in its orientation to knowledge and power are normalized. A critical rhetoric, then, has no easy message for this profession: technical writing teachers understand themselves as reproducing social relations. A discipline founded on a program of service is not ashamed to be of use. Therefore, to develop an effective critical theory for technical discourse, we must move further inside the discipline and the writing it strives to represent. The ethos of the technical professions is not unitary but contradictory and discontinuous. Within those gaps and inconsistencies, on this forbidding terrain, we may find some space for critical thought.

We can begin by looking at a teaching case presented to technical writing teachers. A case, in the pedagogy of technical writing, represents a professional writing situation and assigns the student tasks within it. Teachers construct cases from their own experience or from interviews and fieldwork. Some are fully realized narratives, with multiple, conflicting characters and a body of technical data: a series of assignments, based on the case, can form a semester's work. Reflections on the case method form an important theme in technical writing pedagogy.[7] The case I will discuss, drawn from a large corporation that supplies the auto industry, illustrates how contradictions emerge within professional writ-

6. Carl Herndl, Barbara Fennell, and Carolyn Miller, "Understanding Failures in Organizational Discourse: The Accident at Three Mile Island and the Shuttle Challenger Disaster," in *Textual Dynamics of the Professions,* ed. Charles Bazerman and James Paradis (Madison: University of Wisconsin Press, 1991), 279–305.

7. See John Brockmann, Barbara Couture, Jone Goldstein, Susan Feinberg, Marcus Green, and Charles Sides, eds., *The Case Method in Technical Communication: Theory and Models* (n.p.: Association of Teachers of Technical Writing, 1984).

ing and pedagogy. The case was developed by Ruth Reed, then a corporate trainer of technical writers attached to this corporation; my analysis is heavily indebted to her vivid and frank presentation but does not reflect her views.[8] This case demonstrates the contradictions and paradoxes implicit in ordinary technical documents: the details of the problems it poses reflect the technical apparatus available to writers in 1983 and, more fundamentally, the social relations among those writers and their readers.

The case concerns documentation for computer-assisted redesign of an auto body section. Like any good rhetorician, the author—in this case, a staff technical writer—begins with an analysis of her audience. She locates readers at four levels of the organization. The project supervisor is immediately discounted; the writer imagines him checking the manual over, looking at its design, but not using it or even reading it. There are three other potential readers, each of whom, the writer feels, will require a separate manual. The systems programmer is concerned with the overall operation of the computer, with the translation of program instructions into operations on circuits, and with the simultaneous management of all the programs. The applications programmer will write program for the design task in hand, translating the visual information into logical operations that can be managed on the computer. The final user, the design engineer, does the actual work.

This division of labor generates competing orientations among the three classes of readers; their interactions are presumed to be competitive and hostile. The design engineer appears in the technical writer's account as the enemy. He, alone of these users, is given a nickname, "console jockey." The writer, systems programmer, and applications programmer all assume that design engineers will make their own jobs easier by "tweaking" or "jiggling" the computer, and that such play is a threat to the overall security of the system: "Once the user has it [information used in writing the program] the temptation then is to start manipulating and maneuvering and playing around with those pro-

8. Reed's talk was given at the February 1983 meeting of the Professional Writing Project in Detroit, Michigan, sponsored by Wayne State University and the Fund for the Improvement of Post-Secondary Education. The Professional Writing Project was an invaluable source of information for this essay. It developed a distinct and useful pedagogy for professional writing. The views expressed in this essay are not theirs. See Couture, *Professional Writing*. Direct quotations are from my transcript of Reed's talk.

grams. It's—well, it's irresistible." The effects of pornography have been described in more neutral language but with similar emphasis on the close relation between reading and doing, between licit knowledge and illicit play.[9] The writer therefore imagines writing three manuals: one that discusses memory and systems performance for the systems programmer; another, limited to coding operations, for the applications programmer; and a very minimal working document for the design engineer. The technical writer represents the first two documents, and their users, straightforwardly: these writers need information in a certain functional form. But design engineers are contradictory. On the one hand, their interests are narrow: "The user wants to know—and this is basically all he wants to know—how do I do my job, how do I move that line, how do I rotate that line." On the other hand, as we have seen, the user is insatiably curious. The document produced for the user is thus characterized by what is deleted from it:

> There's no way in the world [the user] should know anything about what the application programmer who wrote the [graphics] program knows. No way whatsoever. In fact, it's often very dangerous for a user to know and to have that kind of information. . . . You have to give each of these audiences [only the] information that audience needs. But you don't start swapping that information from one audience to another. There're simply things people should not, absolutely should not, know. It's an odd kind of thing in this environment because in many ways the user is most ignorant. He knows the least about the computer graphics system, absolutely the least. And yet . . . that's your engineer . . . but yet all he needs, all he should ever have, is what he needs for that job and not, absolutely not, one word more.

Harry Braverman could have invented the term *deskilling,* his word for the evacuation of intellectual challenge from the processes of work, to describe this set of relations, generated as they are by the social relations of the corporation rather than by the demands of technology.[10] A very powerful and expensive tool for generating information has produced a system for segmenting and suppressing information. That system is not

9. See Susan Stewart, "The Marquis de Meese," in *Crimes of Writing: Problems in the Containment of Representation* (New York: Oxford University Press, 1991), 235–72.
10. Harry Braverman, *Labor and Monopoly Capital: The Degradation of Work in the Twentieth Century* (New York: Monthly Review Press, 1974).

imposed by external supervision or by the authority of management but is enforced by relations among workers, particularly by the technical writer, who is likely to be less educated, lower paid, and less upwardly mobile than any of her readers.

Labor has become a mystery that no one understands directly. The systems engineer may understand the computer intimately, but he is indifferent to the product being designed. The user understands the product but not the tool that produced it. The applications programmer and the technical writer play limited and facilitating roles, while the supervisor may have the least detailed understanding of any of the three technical processes under his or her nominal control. The task of understanding and transforming the world becomes a task of rendering the world opaque to language. And since there is no subject who can understand this fragmentation of labor, no discursive rectification is possible. Social processes could realign some worker or group of workers and enable them to understand the design process and its goals, but if they were able to articulate a representation of the whole process, it would no longer be fragmented, no longer be in need of such a discursive integration.

This is a complex writing situation, and it requires complex analytic tools. No single term within Habermas's theory of communication captures its difficulties; we will need to circulate through his texts and his terminologies. In *Knowledge and Human Interests*, Habermas described instrumental discourse as oriented to a goal: the organization of feedback-controlled action, and specifically the elimination of uncertainty in such contexts. Among the texts at hand, the documents produced for the systems programmer and the applications programmer are indeed organized through highly developed feedback systems, with a strong orientation to the elimination of uncertainty. Reed quotes the systems programmer: "Wait a minute. He [the applications programmer] is going to want seventy-five different programs, thousands of lines to code. What's that going to do to my computer?" Habermas's formula for such discourse is apt: "The sentence can be understood as the *formulation* of the plan or intention that guides the *operation*."[11] These technical texts are even more deeply monologic than scientific texts; technical writers are often urged to cultivate the hallmarks of a monologic style—assertions of authority, segmentation of information, imperative

11. Habermas, *Knowledge and Human Interests*, 127.

mood. But whereas in scientific writing a monologic presentation contradicts the intersubjective character of scientific work, technical documents are more often located in the delinguistified operations of system than in the dialogic relations of scientific work. The readers and writers in this case may never meet; even if they did know each other well, their interaction is orchestrated by a compelling structure of hierarchical social relations rather than by intersubjective understanding or shared goals and interests. Rather than concealing an intersubjective orientation to understanding, the monologic surface of the discourse in our case masks systematic misunderstanding and disinformation. The subjective responses of readers and writers, often cordial, are irrelevant; the monologic voice of the writer offers with certainty knowledge that is fragmented and dispersed.

In his later work, Habermas elaborates a theory of communicative competence which flexibly takes into account the social situation of these materials. Habermas's notion of communicative action will be a focus of the discussion of action in chapter 4. Here, my use of the theory is provisional and analytic. Habermas uses *communicative action* to signal his turn from a philosophy focused on consciousness to one focused on intersubjective communication, especially in language. The theory of communicative action also indicates that although discourse includes textuality, it is not to be reduced to textuality. Rather, discourse is implicated in plans and goals, in interactions among subjects who cannot coordinate their actions unless they understand one another. For Habermas, such understanding is achieved among the participants in communication through a shared recognition that speech is subject to criteria of truth, appropriateness, and sincerity. Those criteria are entirely formal: different cultures and different contexts will have divergent views about what counts as a true statement. Further, conversations differ in their orientations: some discourses are directed toward representing the world; others, to the maintenance of community or the disclosure of subjectivity. But in all communicative settings, statements that meet communicative criteria—those understood as true or seen as appropriate to the speaker or perceived as sincere—are preferred to statements that are counted as false or transgressive or insincere.[12]

The formal procedural constraints usually cited as communicative criteria include such maxims as "participants must have access to all roles

12. Habermas, *Theory of Communicative Action,* 1:273–339.

in the discussion," "force and threats are not allowed," "all decisions are based on argument rather than on precedent or prestige." These ideas seem both unattainable and utterly lacking in libido. The just society has been reconfigured via *Robert's Rules of Order*, and we do not even dare hope to see it. Such a response is based, at least in part, on a misunderstanding of the force of the procedural constraints on communicative action. It is immaterial to the critical force of the theory whether or not any instance of communicative action has ever been fully achieved. What *is* achieved, very often, even in the most debased communicative settings, is a redirection of talk based on the counterfactual invocation of these universalizable procedural norms: "We can't decide this without consulting X; he's affected." Just as groups may differ in their understanding of what counts as a demonstration of truth but agree that truth is preferable to falsehood, groups may be unable to recognize all of the ways in which inequality and social domination distort their discussions. But once an opinion is understood as an expression of domination and inequality, agents in a communicative situation will not continue to accept it, even though they may continue to act on it. Norms of communicative rationality affect discussions when they are found to have been violated: by themselves, they do not make the conversation fair, let alone right; invoked counterfactually, they can call any position into question.

In communicative action, agents reach agreements about plans and work out intermediate definitions of their situation and ways of discussing it. They make claims that are reciprocal and subject to validation, they are bound by their words, and their speech acts result in commitment and shared action.[13] None of that happens in the case we have been examining. Work has been removed from the control of all the readers and writers; their relations are displaced and fragmented. The discourse situation is structured on the assumption that no agent will be bound by any commitment, least of all one to the discourse situation itself. No agent is bound by the norms of communicative action. In this situation, the injunction that something ought to be done because an authoritative speaker demands it—an injunction based on power rather than on the relations of communication—is about the best we can do. Such a characterization of the technical discourse situation distinguishes the scene of technical writing from that of scientific writing, where an

13. Habermas, *Postmetaphysical Thinking,* 79–80.

invocation of authority does not, by itself, secure assent or organize action.

Habermas's theory of strategic action captures some elements of our case.[14] Strategic action, like communicative action, requires cooperation among agents and is oriented toward success. Unlike communicative action, it is oriented not to achieving understanding but to successful intervention in the social or physical world. Strategic action, when presented as communicative, operates as a "parasite" on communicative action, leading speakers and hearers to understand themselves as addressed when they are only being motivated. But in this case, all possible speakers and writers, except the design engineer, consent to the deskilling of their discourse in order to reduce uncertainty in their environment. No agreement to sacrifice information for control was reached; no such argument is possible, given the fragmentation of information in the organization. Just as this discourse cannot be rectified, it could not have been ratified by prior consent without contradicting the conditions of its own production.

In a passing remark, Habermas replied to the question of whether the documentation for a word processing program made an implied claim to sincerity: "through the conditions of the sales contract a normative context is established, which appears to justify the normative expectations . . . that the user has toward the computer firm." [15] This remark locates communicative action in the consciousness and motivation of agents, rather than situating it in language and social relations. But the discourses of modernity are likely to have multiple writers, to be embedded in institutions, and to serve no single conscious purpose. To read such texts, the writer needs to be configured as a point of intersection for contradictory impulses and discourses and generalized to include groups and organizations of writers.

It is possible to discern this reconfigured writer in Reed's case. We might read the case as the *Trauerspeil,* the mourning play, of Ruth Reed, the technical writer who reported it. This deeply thoughtful writer was quite aware of the contradictory nature of her work. She insistently represented the manual she would write as "not a word more," as a device to keep the reader "most ignorant," and characterized the excluded knowledge as "dangerous." Whereas the manuals produced were texts

14. Habermas, *Theory of Communicative Action,* 1:285–95.
15. Habermas, *Postmetaphysical Thinking,* 86.

of deskilled labor, the writer's narrative of her work is a text of enlightenment: knowledge is directly configured as power, as disruptive of hierarchy and received social relations, as an object of desire that, latent within the relations of everyday labor, could transform work into disruptive and creative play. The text that transmits knowledge is also marked by negation: it concerns what will not be, cannot be, written, even what should not be written. That impossible negated text is located, for this writer, in an elsewhere that is not constrained by the social relations of the workplace, an elsewhere concretely represented by the professional community of writers and teachers who formed her audience.

The writer represents herself as irrevocably divided. In one moment, the writer enforces—indeed, teaches—the fragmentation and suppression of knowledge. In another moment, before an audience of peers, the writer mourns this suppression. These are not issues of sincerity or complicity: we meet here another version of the divided subject of scientific writing, who appeared in the text as privileged interlocutor with nature and whose location in the discipline was permanently provisional and subject to falsification. The technical writer appears within the texts she produced as the dispenser of homeopathic doses of knowledge; outside them, she produces another, disciplinary text, in which the writer knows what is missing, what is not written, what forms of ignorance she has organized.

Such a writer is organized and inhabited by her desire for a different discourse situation. Such a writer also sadly recognizes in her reader's desire for knowledge an other to which her discourse is imputed. The reader's pleasure in knowing, and in being able to manipulate an apparatus, is imputed to all participants in the discourse situation, even as the situation is designed to frustrate and forbid that impulse. All the participants in this situation structure their writing as if every reader wanted to play all possible roles in the project and in the subject relations surrounding it, and as if any concession to this desire would lead to chaos. Paradoxically, then, this system recognizes some of the basic presuppositions of communicative action: the availability of all discursive roles to all participants and the openness of propositions to negation and contest. We can speak, therefore, of communicative action as an object of desire, present as a negation, even in this bleak situation.

Within this context the claims implied in communicative action become relevant, to both critical understanding and the pedagogy of technical writing. If the participants in this situation desire communicative action, we can ask how they formed such a desire and what their action could look like. Unless an impetus toward full communication is inborn, or essentially human—an assumption that would move Habermas's theory very close to the foundationalism he so cannily avoids—a theory of communicative action needs a more complex articulation between strategic action and communicative action than Habermas has given us so far. Perhaps strategic and communicative capacities are not so clearly separated; perhaps, just as strategic action can be embedded in communication, the aspiration for autonomous discourse can be embedded in distorted and constrained communication. In this case, communicative action, compromised by the needs of dominant groups, emerges, not as well-formed, propositionally differentiated, and institutionally unbound discourse, but as an irresistible desire to tweak a computer.

To see communicative action as embedded in strategic action opens up pedagogical possibilities. It offers an alternative to both messianic and therapeutic pedagogies, to those that propose the teacher as the bearer of correct ideology or those that see her eliciting such ideology from students' experience. Such idealizations cannot *see* the work of teaching writing, of inducting students into advanced practices of language, practices which are dismissed as domination and disinformation. An idealizing pedagogy repeats the generalization staged by a global critique of science. If technical writing serves power, none of it need be thought through, or even read. But it is possible to trace the contradiction between communicative action and strategic action as it emerges in students' texts and readings, using it to reveal and transform discursive practices. Such a strategy asks students and teachers to investigate the specificity of technical discourse, especially as it emerges in the social relations of the job.

Pedagogical practice might examine validity claims as they are enacted, suppressed, or assumed in working situations and consider what happens when those claims are questioned. For Habermas, to question a validity claim is to interrupt a communicative situation and enter into the more difficult terrain of "discourse," a form of discussion that establishes basic principles and reconstitutes a consensus that will once again support communication. Such discourse at the limits is unlikely to emerge in our case: to question a claim in a work setting might lead to strategic discussions that resolve a question prudentially. Only on occasion will such a challenge lead to communicative action. Only when strategic discussions fail is a group likely to move to communication, and their communication is likely to concern, not first principles, but a limited and finite set of questions about the design of auto bodies or the wisdom of letting console jockeys learn coding.

If Habermas opens a door between communicative action and an "upper story" of discourse, I am proposing that a door can also be opened between communicative action and the "lower story" of strategic communication. That door pivots on a central contradiction in the transfer of scientific information in corporate and governmental settings: the text must communicate, but not too much. A scientific practice that has, since its inception, required and fostered the free exchange of information confronts a form of writing that is proud to limit its message to the operational, "and not one word more." [16]

An intersubjective pedagogy for technical writing would begin by teaching students conventional structures, but then would identify the rhetoric of strategic claims to authority, consider the relation between strategic claims and the purposes and goals of technical writing, and suggest how these claims can be contested. The teacher's aim would be not only that students write for success—it would be quixotic and irresponsible to ignore the problems they will face on the job—but to help students become aware of the writing they will do, and also of the writing they might desire or invent. Even in highly conventional and restricted technical discourse, an impulse for communicative action emerges; we can identify the relations of power that block that desire and offer strategies for betraying it into communicative action. An important element in this pedagogy is reflection on the kinds of subjects that technical texts require and create, on their discontinuity with subjects that science constructs, and on the forms of life that such a discontinuous and multiple subjectivity supports.

These are indeed modest goals, and rightly so; technical writing teachers figure in no myths of the vanguard. But if we are to move our understanding of modernity beyond literary and journalistic forms, we must investigate the texts that distinguish our society, with all their contradictions and possibilities. A pedagogy based on this work will not be

16. See Charles Bazerman, "How Natural Philosophers Can Cooperate: The Literary Technology of Coordinated Investigation in Joseph Priestley's *History and Present State of Electricity* (1767)," in Bazerman and Paradis, *Textual Dynamics of the Professions,* 13–44.

heroic; its privileged text is not the intimate journal or the manifesto but directions for working a printing press or a description of treatment protocols at a local clinic. Habermas has described such modest hopes well:

> Of course, "producing" does not mean manufacturing according to the model of realizing intended ends. Rather, it signifies a type of emergence that cannot be intended, an emergence out of a cooperative endeavor to moderate, abolish, or prevent the suffering of vulnerable creatures. This endeavor is fallible, and it does fail over and over again.[17]

The terms of that endeavor, and of its failure, are inscribed in any attempt to understand action. To that attempt, we now turn.

17. Habermas, *Postmetaphysical Thinking*, 146.

CHAPTER FOUR

Action and Rhetoric

· · · · The situation of the rhetorical text, deeply implicated in action, is especially precarious for the texts of modernity. Aristotle could locate the possible sources of persuasion in the credibility of the speaker, the emotions of the audience, and the cogency of the argument: persuasion assumed a coherent audience, a known speaker, and agreement on the qualities of a convincing argument. Persuasion and action were transparently connected; while audiences could be misled or mistaken, Aristotle's rhetorician assumed a direct connection between persuading an audience of a proposition and securing an appropriate outcome.

But modernity fragments audiences and displaces the steering mechanisms of society from the domain of public persuasion. Habermas diagnosed these as problems in differentiation and in the reconstruction of the public sphere. The differentiation of reason is reproduced on the terrain of social interaction; we can trace its outlines in the mutual unintelligibility of the texts of the sciences or the contradictory practices of professional pedagogy. And as Lacan reminds us, securing assent is not the same thing as organizing cooperative activity: public audiences are colonized; their activity can be deflected or displaced. Slavoj Žižek has used the theory of the Lacanian drive to analyze how cynicism, a form of displacement, can inform passive and acquiescent audiences.

Action and the Rhetoric of Intersubjectivity

By calling language and narration *terms* of an intersubjective rhetoric, I
have located such a rhetoric within the territory explored by Kenneth
Burke rather than that of Aristotle. Like the pentad, with its "five
terms" of dramatism,[1] the terms *language* and *narration*—to which I
now add *action*—constitute an object of analysis but are also available
as topics for reflection, either separately or in their relations.

The terms I propose for a rhetoric of intersubjectivity—language,
narration, and action—emphasize the materiality of texts, their location
in time, and their efficacy in organizing social reproduction. They provide us with ways of tracing out the relations of reason and desire. These
terms are not preconditions of texts, categories of rhetorical appeals, or
names for genres. They are nodal points, places where the contradictions within reason and desire concentrate. Whereas the Aristotelian *pis-
teis,* the "appeals" to character, logic, and emotion, figure in contemporary rhetorics as a triangle of discursive forms, satisfying in its stability
but incapable of expansion, the terms in a rhetoric of intersubjectivity
are gathering places in an irregular field, representations of the radical
instability of language.

Action, the third of the terms in a rhetoric of intersubjectivity, connects the discursive space of narration to other methods of analyzing
social life. Whereas language and narration are both central issues in
literary theory and analytic foci that orient rhetoric to textual study, action is anomalous. Action was, of course, a central term for Burke,[2] but
analyses of the text as action also connect rhetoric to social theory and
to other academic disciplines only peripherally concerned with language. Habermas and Lacan use the term in different ways: Habermas,
in the analysis of communicative action; Lacan, in the theory of the
drive. Mediating between, rather than collapsing, these two understandings of action, I begin with Anthony Giddens's relatively neutral
definition of action as a "stream of actual or contemplated causal interventions of corporeal beings in the ongoing process of events-in-the-
world."[3] For Giddens, action includes the possibility of unconscious

1. Burke, *A Grammar of Motives,* xv–xxii.
2. Kenneth Burke, *A Rhetoric of Motives* (Berkeley and Los Angeles: University
of California Press, 1950; reprint, 1969); Kenneth Burke, *Language as Symbolic Action* (Berkeley and Los Angeles: University of California Press, 1969).
3. Anthony Giddens, *New Rules of Sociological Method* (London: Hutchison,
1976), 75. See also Giddens's *Central Problems in Social Theory: Action, Structure*

motivation and can be sedimented into the organized structures of institutions.

This definition suggests two understandings of discourse as action: discourse secures assent, organizing rational agreement, and discourse manages the energies that inhabit subjects and the texts they produce. Communicative action is formed by a structure of assumed and often counterfactual claims to rationality. As mediated by the drive, action is multiple, contradictory, and socially mediated.

The rhetorical analysis of action collocates with the analysis of language and of narration: it raises and organizes questions of signification, of temporality, and of agency that illuminate these terms. The connection between action and language is mediated through Habermas, who sees language as constitutive of communicative action; the connection between action and narration is mediated through Lacan, for whom the drive is a signifying chain articulated in time.

Communicative Action and Practices of Rationality

Habermas sees communicative action as an intersubjective negotiation of validity claims, organized in differentiated discourses, mediated by prior understandings and rules. Habermas defined communicative action in his early essay, "What Is Universal Pragmatics?," as the interaction of at least two people who establish a relationship—usually, but not always, through language. They try to come to a common understanding about the situation in which they are acting through interpretation. They also try to act together, which means they must

---

and Contradiction in Social Analysis (Berkeley and Los Angeles: University of California Press, 1983), 55–56.

In this section, I am not following Habermas's earlier distinction between labor and action, elaborated in "Historical Materialism and the Development of Normative Structures," in *Communication and the Evolution of Society* (Boston: Beacon, 1979). I am not convinced by Anthony Giddens's criticism, in "Labour and Interaction," in *Habermas: Critical Debates,* ed. J. Thompson and D. Held (Cambridge: MIT Press, 1982), 149–61, that the distinction does not permit Habermas to examine the consolidation of power in institutions. This criticism seems to me adequately met in Habermas's later distinction between system and lifeworld (Habermas, "A Reply to My Critics," 267). However, Giddens's later treatment of action in *Central Problems in Social Theory* underscores the need for an understanding of action that includes the unconscious as a ground of motivation. For this reason, his definition seems a more useful place to begin.

agree about how to act. Both interpretation and agreement require language.[4]

Habermas sees communicative action as alternative to both the philosophy of consciousness, based on the autonomous and individuated subject, and Marxist theories of action, based on production. A more rationalized society allows a broader field for communicative action, because assent secured through custom or tradition is replaced by highly differentiated rational evaluations of claims.

Communicative action is both productive and interpretive. It orients actors to their situation and stipulates the possibility of coming to agreement; it also operates a series of interpretive assumptions about intersubjective relations, allowing incommensurable forms of speech to be understood as interventions in a common sociality. Habermas avoids foundationalism by abstaining from claims about obligatory goals or aims of communicative action and by projecting noncommunicative forms of social interaction, such as strategic action, or action secured by tradition rather than by discussion.

Habermas sees the theory of communicative action as an alternative to the paradigm of production—articulated in Marxism—and that of reflection—articulated in classical philosophy. Neither paradigm can be transcended or negated: they must receive a determinate refutation. Action is poorly articulated within the productivist paradigm, since if thought is modeled on the process of production, an unbridgeable gap is created between production and norm-governed social practices. This gap makes it very difficult to motivate arguments for social change, democratization, or even change in the processes of production. Political proposals and arguments appear either as unmediated ethical obligations or as appeals to the force of the masses or the state. But for communicative action, critique is inherent in the relations of discourse, an expression of what is already latent in social interaction—the possibility of transformation:

> the emancipatory perspective proceeds precisely not from the production paradigm, but from the paradigm of action oriented toward mutual understanding. It is the form of interaction processes that must be altered if one wants to discover practically what the members of a society in any given situation might want and what they should do in their common interest.[5]

4. Habermas, *Communication and the Evolution of Society,* 1–68.
5. Habermas, *Philosophical Discourse of Modernity,* 82.

A communicative paradigm is also an alternative to the paradigm of consciousness. There, rationalization implies a reflexive critique, but no uncompromised location mediates subjects' desires for self-knowledge and action. The reflexive critique can be located in the aesthetic, in a social class or political agent, in nature, or in various limit experiences; in any of these locations, it functions as a replacement or representation.[6]

In a communicative paradigm, the other is not a ghost of the absolute but a concrete and determinate interlocutor, all too ready to call the subject into question, and also quite ready to resist reification. If rationality is not an attribute of consciousness but an implicit assumption of communication, then it is not necessary to ground our preference for reason, but it is urgently necessary to specify—and argue about—particular understandings of what is rational. A communicative understanding of rationality connects rational discourse to social consciousness: the social becomes part of the horizon of communication, a resource for understandings, a theme of discourse, and a body of consensually elaborated interpretive patterns.[7]

Such a turn to a communicative paradigm is crucial for rhetorical theory, providing an alternative to the antirhetorical tradition implicit in both the productivist paradigm and the paradigm of consciousness. Plato saw rhetoric as a faulty application of the norms of production to a debased and cosmetic activity; he argued that it should be replaced, depending on the context, by instrumental norms of social control (*Republic*) or by norms of authentic self-expression (*Phaedrus*).[8] Socrates, parodically reciting a confected speech in the *Phaedrus* and then critiquing and retracting his performance, spoke for an oratory that expresses truth spontaneously rather than a rhetoric that guides the labor of language.[9] In the paradigm of consciousness, calculating, goal-oriented subjects cannot generate discourse without placing in question their sincerity and their orientation toward truth. In the paradigm of

6. Habermas, *Philosophical Discourse of Modernity*, 308.

7. Habermas, *Philosophical Discourse of Modernity*, 298.

8. For an interesting treatment of the antirhetorical tradition, see Dilip Parameshwar Gaonkar, "Reflections on the Rhetorical Turn in the Human Sciences," in *The Rhetorical Turn*, ed. Simons. For the evolution of Plato's views on rhetoric in the later dialogues, see Martha Nussbaum, *The Fragility of Goodness: Luck and Ethics in Greek Thought and Philosophy* (Cambridge: Cambridge University Press, 1986), 200–235.

9. Plato, *Phaedrus*, trans. R. Hackforth (Indianapolis: Bobbs-Merrill, 1960). References to the *Phaedrus* will be given parenthetically in the text.

production, rhetoric, as ornament and incitement, falls into the unthinkable gap between norm and action. Rhetoric is therefore, as it would become for Kant and Locke, a collection of shabby tricks. In either paradigm, rhetorical analysis is admonitory or rectifying of the deceptive text, exposing its dubious propositional content and manipulative illocutionary force.

But if production and representation of the world are included within a paradigm of communication, then the rhetorically formed text is no longer a scandal. Language is not adjunct to a projected representation of a truth outside speech. Rather, production and representation are understood as actions organized in language. The completed product of labor is no longer privileged as central objectification of the human agent. The human agent is objectified, not in production or—hopelessly—in reflection, but in discourse, so that rhetorical elaboration and the technical control of discourse are labors of language rather than disreputable ploys.

The weaknesses of the theory of communicative action, from the point of view of rhetorical theory, are equally striking, and quickly stated. For Habermas, language is reduced to a neutral carrier of communicative intent. But language, the constituting structure of communicative action, is not its accidental presupposition or neutral conveyer. Further, Habermas mediates the social location of communication through social evolution, the organization of communication as a learning process and as a motor of historical change. Habermas's evolutionary understanding of communicative action is problematic, even ethnocentric, especially given his tendency to schematize levels of cultural development.[10] Far from sponsoring a dialogic, contestatory, or even interesting relation between the specific structures of rationality associated with technological cultures of Europe and North America and those that characterize other regions of the world, a learning process that assumes hierarchies of development replaces communicative action with paternalist guidance. Moreover, it is not self-evident that communicative action is a socially effective learning process. Just who is the learner? What has been learned? Not only the disasters of the twentieth century but contemporary revivals of nationalism and religious funda-

10. See the use of Kohlberg in the final chapter of *Communication and the Evolution of Society.* For an explicit treatment of this issue, see Habermas's "Struggles for Recognition in the Democratic Constitutional State," in *Multiculturalism,* ed. Charles Taylor and others (Princeton: Princeton University Press, 1994).

mentalism, and even new social movements critical of modernity all seem resistant to an evolutionary concept of communicative understanding.[11] The discontinuity, disparity, and heterogeneity of contemporary social practices challenge current critical theory, just as fascism, tragically, challenged the first generation of the Frankfurt School. Movements for social change can be normatively secured, but this possibility does not guarantee any such security for any specific social movement, no matter how benign. What connects Habermas's notions of system, lifeworld, and differentiated reason to his notion of communicative action is an understanding of language as a symbolically mediated and historically situated practice of rationality and reflection. Followed consistently, such a theory places language at the center of communicative action— where, after a "communicative turn," we might have supposed it would necessarily be.

The Differentiated Domain of Communicative Action

The incommensurable discourses of academic disciplines raise particular problems for communicative rationality that are best addressed within the framework of differentiation. Differentiated forms of reason are grounded in practices of discourse, as participants give an account of their thought and practice in dialogue with others. Differentiated forms of reason are secured, but only provisionally, by the integrity of the speech situation in its openness to the unforced force of the better reason. No metaphysical power is claimed for any of the differentiated forms of discourse—neither for science nor for political discourse nor for self-disclosure. Without the pressure of a metaphysical claim, the theory of communicative action has no recourse to negative metaphysics: although it secures no religious claim, it "will even coexist abstemiously" with religious discourse.[12]

The theory of communicative action values difference not as Other— that is, self-referentially—but rather in relation to the conduct of discourse. An expansion of the terrain of difference broadens its possibilities, develops its power to sustain disagreement, and constructs a public sphere for communicative action. Differentiation of discourses supports

11. See Nancy Fraser, *Unruly Practices: Power, Discourse, and Gender in Contemporary Social Theory* (Minneapolis: University of Minnesota Press and Polity Press, 1989).

12. Habermas, *Postmetaphysical Thinking*, 145.

the individual differentiation of subjects, the coming together of groups of like-minded individuals to work out forms of talk within which very serious disagreements can be contained and resolved.

Such an understanding of communicative rationality grounds the experience of moral choice in dialogic relations. Norms are established, and renegotiated, just as subjective identity is formed, in the intersubjective relations of recognition and argument. It is possible, therefore, to frame normative and political questions within the framework of communicative ethics and avoid reduction to either decontextualized individual entitlements or a Nietzschean exercise of power.[13] Modernity supports individuation, but it also transposes the experience of the ethical to contested issues of intersubjectivity. And the complexities of differentiated discourse are not easily translated to a common language in the public sphere. Moral questions can no longer be limited to the ethical dilemmas of individual lives: in *Multiculturalism,* a collection of essays on contemporary communicative ethics, ethical questions include Quebeçois language policy and German immigration law.[14]

Contemporary advanced societies are shaped by a disjunction between system and lifeworld, in which lifeworld is increasingly colonized by system. For Habermas, the lifeworld is the domain of customary interactions and also the context for communicative actions. System refers to the reified, semiautonomous sphere that arises out of the lifeworld, including the money system and administrative mechanisms.[15] System colonizes lifeworld; new social movements can be seen as attempts to contest such colonization. But system cannot intervene in the lifeworld to generate meaning; granting the exigencies of ideological reproduction, the delinguistified steering media can use the structural violence of system only to create compulsion, never motive:

> Through processes of regulation and intervention, the lifeworld context is subject to monetary and legal measures. But the communicative structures of the lifeworld can fulfill the functions of cultural reproduction, social integration, and socialization when individuals themselves can generate motive and reasons for action via argumentative processes. There can be no "administrative production of meaning," for meaning

13. See Habermas, *Moral Consciousness and Communicative Ethics;* Habermas, *Justification and Application.* Essays in Taylor and others, *Multiculturalism,* grapple with this problem.

14. Taylor and others, *Multiculturalism,* 50–64 and 135–42.

15. This discussion draws heavily on Benhabib, *Critique, Norm, and Utopia.*

and motives can only be created through the power of conviction as experienced by participants themselves.[16]

The colonization of lifeworld by system and the inability of system to support cultural reproduction both imply that rationalization is a contradictory process. Forms of rationality become much more finely articulated, and personal inflections of social discourses are much more deeply individuated (provoking a more peremptory demand for meaning and for the rational justification of cultural norms and practices). But rationalization simultaneously erodes the practices of the lifeworld that might have generated rational justification. Since his very early work *Legitimation Crisis*, Habermas has identified the centrality of this "crisis of meaning," which might either demystify power, realign system and lifeworld, and expand the sphere of communicative action, or else lead to reimposition of traditional cultural norms.

Communicative Action in a Public Sphere

These outcomes, like so much else, depend on the discursive terrain available to us. If we desire a rationalization of the forms of common life, where can that desire be developed, reflected upon, and proposed as a common project? Habermas locates such discourse in the public sphere, an ensemble of relations among writers and readers, removed from the official discourse of the state.[17] In the public sphere, the problems of politics, society, and culture are represented in general terms and opened to rational discussion. Habermas saw the elaboration of a public sphere in the Enlightenment as an oppositional event which reorganized political discourse. In contemporary life, the public sphere is attenuated, or "refeudalized": the boundaries between state and society, public and private, are blurred. Public business is done by negotiation among competing interests rather than by a search for rationality and is associated with spectacles of mass culture and mass consumption. The theory of the public sphere expresses a desire for a specific form of communicative action, one that supports political agency.

For rhetorical theory, which concerns itself with the deployment of available means of persuasion, notions of system, lifeworld, and public sphere distinguish social actions that rely on reasoned justification and

16. Benhabib, *Critique, Norm, and Utopia*, 249.
17. Habermas, *The Structural Transformation of the Public Sphere*.

reciprocal argument from those that do not. Habermas offers a theory of discourse that avoids such absurdities as the belief that all social relations are subject to argument and rules out the nihilist renunciation of discourse to contest for power. We have reason to widen the sphere of rhetoric, to expand the scope and complexity of our understanding of communicative action. With the blunting of class struggles, militancy and spontaneous desire seem as likely to prompt bloody, pointless national and religious struggles as to generate an emancipatory praxis. The theory of communicative action can help us understand, rather than idealizing, new social insurgencies that are succeeding working-class and socialist movements, and it can help us shape a theory of political agency appropriate to this phase of modernity, one that does not simply attach itself to social movements as agents of change, just as earlier theories attached themselves to classes or national groups.

But the concepts of communicative action, differentiation, and the public sphere, however useful they are in the analysis of rational arguments, are not sufficient for the understanding of action. What we need can be found in Lacan's notion of the drive.

The Drive, Action, and Systems of Differences

The drive is the classical psychoanalytic topic for the discussion of the impetus and provocation of action. Although Lacan has no explicit theory of action,[18] he has a great deal to say about the drive, which is for him a monumental topic, locating action in desire and branching into ancillary treatments of aggression, the symptom, and repetition.

Lacan insists on the sexual organization of the drive because the drive—and the transformed actions it enables—is organized in sexuality as a system of differentiation and signification, rather than because of any necessary eroticism of the object.[19] The drive is formed by negation: it is neither a personal expression nor a description of its object. The

18. See, however, the suggestive parenthetical remark in which Lacan specifies "ordered and significant actions" as "action in the real sense, that of speech" (*Seminar II*, 297).

19. Lacan bases his position on Freud: "The sexual instinct and the sexual object are merely soldered together—a fact which we have been in danger of overlooking in consequence of the uniformity of the normal picture, where the object appears to form part and parcel of the drive. We are thus warned to loosen the bond that exists in our thoughts between drive and object" (Sigmund Freud, "Three Essays on Sexuality," in *The Standard Edition of the Complete Psychological Works of Sigmund Freud,* ed. James Strachey [London: Hogarth, 1953], 7:125–45).

drive represents the object as desirable and desiring, incorporating it into gender as a system of differences. The impetus of the drive emerges as action, transformed by conscious intention, transference, or derailments of identification. Action is always, therefore, saturated with a system of meanings prior to and external to both subject and object of the drive.

Since Freud, it has been usual to speak of the *aim* of a drive. Lacan demonstrates that this aim is continually displaced, necessarily implicated in the subject's history of exchanges, omissions, and lapses of memory, articulated as a commerce with various others and with the real. The aim of the drive is always erratic, always under negotiation with potential objects, for whom something quite different, and equally oblique, is at stake. The very constitution of the drive is borrowed: it takes its shape from something else. What is desired, the object of desire, the aim of the drive, are all bound up in the linguistic structures of the subject. The drive therefore implicates action in communication. As Laplanche puts it, "On the one hand there is from the beginning an object, but . . . on the other hand sexuality does not have, from the beginning, a real object."[20]

But although the drive is complex, it is neither contingent nor indeterminate: the relations of a subject with a historical and social given are not accidental but ideologically and symbolically mediated in structures that are all too stable. Definite but inaccessible to consciousness, these structures will be expressed in multiple, contradictory formulations:

> desire is situated in dependence on demand—which, by being articulated in signifiers, leaves a metonymic remainder that runs under it, an element that is not indeterminate, which is a condition both absolute and unapprehensible, an element necessarily lacking, unsatisfied, impossible, misconstrued, an element that is called desire.[21]

The lack, the need for satisfaction, an impossibility and misconstruction, deliver the drive over, both in aim and in object, to a terrain of intersubjectivity, where error and indeterminacy continually proliferate and unstably define one another. The metonymic remnant of the demand scavenges among leftovers and misconstructions of other desires for a

20. Jean Laplanche, *Life and Death in Psychoanalysis,* trans. Jeffrey Mehlman (Baltimore: Johns Hopkins University Press, 1976), 19.
21. Lacan, *Four Fundamental Concepts,* 154.

less costly error, one that is less time-consuming and more reliably plea-
surable. An understanding of the drive reconfigures the relation between persuasion and action from Aristotelian transparency to complex
overdetermination. The drive is already both action and thought; it is
also an action that eludes thought, and a thought that is only indirectly
expressed in action.

In social theory, deflected and displaced relations between thought
and action are usually analyzed as ideology, a useful way of describing
dislocations of the public sphere, especially if ideology is firmly uncoupled from any notion of concealment or conscious deceit. Slavoj
Žižek provides such an understanding of ideology. He sees it as a form
of institutionalized and sedimented action which no longer requires belief. Commodity fetishism, for example, presents money as if it were
wealth; individuals do not believe that money is a magical embodiment
of labor and material, but they *act as if* money were magic. Analogously,
totalitarian ideology no longer pretends to take itself seriously, no
longer makes demands on citizens for belief, but only requires that they
act as if they believed. Žižek poses the question to conventional understandings of ideology: where is the illusion here?[22] Cynicism enables illusory action to continue, while preserving the satisfaction of having
resisted deceit.

If belief is uncoupled from action, it can also be delegated: other
people can believe for us, just as the chorus in *Antigone,* according to
Lacan, feels for us,[23] just as the studio audience or the laugh track of a
situation comedy, according to Žižek, enjoys for us.[24] The unconscious
occupies a deeply paradoxical position: it is internal to the subject but
unknowable to her. There, ideology exercises its force "only insofar as
it is experienced, in the unconscious economy of the subject, as a trau-
matic, senseless injunction."[25] Žižek holds that this trauma gives Law
its authority and ideology its enjoyment. His point recalls Lacan's passing remark that in masochism, pain becomes a good, an object of exchange.[26] Ideology allows the subject to escape the real, whether the real
threatens as history (eluded through easy historicism) or as the desired

22. Slavoj Žižek, *The Sublime Object of Ideology* (London: Verso, 1989), 32. See
also his *Tarrying with the Negative: Kant, Hegel, and the Critique of Ideology* (Durham, N.C.: Duke University Press, 1993).

23. Lacan, *Seminar VII,* 241–87.

24. Žižek, *The Sublime Object of Ideology,* 35.

25. Žižek, *The Sublime Object of Ideology,* 43.

26. Lacan, *Seminar VII,* 240.

object. Ideology supports a concern with consistency, commitment to projects related to the ego ideal, and pleasure in renunciation.

The discourse ethics that proceeds from Lacan's analysis is formal and uncompromising. It enjoins us not to give way regarding our desire, without regulating, or even addressing, what it might be good for us to desire. Lacan's ethic is utterly without positive content. Remarkably enough, it has deep affinities to Habermas's communicative ethics, foregrounding the centrality of intersubjectivity and renouncing any unmediated access to the rational or the desirable. We are (almost literally) the last to know what our desire is, and therefore we cannot know, without reflection, when we are giving ground relative to it. Lacan offers scattered clinical hints about how analysands go astray, but no strategy, neither reflection nor spontaneity, neither renunciation nor the fulfillment of fantasy, is favored as likely to implicate us in anything but continued displacement and error. ("This endeavor is fallible, and it does fail over and over again.") For Lacan, error and the symptom cannot be transcended; they can only be gone through, a process Žižek generalizes as "going through the social fantasy."[27]

"Going through" the fantasy or symptom is a form of communicative action. It opens to individuals and groups the possibility, not of grasping desire directly, but of perceiving its displacement, not of unmasking ideology, but of discerning its surfaces. These perceptions are not about delirious access to the real but suggest a kind of language that insists on its own materiality, its intersubjectivity, its distance from both the real and the ideal speech situation.

Where will we find such a language? Habermas would not have recognized an image of communicative rationality in Žižek's privileged example of "going through"—the android in the movie *Bladerunner* saying, "I am a replicant."[28] Still less would he have found the Lacanian short session, with its rigid and asymmetrical discourse roles, an ethically exemplary discourse. But the dislocation of language from the public sphere and the dissociation of persuasion from action will require us to invent ways of talking that do not resemble the conversational disputes of the Enlightenment salon. We are more likely to find a critical discourse at the edges and folds of expert or popular forms than in a fragile space removed from either of them. If Habermas tells the happy story of communicative action as a practice of reason, capable of sustaining

27. Lacan, *Seminar VII*, 87–138; Žižek, *The Sublime Object of Ideology*, 124.
28. Žižek, *The Sublime Object of Ideology*, 41.

more and more intense differentiation, available for reflecting on a broader and broader social terrain, Lacan tells the sad story of action as necessarily implicated in error, necessarily unsuccessful, bringing us into a relation with the other marked by domination and frustration.

Psychoanalysis, Language, and Agency

Psychoanalysis can be seen as a communicative practice open to reason (and to other forces) and capable of effecting change.[29] Since this book is not a therapeutic text, I will take psychoanalysis as emblematic of such practices rather than as the unique instance of them: the analysis of psychoanalysis should be extended, with important changes, to such discursive forms as critique, political analysis, experimental literature, and disciplinary self-reflection. Although psychoanalysis (like experimental literature, unlike disciplinary self-reflection) is not simply a cognitive process, it is an intersubjective relation organized in language. It was also, in Lacan's practice, marked by negation and elision. We know little about Lacan's sessions except when, and how, he stopped them—the tactics of the short session. Although he was, throughout his working life, occupied with analytic technique and analytic discourse, Lacan left us a thin record of his own practice. We have no case histories and sparse examples of his work with patients. There is a transcript of one instance of Lacan's practice, a clinical interview in which the psychoanalyst interviews a patient in front of a class.[30] This genre is didactic rather than therapeutic: the interview is part of students' training rather than an episode in the cure. In the interview, we read the discourse of the university rather than that of the analyst.

Lacan understood analytic discourse as action productive of meaning: "On peut dire que l'action psychanalytique se développe dans et par la communication verbale, c'est-à-dire dans une saisie dialectique du sens" (We could say that psychoanalytic action is developed within and by means of verbal communication, which is to say in a dialectical grasp of sense).[31] The clinical interview translates this "dialectical grasp of sense"

29. See Roy Schafer, *Retelling a Life: Narration and Dialogue in Psychoanalysis* (New York: Basic, 1992), for a critique of cognitivism in the understanding of psychoanalysis.

30. The interview is included in Schneiderman's *Returning to Freud*, 19–41. Subsequent references to this article are given parenthetically in the text.

31. Jacques Lacan, "L'agressivitée en psychanalyse," in *Écrits* (Paris: Seuil, 1966), 102 (my translation).

into academic language. And while the picture is not pretty—Lacan, as an interviewer, is terrifying—it is illuminating.

From the opening words of this interview with the psychotic Mr. Primeau, understanding is linked to aggression, error, denial, and contests for mastery.

> Dr. Lacan: Sit down, my good man. You have found a great deal of interest here. I mean that people are really interested in your case. You spoke with your psychiatrists. Many things have been somewhat clarified. Tell me about yourself. (Mr. Primeau is silent.) I don't know why I would not let you speak. You know very well what is happening to you. (19)

Lacan, introducing the patient, does not call him by name but instead demands his speech. Lacan interpret's Primeau's silence as a response, something on the order of "I, Primeau, have been prevented from speaking by Lacan." Lacan denies any such prohibition and recalls Primeau to his immediate location: he is in the amphitheater; he knows the drill.

We might note further the displacement of address in this interview. In the dialogue between analyst and patient, the patient's answers to questions tell the analyst nothing: all questions are in principle already answered.[32] The analyst, symmetrically enough, addresses the patient without effect. The "real" audience is silent, spectating. That audience is supposed to learn something unsaid, a diagnostic commentary extrapolated from the analyst's line of questioning and also, perhaps, a professional *habitus* transmitted in the analyst's illocution. We are in the unfriendly territory of Lacan's first seminars.

The discursive situation, then, is marked by its institutional setting; the action of the discourse is deflected, and the conversation represents an unspoken monologue. Lacan is quite frank with Mr. Primeau about this setting and its limits; he does not tell Primeau that the audience wants to help him. He names quite exactly the audience's business with Primeau—they are interested—and locates his own demand for speech within this interest. The institutional situation enforces publicity for both the speaker and his interlocutor, reinscribing every utterance as a performance.

32. James Britton, in *The Development of Writing Abilities, 11–18* (London: Macmillan, 1975), describes this strange discourse, which pretends to be informative, as "transactional." He finds that it characterizes the vast majority of student writing.

In the wider public relations that the institution organizes, questioner
and respondent are deeply unequal:

> Mr. Primeau: Since you are a very well-known personality, that
> made me anxious.
> Dr. Lacan: How do you know that I am a well-known
> personality?
> Mr. Primeau: I tried to read your books. (28)

This is not at all Habermasian communicative action. Primeau's discourse is deployed as evidence rather than understood intersubjectively;
discursive roles are frozen and unequal, inhabited by social constraints
quite different from the unforced force of the better argument. And
Lacan defends his privilege adroitly: Primeau acknowledges, quite cou-
rageously, that there is something intimidating about a cultural hero
asking you, in front of scores of spectators, whether you are still hearing
voices. Lacan interprets this acknowledgment as another symptom. Primeau's recognition of the asymmetries of power, and of his own displaced speech in the interview, become further evidence of his illness.
Which, of course, it is.

But the news is not all bad. The very inequality between speaker and
audience establishes a polarity that can be exploited. Neither doctor nor
patient can speak with full intelligibility, but some forms of efficacy are
available to each of them. Speaking within an institution that does not
pretend to hear him, the anxious patient identifies Lacan as someone
who has already spoken but who cannot be understood—he writes un-
readable books. Caught within the unequal discursive relation that consigns him to answering questions and the audience to listening silently,
Primeau can use the audience as a mirror:

> Mr. Primeau: Yes, she resembled her a little. But Claude did not
> wear makeup. This lady has put on makeup.
> Dr. Lacan: Do you ever put on makeup yourself?
> Mr. Primeau: Yes, it happens that I put on makeup. It has hap-
> pened to me, yes. (He smiles.) (30)

The makeup that Primeau regrets seeing on the lady in the audience
("It's a shame that she is wearing makeup") is the makeup that happened to him, a misfortune that it is appropriate to smile in the face of.

The institutional setting is not benign, or even humane; it is simply
available for the production of meaning. There, Lacan demands speech
and denies having forbidden it. From the first, he deploys the institutional setting of the interview and the inequality it effects to produce

meaning and display knowledge. Lacan offers us, here and in the seminars, two modes of agency: an agency organized by the drive, at odds with its object and mistaken about its aims, or an agency mediated by analysis, in which the subject is repeatedly elided, but knowledge—of the subject as effect of language—is available. In both cases, agency is uncoupled from knowledge, which is barely possible, costly, and deeply implicated in error, particularly in the identificatory stabilization of the ego: "Or cette stagnation formelle est parente de la structure la plus générale de la connaissance humaine: celle qui constitue le moi et les objets sous des attributs de permanence, d'identité et de substantialité, bref sous la forme d'entités ou de 'choses'" (Now, this formal stagnation produces the most generalized structure of human knowledge, that which constitutes the ego and its objects under the attributes of permanence, identity, and substance, in short under the form of beings or of "things").[33] Knowledge formed in the subject's incorporation of his or her aggressiveness is paranoid. The desire to know is linked to a terrified attempt to stabilize, to keep "in place" the subject's own body as the object of punishment, revenge, and dismemberment, by those who have accompanied the subject in his or her embodiment.

In the clinical interview, the accents of paranoia distinguish both speakers. Primeau, who confesses only to having *tried* to read Lacan, gives his psychosis a Lacanian inflection: "I am constantly making the imaginative flow" (20); "all speech is signifying" (23); he offers to show Lacan his "*écrits*" (41). Having been made anxious by Lacan's celebrity, he can also take it over, using Lacan as a disembodied form that sends him messages, imposes sentences into his line of thought. Primeau forestalls his conversation with Lacan the analyst by conducting a prior conversation with Lacan the writer, whom he can incorporate by identification.

And Lacan generates a different kind of stabilizing knowledge, first of all, in his demand for speech. That demand is repeated—to take up, for the moment, the paranoid accents of the text—no fewer than six times in the first pages of the interview. Chillingly, Lacan sends Primeau on his way with a cheerful prognosis, and then observes to the class: "Today we have seen a 'Lacanian' psychosis. . . . I don't see how he is going to get out of it. There are suicide attempts which end up succeeding. Yes" (141). Primeau is reduced to a dismal formula.

33. Lacan, "L'agressivité," 111 (my translation).

Primeau's aggression is expressed in his appropriation of Lacan; Lacan's aggression produces his institutionally efficacious knowledge of Primeau. In both cases, aggression produces knowledge through a dangerous, possibly fatal, identification. Primeau sees his psychoses operating in Lacan's registers; Lacan recognizes his own voice in Primeau's telepathic hallucinations. Lacan denies none of these stabilizing identifications, no matter how implausible: "You thought you were the reincarnation of Nietzsche? Yes, . . . why not?" (37). The interview creates a body of knowledge in an institutional setting, generated by inequality and given force and stability by the energy of aggression. Primeau is little more than a discursive prop organizing this knowledge, representing one of the possibilities of a discourse: that it always imputes meaning to another. The clinical interview, in this case, is an institutionally situated form of knowledge that demonstrates how meaning is deflected and how understanding might take root in the gaps and necessary errors of the discourse.

The seizure of knowledge, of course, cannot be accomplished once and for all. Like the tactics of negation and the demand for speech, it is iterated, felt as a fluctuating pressure within the discourse in the moments when the analyst moves from the position of the one who knows to that of the one who desires knowledge. In discussing whether he is receptive to Primeau's telepathy, Lacan says:

> I am not very receptive, since I am showing you that I flounder in your system. The questions that I asked you prove that it was precisely from you that I wanted to hear your explanations. I have thus not received the important part of what we call provisionally "your world."

Lacan's demand for Primeau's speech gives way to a confession of his need for it—he cannot receive Primeau telepathically. Speech is something that he desires from Primeau, not something that he, omniscient, already knows; desire provokes a conversation with someone who can tell us something new. Lacan's need is demonstrated in error, in his "floundering." When his need has been met, Lacan will still be in error, since he will possess—and therefore be possessed by—what he must call "Primeau's world," a world of error. Error is not a momentary complication, retarding for a moment the harmonious happy ending, but the necessary accompaniment of a knowledge rooted in aggressiveness, deflected from aggressiveness only by a mistaken desire. Error incites the action of discourse, implicating it in the subject's system of drives, ensuring that all forms of talk, including the discourse of the university, will be erroneous, productive, and endlessly proliferating.

In the space of the delusive identifications and diagnoses that generate knowledge, the clinical interview is undertaken through patent errors, diagnoses made only to be bracketed ("what we call provisionally 'your world'"), through an avowal of desire ("it was precisely from you that I wanted to hear"). Psychoanalytic action, particularly in this educational setting, does not cure Primeau. Everything that we know and see in the interview, whether we stand in the place of the initial spectators or reconstruct it more dialogically, has been produced within institutional structures of identification, mirroring, and continued aggression. Psychoanalytic action is represented here as a specific relation: Lacan asks Primeau for something, calls on him as a subject. Or, as Lacan puts it in the essay on aggression, "Seul un sujet peut comprendre un sens, inversement tout phénomène du sens implique un sujet" (Only a subject can understand a meaning, and conversely, every phenomenon of meaning implies a subject).[34]

This interview enacts the bad news that understanding is situated institutionally. However strenuously we seek situations in which all speakers have access to all discursive roles, our institutional settings establish relations of inequality and domination. Those settings invoke knowledge as something that has already been produced and enforce identificatory stereotypes that stabilize the paranoia of the speakers. Images unroll, giving way only temporarily to a specific kind of talk that Lacan identifies with psychoanalysis, which we can take as a metonym for discourse that produces a conjunction of subject and meaning.

Psychoanalytic discourse is hedged about with error. It is not the direct apprehension of one soul by another; it is infected with technique, impelled toward scientific reproducibility, located in time, fallible, and only uncertainly transmissible. The slender supports of technique and accountability permit nothing more remarkable than a kind of talk: speaking a desire that is not the Other's, a desire that displaces the subject and deranges its knowledge. Unlike knowledge stabilized by aggression, this inscription of desire changes the subject, changes the relations among subjects. Lacan spoke of "action in the real sense, that of speech"; speech which establishes the subject as agent, locates that subject in time, and permits him or her to become implicated in a stream

34. Lacan, "L'agressivité," 102.

of causal interventions in the ongoing process of events-in-the-world and which does not simply displace a desire assigned to an Other.[35]

On this terrain, universality is not a guarantee of communicative desire for truth but evidence of the stasis of discourse; the mobility of desire counts for more than the subject's willingness to be convinced by the stronger argument. For Habermas, action takes place in a world where error begs to be corrected; for Lacan, it takes place in a world where error is intractable, and where its correction is not necessarily an improvement. Both theories describe the world in which we live and speak.

Rhetoric and the Economies of Reason and Desire

I have defined the three rhetorical terms *language, narration,* and *action* as nodes in a network that establish important relations in a rhetoric of intersubjectivity. These relations are structured by the institutions and disciplines through which modernity organizes knowledge. The question of rhetoric's own institutional situation naturally emerges: we confront its ambiguous status as art, pedagogy, discipline, and protocol of production.

Rhetoric has long enjoyed and suffered from such status ambiguities. Both rhetoric's place among the disciplines and the line of its transmission are contested.[36] Much of what we know about the early rhetors and the Sophists is drawn from critiques of their methods or from analyses of their speeches rather than from programmatic statements. In spite of wave after wave of historical "rehabilitations," the Platonic character-

35. Lacan, *Seminar II,* 297.

36. See Takis Poulakos, ed., *Rethinking the History of Rhetoric: Multidisciplinary Essays on the Rhetorical Tradition* (Boulder: Westview Press, 1993), and Victor J. Vitanza, ed., *Writing Histories of Rhetoric* (Carbondale: Southern Illinois University Press, 1994), both of which include important accounts of these contests.

There is also an extensive literature adapting classical rhetoric for composition or rejecting its influence. For adaptations of classical rhetorical theory, see, among others, Edward P. J. Corbett, *Classical Rhetoric for the Modern Student,* 2d ed. (New York: Oxford University Press, 1971); George A. Kennedy, *Classical Rhetoric and Its Christian and Secular Tradition from Ancient to Modern Times* (Chapel Hill: University of North Carolina Press, 1980); and James Kinneavy, *A Theory of Discourse* (Englewood Cliffs, N.J.: Prentice Hall, 1971). For critiques of this tradition, see James Berlin, *Rhetoric and Reality: Writing Instruction in American Colleges, 1900–85* (Carbondale: Southern Illinois University Press, 1987), and C. H. Knoblauch and Lil Brannon, *Rhetorical Traditions and the Teaching of Writing* (Upper Montclair, N.J.: Boynton/Cook, 1984).

ization of Sophistic rhetoric as a corrupting educational practice and a
debasement of civic discourse still haunts contemporary usage of the
term.[37] Rhetoric appeared for antiquity—and perhaps appears for us—
as a discipline claiming extravagant powers for itself that is denounced
as dangerous or useless by philosophy.[38] Rhetoric's pedagogical claim of
forming citizens and its political claim of resolving disputes, like the
philosophical critique of rhetoric as deception and distortion, are contagious: they reemerge at intervals from Plato, through the Enlightenment philosophers from Locke to Kant, to the present. It is difficult to
believe that such characterizations indicate the same human activity,
let alone the same academic discipline; they suggest that rhetoric is not
something stable and knowable but a contested practice, variously theorized, that requires a pluralist definition.[39] The construction, appropriation, or rejection of a "rhetorical tradition," like the cognate construction of the Shakespearean canon, has been a central tactic in forming
and reforming English as an academic discipline.[40]

Rhetoric is for us an academic discipline, specialized and institutionally situated, located in a number of university departments. It sponsors,
in complex ways, several essential and undervalued pedagogical practices: the teaching of writing, the teaching of speech. It also claims
among its objects of knowledge texts recording premodern oratorical,
literary, and pedagogical practices, texts remarkable for their scope, variety, and ambiguous cultural status. (These are also perhaps the only
texts of antiquity that it is intellectually respectable to dislike.) As heirs
of this canon, we read both praise and criticism of rhetoric with a certain
sense of dignified flattery: Plato never denounced linguists or sociolo-

37. See the useful summary of this history in Jane Sutton, "The Marginalization
of Sophistical Rhetoric and the Loss of History," in *Rethinking the History of Rhetoric*, ed. Poulakos, 75–90, and Takis Poulakos's discussion in "Human Agency in the
History of Rhetoric: Gorgias's *Encomium of Helen*," in *Writing Histories of Rhetoric*, ed. Vitanza, 59–80. For a provocative account of the Sophists, and a rejection
of the narrative teleology that relegates them to precursors of Plato and Aristotle,
see Susan C. Jarratt, *Rereading the Sophists: Classical Rhetoric Refigured* (Carbondale: Southern Illinois University Press, 1991).

38. Janet Atwill, "Instituting the Art of Rhetoric: Theory, Practice, and Productive Knowledge in Interpretations of Aristotle's *Rhetoric*," in *Rethinking the History
of Rhetoric*, ed. Poulakos, 91–119.

39. For examples of pluralist understandings of rhetoric, see C. Jan Swearingen,
Rhetoric and Irony: Western Literacy and Western Lies (New York: Oxford University
Press, 1991), and Herbert W. Simons, "The Rhetoric of Inquiry as an Intellectual
Movement," in *The Rhetorical Turn*, ed. Simons, 1–31.

40. Grady, *The Modernist Shakespeare*.

gists as dangers to the commonwealth. Who was to know there was so much meat on those dry bones of composition teaching?

Our bemusement, of course, also reflects our desire for social agency and for an efficacious means of understanding the discourses that organize our working days. In the passionate praises and denunciations of the rhetoric of Athens, we are delivered from the fears that haunt every disciplined practitioner: that what we do will not, in the end, mean very much. I am not exempt from these fears; I will therefore frame this discussion of rhetoric as a modern discipline by returning to the *Phaedrus,* a premodern text, and examining responses to it by two contemporary rhetoricians: Jasper Neel's *Plato, Derrida, and Writing* and Brian Vickers's *In Defense of Rhetoric.*[41] My reading is indebted to Nancy Struever's sense of rhetorical positions as programmatic and performative and to Martha Nussbaum's analysis of the *Phaedrus* as a moment in the development of Plato's positions on rhetoric and on embodiment.[42] In reading Plato, Neel, and Vickers, I will be working toward an understanding of the rhetoric of modernity as a temporally situated means of analyzing the discursive economies of rationality and desire.

The *Phaedrus* can be read as a meditation on the relations between reason and desire, an attempt to securely distinguish them, and a rejection of rhetoric as a technique for containing them. Reason and discourse are, as we have seen, eroticized. Socrates assigns his speech in praise of love to a fictional philosopher, Stesichorus, from the town of Himera, a name which means "desire" (56). Within the dialogue, Socrates argues that rhetoric awakens the passions of the audience with arguments about probable events rather than cultivating their desire for truth. Rhetoric represents a dispersed, ungovernable, and intractable image of precisely that commutability of reason and desire that, in a different key, distinguishes philosophy.[43] Against this errant rhetoric,

41. Jasper Neel, *Plato, Derrida, and Writing* (Carbondale: Southern Illinois University Press, 1988); Brian Vickers, *In Defense of Rhetoric* (Oxford: Clarendon, 1988). My reading takes place within the context of Jacques Derrida's treatment of the *Phaedrus* in "Plato's Pharmacy," in *Dissemination,* 61–171.

42. Nancy Struever, *Theory as Practice: Ethical Inquiry in the Renaissance* (Chicago: University of Chicago Press, 1992); Nussbaum, *The Fragility of Goodness,* 200–233.

43. Readings of the *Phaedrus* that see it as a rehabilitation of rhetoric include Martha Nussbaum, "'This Story Isn't True': Madness, Reason, and Recantation in the *Phaedrus,*" in *The Fragility of Goodness,* 200–233; Charles L. Griswold, *Self-Knowledge in Plato's "Phaedrus"* (New Haven: Yale University Press, 1986); and David A. White, *Rhetoric and Reality in Plato's "Phaedrus"* (Albany: SUNY Press, 1993).

Socrates is made to propose a rhetoric of divisions and parts, a fitting tool for the philosopher who undertakes the necessary work of persuasion.

We can read against the grain of this proposal, taking our cue from Anne Lebeck's injunction to read the dialogue "as if it were poetry, more specifically, as if it were a choral lyric in a tragedy."[44] In such a reading, Plato's figures of the soul are central to the poetic structure of the text. Sometimes Plato imagines the soul as a charioteer and two winged horses (28), and at other times he speaks of it as a being that "begins to grow wings" (33). We can read these figures as images of reason's vulnerability to the contagion of desire. Placed within a body, the soul is drawn by the beauty of the beloved to recall divine knowledge and grows wings to reascend the heavens. Knowledge is the reward of love; the soul's awakening to remembrance of the divine is represented as a bodily transformation:

> Next, with the passing of the shudder, a strange sweating and fever seizes him: for by reason of the stream of beauty entering in through his eyes there comes a warmth, whereby his soul's plumage is fostered; and with that warmth, the roots of the wings are melted, which for long had been so hardened and closed up that nothing could grow; then, as the nourishment is poured in, the stump of the wing swells and hastens to grow from the root over the whole substance of the soul. (96)

Like the allegories Socrates had dismissed earlier in the dialogue, this fable can be read in more than one way. Traditionally, the white horse is associated with reason and the dark with appetite; the dialogue is read as opposing reason to passion and arguing for the superiority of reason and the need to control, and finally renounce, passion.[45] But both the light and dark principles within the soul are represented as horses—Soc-

44. Anne Lebeck, "The Central Myth of Plato's *Phaedrus*," *Journal of Greek, Roman, and Byzantine Studies* 13 (1972): 267–70 (quotation from 267).

45. For example: "The *better horse* is the rational power, which may examine either universals or particulars. Its companion, the [irrational] appetite, is also called a horse. In ourselves and the gods alike, the better horse and the charioteer participate in identity more than in difference, in rest more than in motion. The *worse horse* is the imagination together with the nature (that is, the vegetative power) and the appetite, the companion of both" (Marsilio Ficino, *Commentarium in Phedrum*, in *Marsilio Ficino and the Phaedran Charioteer*, Michael B. Allen [Berkeley and Los Angeles: University of California Press, 1981], 98). See also Griswold, *Self-Knowledge in Plato's "Phaedrus,"* 94–96; Hackforth's translation of the *Phaedrus*, 107; for an alternative reading, see Ronna Burger, *Plato's "Phaedrus": A Defense of a Philosophic Art of Writing* (University: University of Alabama Press, 1980), 65.

rates does not imagine a horse yoked with an ass, and the dark horse is not alien to the soul. The two horses respond, albeit differently, to the same master and undertake the same activity—drawing closer to the beloved and ultimately to the divine.[46] Indeed, without the rudeness and forwardness of the dark horse, the charioteer would be frozen forever in decorum and never achieve union with the beloved, who would never be provoked into growing wings of his own. It is the bad horse that first approaches the beloved; the bad horse persists in pursuing the beloved, to the "shame and horror" (104) of the good, and finally, when the passion has become mutual, claims "a little guerdon for all his trouble" (106). The allegory represents reason at the mercy of desire: without the peremptory dark horse, the good horse of reason is stranded and immobile, and the beloved soul is never transformed.

The dialogue, in both its frame and its central fable, celebrates philosophy as a practice of discourse in which the dangerous commutability of desire and reason is tamed: the philosopher's desire for truth is eroticized but contained by dialogue and aspiration for the eternal. Not so for the lover, the rhetorician, and the writer. When the virtuous youth is corrupted by the arguments of an unscrupulous lover, discourse has exchanged reason directly for desire. Similarly, the lover of discourse, blinded by the desire to perform, speaks against what is most precious to him; the rhetorician sways the multitude, arousing their passion with arguments drawn from probability, and the written text is maltreated and abused, bent to the reader's desire.

In all these images of passion confounded with reason, discourse is explicitly located in time. For the *Phaedrus*—or at least the myth Socrates includes in his retraction—time is overcome in the anamnesis which rewards philosophic contemplation: a visual recollection of the hyperuranian beings previously glimpsed in the soul's struggle. Such a recollection stands against the particularly rhetorical uses of memory, which are heavily and paradoxically mortgaged to time. Socrates' retraction is followed by a discussion of technical rhetoric, for which memory was a performance skill: the orator's ability to recollect the speech he has

46. G. R. F. Ferrari, in the provocative *Listening to the Cicadas: A Study of Plato's "Phaedrus"* (Cambridge: Cambridge University Press, 1987), 192–93, details the linguistic complexity of this passage. The dark horse is described as using discourse and persuasion to effect his goals, and the charioteer resorts to violence, including the particularly equine action of "rearing back." Ferrari reads this transfer, however, as cautioning against an identification of discourse and reason: the dark horse is using persuasion only instrumentally.

not yet given and to perform the text produced by study as a spontaneous utterance. Rhetorical memory is a technique that conceals labor, a
work in time that creates its own past, eliding the labor of composition.
Embedded in memory, every performance of the oration becomes a
quotation of an inaccessible source. The speech is a kind of Lacanian
symptom, the trace of an object that we first see as it vanishes. Rhetorical memory, therefore, doubles and falsifies the work of philosophic
recollection. It offers a premodern anticipation of Žižek's cynicism: the
audience knows that the orator's speech has been conned but receives
it, all the same, as a spontaneous outpouring. For the *Phaedrus,* the
scandalous force of rhetorical memory is associated with writing, beginning with the eroticized script Phaedrus conceals, ending with the myth
of Theuth, in which writing is presented successively as an improver of
memory, the destroyer of memory, an aid to memory, and a refreshment
or pastime for memory. And since these strictures can only be read in a
dialogue which never, as far as we know, existed except in writing, they
remind us forcibly that we are reading, that we are separated from the
text by time.[47] But the text declares: "Nothing that has ever been
written in verse or prose merits much serious attention" (161). Temporality, and writing, are to be stabilized in a practice of recollection that
simultaneously employs and denies them. Rhetoric, rather than subor-
dinating or containing the temporal, uses temporality as a resource, relying on the momentary passion of the speaker, the inexperience of the
auditor, the temper of the crowd, and the pale reflection of the written
record. Rhetoric is an intractable double of philosophy, compromised
by temporality and committed to the probable rather than the certain.

Socrates does not imagine that souls yoked to bodies can exempt
themselves from time, even in the exercise of philosophic leisure. Therefore, Socrates does not entirely or consistently condemn rhetoric—except as a pedagogy. He does not renounce the use of rhetoric: both
Socrates and Phaedrus use rhetorical categories such as arrangement
and appropriateness to evaluate Lysias's speech, Socrates' rejoinder, and
the devices of technical rhetoricians. Like the dark horse, rhetoric is necessary in a world where truth is not transparent, where decisions are
made passionately, and where speech and writing are not divinely in-
spired but must be shaped and labored. Socrates describes himself as

47. Lebeck, "The Central Myth of Plato's *Phaedrus,*" 288. On the composition
of the *Phaedrus,* see Gerrit J. De Vries, *A Commentary on the "Phaedrus" of Plato*
(Amsterdam: Hakkert, 1969), especially 18–22.

"one who has a passion for listening to discourses," with whom Phaedrus can "share his frenzied enthusiasm" (22): the dialogue offers rhetorical texts as objects of passion. But philosophers are to reject, repeatedly and on many levels, what the rhetorician embraces: time, expressed
in attention to the situation presently at hand, in arguments drawn from
the probable, from what usually happens and is often the case, and in
the techniques of writing and memory to contain the power of time over
speech.

The rhetorical embrace of temporality becomes most dangerous for
Socrates when it organizes pedagogy. Socrates is scandalized by rhetorical instruction oriented toward technique and analysis.[48] By forming the
youth's soul, pedagogy reaches into the future, developing in both the
individual youth and the city as a whole a facility with rhetoricized discourse. Socrates saw such education as tampering with the eternal, with
the domain of philosophy. He did not accept or use this rhetorical practice and never treated it with anything but contempt and ridicule in the
dialogues.

Rhetorical discourse does not suppress passion: passion is given fright-
ening power, as if it persuaded magically. In a dialogue which imagines
passion as a powerful impetus moving the soul toward beauty, rhetoric
eroticizes reason and seduces it into temporality. Even the dialogue's
careful distinction between a passion for speech and speech directed by
passion does not redeem rhetoric.

As present-day rhetoricians respond to Plato's critique—and it is
striking how often they do—they reach quite remarkable levels of
scandalized engagement. Such treatments show why rhetoric is so intractable for us, and what exchanges between reason and desire it organizes. Brian Vickers, whose *In Defense of Rhetoric* deploys a daunting
familiarity with a broad range of rhetorical literature, argues for a traditionally humanist understanding of rhetoric as a verbal art essential to
literary production. Jasper Neel, in *Plato, Derrida, and Writing,* works
out a Sophistic critique of the *Phaedrus* in support of process-oriented
writing instruction. Although these authors have little else in common,
both of them approach with scandalized incredulity Plato's arguments
against rhetoric. Plato has given rhetoric such a bad name, they find,
and used such flimsy arguments. First Neel:

> Yes, I do think that writing is the origin of the soul and of dia-
> lectic, and I think it functions to tell not only readers but also

48. See Kennedy, *Classical Rhetoric,* for an account of rhetorical instruction.

writers something they did not know. And I think Plato knew that too. He could never accept the fact that instead of his writing, writing wrote him. It is, however, high time we dismiss his *Phaedrus* as a serious document about writing, for the text is deceitful and false. It attempts to say the opposite of what its author knew to be true and hated with all his heart.[49]

What is this text that clearly communicates to a critic what its author knew but wanted to conceal? We hear similar tones in Vickers, reflecting on Plato's summary of technical rhetoric in the second part of the *Phaedrus:* "Plato's hostility to rhetoric is so great, and his misrepresentation of it so extreme, that it is impossible to take his accounts as reliable history or exposition."[50] Plato is seen as failing in philosophic neutrality, as attempting to persuade us of the danger in rhetoric's project of persuasion. Both Neel and Vickers find in Plato all the animus, all the deceit, that Plato imputed to the rhetoricians: they see in Plato the worse case made to appear the better; knowing the truth, Plato has used falsehood to persuade a multitude; Plato's discourse is motivated by interested passion, "animus," rather than the desire for truth.[51]

If the *Phaedrus* convicts rhetoric of a deceptive victory over time, Neel finds in Plato an indefinite postponement of the rhetorician's appointment with the best available alternative. Undecidability, in this debate, moves from writing, to rhetoric, to the *Phaedrus,* to philosophy. Neel and Vickers, in accusing Plato of the doubleness and deceit that Plato criticized in the Sophists, accede to the categories of evaluation of the *Phaedrus:* truth rather than secular efficacy; sincerity rather than control of persona; orientation to the unchanging rather than conscious positioning in the temporal. Such concessions make it difficult for either Vickers or Neel to win their argument with the dead.

But perhaps this is an argument they need not win. Rhetoric may be the threatening Platonic double or the accommodating Aristotelian *antistrophos* of philosophy[52]—but the discourses of modernity are adept at managing such reflections. Differentiated discourses are insulated from each other even when they treat similar topics, as prosody is isolated from phonology. Both philosophy and rhetoric are free to propose hi-

49. Neel, *Plato, Derrida, and Writing,* 78.

50. Vickers, *In Defense of Rhetoric,* 15.

51. For an analysis of argument and pathos in the antirhetorical tradition, see Page duBois, "Violence, Apathy, and the Rhetoric of Philosophy," in *Rethinking the History of Rhetoric,* ed. Poulakos, 119–34.

52. Aristotle, *Rhetoric,* trans. George Kennedy (New York: Oxford University Press, 1991), 28.

erarchies which privilege philosophic or rhetorical discourse; there is little fear that these hierarchies will confront each other. Even within a single academic discipline, hierarchical arguments among fields—say, aesthetics, literary criticism, rhetoric, and composition—are far more often assumed than joined. The Platonic quarrel with rhetoric, then, is not open to a dialogic rejoinder. To advance, now, something called "rhetoric" against something called "philosophy" is an empty exercise. No one is there to fight back. No one will ever be there to fight back.

To argue about the relations between contemporary composition or literary criticism and the various rhetorics of antiquity, then, is itself an act of rhetorical memory. And the *Phaedrus* (eliding for the moment the distinction between recollection and memory) offers us a remarkable anthology of memorial styles. The recollection of hyperuranian beings, glimpsed beyond the spheres, corresponds to what Kathleen Welch acidly calls "the Heritage school," which organizes the history of rhetoric as an unbroken transmission from Aristotle to contemporary theory.[53] The remembered and recited speech of Lysias, a reversal of commonsense evaluations, arguing democratically for the underdog, corresponds to revisionist rhetorical historiography. And the garden of Adonis, that overheated and ornamental seminary, corresponds to postmodern subversive historiography.[54] The disciplinary act of recovering and interpreting the various rhetorics of antiquity is an institutionalized repetition of the orator conning his speech, a way of recalling something that has not yet happened in order to organize a future course of action. And this repetition is not an error: only such a constructed memory could mediate among the expert discourses of modernity or remember into being the attenuated public space in which they can be adjudicated or offer the attention to desire that will soften rigid, symptomatic structures of language.

In both Neel and Vickers, such a model of memory and such a connection to action are assumed but not opened to reflection, as in the cynical proverb quoted in Vickers's introduction: "We like cheese well enough, but we still cover it up."[55] For Vickers, rhetoric is an academic

53. Kathleen Ethel Welch, "Interpreting the Silent 'Aryan Model' of Histories of Classical Rhetoric: Martin Bernal, Terry Eagleton, and the Politics of Rhetoric and Composition Studies," in *Writing Histories of Rhetoric*, ed. Vitanza, 38–48.

54. For an illuminating discussion of these approaches, see Victor J. Vitanza, "'Notes' toward Historiographies of Rhetorics; Or, Rhetorics of the Histories of Rhetorics: Traditional, Revisionary, and Sub/Versive," *PRE/TEXT* 8, nos. 1–2 (1987): 63–125.

55. Vickers, *In Defense of Rhetoric*, i.

discipline that combines an analysis of argument with a polysemous understanding of trope; its force is largely analytic. For Neel, rhetoric is a means of instruction in writing that focuses on the process of generating meaning in written texts; its force is largely pedagogic. Both theorists elide precisely that commerce and exchange between rationality and desire which rhetoric organizes, precisely that movement between expert and public discourse, between a constructed past and a projected future, which is the domain of rhetoric.

Such images suggest possibilities of pleasure connected to rhetoric's status as a specifically verbal art, a material practice of language. In both Neel and Vickers, the pleasure is a little recondite:

> If you cannot pick up a list of the figures and read it through avidly, thinking of all the instances of their application and re-creation in Petrarch or Racine, Shakespeare or Milton, then you have not yet thought yourself back into a Renaissance frame of mind.[56]

> Just before he and Phaedrus leave the shade of the plane tree, Socrates finally dismisses writing as nothing more than amusing play . . . [but] writing for Plato was not play, not by a long shot. If anything, writing was play only through its opposition with the impossibility of anything else. Writing is, as they say, the only game in town.[57]

Rhetoric is associated, for different reasons, with play and pleasure in the structures of the written text. However "classical rhetoric" is defined—and Neel and Vickers define it quite differently—it is seen as a practice of language which includes both rationality and pleasure, as a highly structured activity directed at no discernable goal, as a game. In "the Sophists" or "the Greeks" or "classical rhetoric," a contemporary theorist reads an image of a discursive practice that is not differentiated, in which reason and desire are not at odds.

What is at stake, I think, is the anxiety that accompanies differentiation. For critical reflection since Adorno, the assumptions, relations, and gaps among the discourses of modernity have been central problems, made more intractable by the autonomy distinguishing disciplinary discourses. Further, differentiated discourses determine legal and political relations in ways that are not easily regulated by a compromised public sphere. Rhetoric, especially the rhetoric of the Sophists, appears as an

---

56. Vickers, *In Defense of Rhetoric*, 283. Vickers's appendix includes just such a handy list.
57. Neel, *Plato, Derrida, and Writing*, 64–65.

alternative point of origin and promises a general discursive art, a way out of the dilemmas of differentiation, which is something worth defending. Rhetoric in general and the Sophists in particular are constructed as a specular image available for identification, as an other which announces alternative possibilities for our future: we find in the Sophists images of well-paid professionals who operate outside disciplinary boundaries and who suggest that we can practice the discourses of differentiation (indeed, what else could we do?) and also aspire to public efficacy. The rhetoric that scandalized Plato offers an image of discourse in which reason and passion are not at odds.

The discourses of modernity, however, establish quite different relations between pleasure and reason, desire and discourse. They require a rhetoric that accepts partial and probable knowledge, not as an epistemic condition or an antistrophe to dialectic, but as a necessary reflex of the differentiation of discursive practices. A rhetoric for modernity imagines reason and desire not as two beasts of burden, however yoked together, but as connected systems of signification, each essential to the power of the text.

A Rhetoric for the Discourses of Modernity

Rhetoric traditionally recognizes temporality and contingency and values probable conclusions argued from uncertain evidence. But since all the discourses of modernity are temporal, contingent, and concerned with probabilities, a rhetoric of modernity has no "counterpart"; it is concerned with the conditions under which, in contemporary societies, things manage to get said at all.

The Socrates of the *Phaedrus* distinguished philosophy from rhetoric by its subordination of the erotic relations of discourse to the stabilizing aim of discerning truth and forming the soul; rhetoric, on the other hand, is content to use passion as one of the available means of persuasion. (The narrative of the *Phaedrus*, as we have seen, is much less secure in distinguishing means from ends.) For the discourses of modernity, no such stable distinction between desire and rationality is conceivable. A rhetoric for these discourses articulates both the practices of rationality and the practices of desire intersubjectively. Arguments are understood as discursive relations within speech communities, in which claims are opened to correction and argument; desire is understood as the subject's construction of a place in the ensemble of identificatory relations and projects. Practices of rationality can take the relations of desire as their subject or employ those relations as one of their motives; desire can be articulated in the discourses of rational practices. The discourses of modernity transfer energies of rationality and desire from one system to another. They cannot be reduced into each other or collapsed together; they require distinct analytic approaches.

It is the work of a rhetoric of intersubjectivity to organize these approaches and to suggest the terms by means of which the discourses of modernity can be understood in their doubleness and connection. A rhetoric for modernity cannot move directly from analysis to production. No general art can teach students to write the differentiated discourses of modernity, although an analytic discipline can specify disciplinary understandings of what counts as good reason. As an analytic discipline, rhetoric considers the text as language, narration, and action; it finds in the various rhetorical canons a rich body of exemplary texts, but it neither claims them as models nor rejects them as dangerous. The rhetoric of modernity begins with an analysis of language because language, including both the material level of the signifier and the illocutionary level at which speakers enact their relations, carries the dual inscription of the discourse as a performance of rationality and an enactment of desire. The text is understood as written: it is an object of labor, articulated over time, subject to both writerly revision and readerly interpretation. Plato's rhetoric descends to writing and serves philosophy (just as the dark horse is yoked to the light, just as rhetoric uses the passions to persuade), but modernity interrupts this orderly hierarchy. The incommensurable forms of reason cannot be yoked to one another's service or reduced to a common goal which subordinates some elements of the text to others.

A contemporary rhetoric analyzes the language of the disciplinary text to examine its choice of signifiers and the relations it effects between its signifiers and constructed objects of knowledge. The text offers itself as a representation of objects in the world, objects that have been constituted cooperatively with other practitioners of a discipline, objects that organize cooperative action. But the text cannot simply reproduce the current languages of a discipline. It must produce something new, often a new way of writing. The material labor of writing, located in time and space, commits the writer to relations of membership, locates her ideologically, and implicates writer and reader in an intersubjective relation.

Further, as the vehicle for the primary formation of the subject, language also locates the subject's desire in relation to real and imaginary objects. Since language is organized as a structure of division and deferral, the subject's desire does not read itself transparently in the language of the text. Instead, the text, even as it promises disclosure, defers, displaces, and deflects that desire. The text implicates reader and writer in an economy of desire which will never achieve stasis; a rhetoric of intersubjectivity will find remnants of discourses which have been transformed, foreclosed, or abandoned rather than triumphant gestures of closure.

The second rhetorical term, narration, sponsors an analysis of these relations as they are extended in time and as they articulate relations between the narrator of the story and its audience. The structures of narrative permit the labor of writing to arrange and redirect temporal relations. They also structure the text's performance of desire, characterized by deferral and deflection. Narration can be discerned in the differentiated texts of modernity on several levels. It may organize the "content" of the text. A legal document, for example, will include a narrative of "facts" and a narrative of precedents, a secular narrative and a disciplinary narrative. Similarly, a scientific text includes both a narrative about nature and a narrative about science. Within these larger narrative figures, smaller episodes are organized: accounts of experiments or proposals for them, typical instances or examples, contrasts between the historical past and the enlightened present, procedures and directions. In all these accounts, the text poses and answers its central questions: What is agency, and who can become an agent? What counts as an explanation of why something has happened? What counts as something happening? The narrative structure of the text organizes its subjects, objects, episodes, and their connections.

The narrative of the text also positions it in relation to other writings, within a conversation, to use Richard Rorty's terms, that is only known textually.[58] Differentiated conversations present alternative narrative representations of the central moves and significant speakers in a discipline. One of the text's persuasive tasks is to tell the story of the discipline's conversation, so that the text itself is its culminating episode. The text also invites its reader to take up the role of the receiver of a narration, or

---

58. Richard Rorty, *Philosophy and the Mirror of Nature* (Princeton: Princeton University Press, 1979).

in Prince's term, the narratee.[59] In a disciplinary narrative, readers may also be characters in the text's story of the growth of knowledge; in other discourses of modernity they may be the objects of regulation or implicated in legal or administrative proceedings. The telling of stories has always been understood, rhetorically, as a dangerous business: the traditional figure of *narratio* derives from an advocate's presentation of the facts of a criminal case. Under conditions of modernity and differentiation, the relation between the teller of the tale and its audience can be equally intense—and the high-stakes game of narration can be played out over a disciplinary or procedural narrative for decades.

The rhetorical analysis of narrative includes an analysis of the subject as formed in the languages of deferral and displacement, the languages of the unconscious. A rhetoric of intersubjectivity is not concerned, however, with psychoanalyzing writers or readers. Paradoxically, there are few things about a text less personal or individual than its structure of desire, which is almost always an inflection of the "common lot." The structure of desire in a text concerns rather its constitution of a subject who is understood to produce the discourse, and of that subject's relation to knowledge, to the objects of knowledge, and to the reader invoked by the text. Those relations are often deployed in a narrative—of discovery, of origin, of triumphant or fruitless labor. A rhetorical analysis addresses such narratives, not to debunk them or to uncover some shortcoming in them, but to understand what they ask us to do, what the writer has done with the resources—of both textual and secular, inner and outer worlds—at her disposal. Our business in understanding narrative as a structure of desire is neither therapy nor diagnosis but the rhetorical labor of memory. We want to remember what the text forgets into itself, not because it wants to deceive us, but because it is a text.

The final term in a rhetoric of intersubjectivity, action, relates the text to the domain of coordinated social activities. The text is understood as persuasive because of its implication with the drive and its location in a social system of constraints and projects. A rhetorical analysis of action sees action as organized within and without the text. The text does something, moves something, in the world, whether by organizing collective activity or by reshaping the resources of the language. It is located in an institution or refuses an institutional location. The text

---

59. Gerald Prince, *Narratology: The Form and Function of Narrative* (The Hague: Mouton, 1982).

speaks not only about its subject but also about organizing social action, about reproducing society as a domain of knowledge and understanding.

And the text also acts beyond its referential or operational force: it enacts the subject's demand for recognition or the possibility of opening that demand to consciousness and change. The discourses of modernity mobilize the subject's search for a communicative discursive situation, one that redeems the counterfactual claims implied by every speech act and permits efficacious action. This search is organized as an inquiry into what is permitted, an investigation of speech as necessarily displaced—by quotation, by a refusal to speak or to permit speech, by a refusal to hear, by answers that are not rejoinders. Like Lacan's interview with Primeau, the search for full speech will not necessarily strike us as humane or polite; what is at stake is not the confirmation of the subject's desire but a confrontation with that desire as something spoken through the subject. Like Habermas's ideal speech situation, desire is counterfactually present in speech; it is known only obliquely, as an absence. A specifically rhetorical analysis of the text as action makes absence visible and demonstrates it within the disciplinary norms of textual studies rather than within those of psychoanalysis or of political critique.

All three of these rhetorical terms—language, narration, and action—address the discourses of modernity as differentiated practices of reason. A contemporary rhetoric cannot claim a general purchase on all available forms of knowledge; nor can it be confined to inexpert discourses, or the domain of general knowledge. A contemporary rhetoric is a distinct discipline among other text-based academic disciplines, addressed to all the forms of textuality that operate persuasively and to all their means of persuasion. It is both an analytic and a productive art, but it does not substitute rhetorical issues for the properly disciplinary questions that might be posed of a text. Its relation to production is mediated by the academic practices of composition.

Rhetorical issues, as organized by the three terms we have been examining, are complex and significant and concern many levels of textuality, from material inscription and dissemination to the history of a discipline or genre, from construction of a reading subject to construction of statistical evidence. In all of these analyses, a rhetoric of intersubjectivity is concerned with the relations between rationality and desire, with the way in which these two systems are integrated, connected, and separated within the text. Aristotle's proposal that texts undertake difficult persuasive projects by mobilizing the passions of auditors marked rhetoric as a scandalous or powerful discipline. A present-day rhetoric must trace out much more complex relations between emotions and arguments and can claim no predictive power—or even any particular moral force—in doing so. All that can be argued, all that needs to be argued, is that rhetoric opens to reflection the ways that we, and other readers, are persuaded, by ourselves and other writers. Without doubting the credibility of the text, a rhetorical analysis could show that all the claims made in a particular discourse are deeply implicated in relations of desire, are predicated about objects that have no being outside the discourse, and are profoundly and unconsciously implicated in the temporality of the text. Such disclosures move us to think about discourse and desire, about textuality and time, but not necessarily about the claims of the text, which are appropriately tested and decided by a quite distinct discursive formation, that of their discipline, or, under the most fortunate circumstances, of a reconstituted public sphere.

CHAPTER FIVE

Reason and Desire in Public Discourse: Reading the MOVE Report

•   •   •   •   Scientific texts inhabit the forbidding territory of mature disciplines; they are fully differentiated and armed with deeply operational claims to represent nature. Public policy discourse provides a counterpart (an antistrophe?) to the texts of science. Legal documents, government reports, and serious journalism effect specific technical operations of organizing and administering action and respond to broad public concerns. Public policy discourse shares with scientific and technical writing some very general constraints, notably the central explanatory frame of instrumental reason and the formation of an audience of experts, but that audience coexists with a "general public" that reads, thinks about, and holds opinions on issues of policy. Public policy writing is therefore linked to the writing of history and to the tradition of political writing originating in the Enlightenment.[1]

Public policy writing shows us how the discourses of modernity constitute the public; it is a set of diverse practices rather than a coherent body of texts. As with scientific documents, my interest in these texts will be to rhetorically theorize the work of reading, seen as a practice located in time and implicated in error and displacement. When we read public documents within the problematics of reason and communicative action, the issues associated with them are discussed in relation to the

---

1. See the discussion of history in chapter 1 and the works cited in n. 80 of that chapter.

public sphere. Habermas investigated the public in his early *Structural Transformation of the Public Sphere* (1962) and in his more recent *Moral Consciousness and Communicative Action* (1990). These theories were debated in the scholarly conversations recorded in *Habermas and the Public Sphere,* edited by Craig Calhoun (1992), and in *The Phantom Public Sphere,* edited by Bruce Robbins (1993).[2] Here, the public appears as a discursive domain constructed during the Enlightenment and organized by readers, writers, and speakers who participated as individuals without official status and addressed the affairs of public life with the tools of rational persuasion and secular argument available to all writers and speakers. *The Structural Transformation of the Public Sphere* ends with a lament for the corrosion of the public sphere by mass media; in his more recent work, Habermas has seen the possibility of constructing a public sphere which uses such media to increase avenues of participation.

For public policy discourse, the issues of the public sphere and its absence are connected to the traditional rhetorical issues of audience and genre. Just as the Greek rhetorician was counseled by Aristotle to consider to whom he was speaking, their characteristics, and their disposition to the case at hand, a contemporary rhetorician considers how subjects are formed as readers, what stories they have learned to hear, and what forms of agency are open to them. Public policy discourse is sometimes addressed to a general public; sometimes it is composed for other experts in a field of administration. The rhetoricians of the Document Design Project were among the first to systematically study this anomaly in the address of public documents, under the topic of "writer based prose,"[3] which records the procedures of an expert administrator rather than explaining their relevance to a client. More recent studies

2. Craig Calhoun, ed., *Habermas and the Public Sphere* (Cambridge: MIT Press, 1992); and Bruce Robbins, ed., *The Phantom Public Sphere* (Minneapolis: University of Minnesota Press, 1993). For scholarship in rhetoric on the public sphere, see Thomas Farrell, *Norms of Rhetorical Culture* (New Haven: Yale University Press, 1993). For media studies that approach issues of the public descriptively, see Kathleen Hall Jamieson, *Eloquence in an Electronic Age: The Transformation of Political Speechmaking* (New York: Oxford University Press, 1988). Habermas's theory of the public has been extended, critiqued, and developed by Oskar Negt and Alexander Kluge in *The Public Sphere and Experience: Toward an Analysis of the Bourgeois and the Proletarian Public Sphere* (Minneapolis: University of Minnesota Press, 1993).

3. Flower, Hayes, and Swarts, "Reader-Based Revision of Functional Documents."

of professional communication use an ethnographic, rather than cognitive, framework and see the writer as disposed within a network of multiple, conflicting goals. Some of the distinctive forms of "bad writing" associated with public policy discourse—jargon and obfuscation, euphemism, journalistic reductions of complex issues—are read as symptoms of these conflicting communities of readers and writers. (See, for example, the essays in Charles Bazerman and James Paradis, eds., *Textual Dynamics of the Professions: Historical and Contemporary Studies of Writing in Professional Communities.*) Both these trends in the study of professional writing express, within the discipline of rhetoric, modernity's unease with differentiation.

Like all other endemic errors, the "bad writing" associated with government documents, legal texts, and academic writing in the social sciences demonstrates a difficulty in intersubjective rhetorical relations. The writing of public policy is torn between two contrary aspirations: to develop a specialized disciplinary formation and to engage whatever remnants or approximations of a public sphere are available.

Texts addressed to a broad audience do not necessarily sustain the public; nor is expert discourse necessarily undemocratic. I have found no defenders, of whatever political persuasion, of the rhetoric of George Bush's 1988 Willie Horton ads, which held presidential candidate Dukakis responsible for the crimes of a furloughed prisoner, even though these commercials were broad and powerful in their address. And social movements have relied on expert arguments to support comparable worth, education reform, community policing, and a wide range of varied political interventions. Both broad political discourse and the expert writing of public policy studies can have varying effects on the vitality of the public sphere. The text I will analyze, the MOVE report, is a document written in public crisis and addressed to the population of a city; it is deeply engaged with the issue of finding or making a public sphere in which it might be read and understood.

Our own interest in the existence of a public sphere is deeply involved with our desire for historical agency as intellectuals. We try to change people's minds through rational discourse and through all of the other devices of rhetoric: humor, the reinterpretation of classic texts, analysis, the search for stories, the renovation of a language in poetry. We even try to change people's minds when we write that society is constituted in an array of power relations and that rationality is created only within them, or when we hold that theoretical positions have no consequences at all. We undertake this labor of persuasion, not because we think that society is transparent to rationality, but because we must live with the outcome of socially constructed decisions, because we want to influence them, and because we do not want them to be determined by force. As Habermas put it:

> There seems to be in the minds of many of my interlocutors over the past years an alternative I've never quite understood: that when there are differences, we also have the choice of escaping these repressive procedures [of public discourse] and just going off in peace. That's not a meaningful alternative choice. There are problems that are inescapable and can only be solved in concert. Who, then, makes up the concert?[4]

Our labor of persuasion is organized to prevent the concert from being made up arbitrarily. And not us alone: discourse is the only alternative to marginality and silence for those without money and power, the only place where money and power are open to question.

But of course the public is not so simple. Not only is the public sphere, as Habermas projected it, fragile; it also, from its inception, marginalized and excluded other discursive formations, such as the plebeian alternative publics, circles of readers, or informal associations that included women. Nor is exclusion avoidable; even in the most benign political situation, the public sphere will always be imperfect because it is articulated in time, under conditions of necessity and pressing action. Not all speakers will develop their positions; not all relevant positions will be heard; communication will be modulated by mass media to which not all speakers will have access. The public sphere is fundamentally contradictory, since it is formed by speakers who have recognized one another as rational agents and as members of the group competent to discuss matters of public policy and politics. Such recognition is always, has always been, predicated on the identification of others who are incompetent, excluded from the public, whose voices do not count.

That contradiction renders the theory of the public sphere problematic but not useless.[5] We need a precise understanding of the relation between inclusion and exclusion under conditions of contemporary po-

4. Jürgen Habermas, "Concluding Remarks," in *Habermas and the Public Sphere*, ed. Calhoun, 467.

5. See the essay by Habermas, "Further Reflections on the Public Sphere," in *Habermas and the Public Sphere*, ed. Calhoun, 421–61; and also Seyla Benhabib, "Models of Public Space: Hannah Arendt, the Liberal Tradition, and Jürgen Habermas"; Fraser, "Rethinking the Public Sphere"; and Michael Warner, "The Mass Public and the Mass Subject"; all in *Habermas and the Public Sphere*, ed. Calhoun.

litical discourse and an understanding of how, given the contradictions between lifeworld and system and given the differentiation of disciplinary discourses, we can broaden the sphere of public discussion to include more speakers, to address more issues, and to sustain more developed arguments.

All these contradictions can be traced out in the MOVE report. Particularly, we can find in that document a discursive attempt to create a public sphere in which the tragedy of MOVE can be understood, and an ideological attempt to erase tragedy, to substitute a normalized story of transgression and punishment for a political understanding of marginality, inclusion, and violence. These contradictory projects correspond to contradictory moments in the theory of the public sphere; we can trace them out in an analysis of language, narration, and action, central rhetorical terms.

The project of creating a public sphere is not simply an attempt to create good feeling: in this case, by calling for "healing" and "reconciliation" after the MOVE disaster. Although participation in the public sphere has always provoked strong emotions and provided strong satisfactions, the public sphere is also a domain of reflection. The development of the public implies both prudential reflection—problem solving, the anticipation of difficulties—and other demanding modes of thought about the nature of our common civic life. In the case of these events, the borders between quotidian issues of participation and inclusion and tragic issues of life and innocent death are not easy to trace.

Our central text will be the report of the Philadelphia Special Investigation Commission, formally titled *The Findings, Conclusions, and Recommendations of the Philadelphia Special Investigation Commission,* which is also known as the MOVE report (March 6, 1986).[6] The MOVE report comes to us with an armamentarium of associated texts: the archives of the commission, including various drafts of the report; the transcripts of the five weeks of public hearings that prepared for the report; the documents produced by the commission in the course of its investigation; hundreds of hours of interview transcripts produced by

6. Philadelphia Special Investigation Commission, *The Findings, Conclusions, and Recommendations of the Philadelphia Special Investigation Commission* (Philadelphia, Mar. 6, 1986). The report was reprinted in *Temple Law Quarterly* 59, no. 2 (1986). Quotations in the text are taken from the official report and are identified by finding or recommendation number. I have generally normalized the typography of the findings; in the report, the main finding is in uppercase, and the subordinated "dot points" are indented in smaller type below. I quote finding 15 in its entirety below and reproduce, as closely as possible, its format.

private agencies; sustained press coverage of the MOVE disaster and of the commission's own work.

To read the report that was distilled from these texts will demonstrate the strengths and limits of Habermas's categories, which have been both fruitful and problematic in their historical applications. It is remarkable, in fact, how often critiques of Habermas turn on the questions of historical specification (usually invoking the topics of the idealized, the historically specific, or the origins of the public sphere).[7] And just as often, defenses of Habermas renounce any project of historical description, sometimes by valuing the "critical" above the "empirical," sometimes by arguing for a productive disjunction between them, as in Lloyd Kramer's statement:

> Habermas provides the model of a historically informed, critical theorist who sees historical study as a method for challenging and transforming the present as it rediscovers and reinterprets the past. Most historians may be willing to deal with Habermas' work on the first, empirical level, but it seems clear that his own interest in history relates more to this second, critical level.[8]

Habermas's "own interest," to collaborate with this entombment of a thinker whose work is still very much alive, does not actually seem to be so univocal. He sometimes presents his work as a research program, to be filled out by various scholars, including historians. At other times, history offers the possibility of falsifying a theoretical position; historical research has often prompted Habermas to modify his thinking, or at least vary his emphasis. Habermas has usually responded to questions about particular political situations by resisting any unmediated movement from critical categories to tactics for contemporary situations, preferring to point out how a political situation raises problems that have been insufficiently theorized.[9]

We might be guided in the dilemma of understanding the public without idealization by the methodological issue that Lloyd Kramer raises in "Habermas, History, and Critical Theory." How can a historical description—and that category should include discussions of current

7. For critiques of the historical discussion in Habermas, see essays by Baker, Ryan, and Eley in *Habermas and the Public Sphere,* ed. Calhoun. For Habermas's rejoinder, see his "Further Reflections," 424.

8. Lloyd Kramer, "Habermas, History, and Critical Theory," in *Habermas and the Public Sphere,* ed. Calhoun, 239.

9. See, for example, his interview "Ideologies and Society in the Post-war World," in *Habermas: Autonomy and Solidarity, Interviews,* ed. Peter Dews (London: Verso, 1986), 46.

history—strengthen and focus political critique? We cannot treat history and critical theory as interconvertible currencies of knowledge—each discovery of domination generating a proportionate dose of critique. Differentiation implies that there is a price for all such exchanges. The problem of mediating the actual and the critical is perennial in the works of the Frankfurt School and its successors. It resists both general resolution and management through a reified autonomy of the isolated case: no historical event comes to us with its critical force inscribed on its face; none, on its face, forbids critical interpretation.

It is at this juncture that Lacan, theorist of the ideological and erotic force of narrative, becomes essential. Critical theory establishes its distinct interpretation of events precisely by eliding their narrative connections and foregrounding their structural similarities; Odysseus becomes Sade becomes the culture industry. Lacan redirects our attention to the connections that descriptive history and critical theory both establish among the elements of a signifying chain and to the satisfactions that such connections propose for readers through their resonances with other forms of articulation among signifiers, speakers, and hearers. Lacan, in other words, enables us to trace in texts the logic of desire. The text expresses and conceals a desire to be decoded according to the method Lacan derived from Freud:

> what is involved is a reading, a qualified and skilled translation of the cryptogram representing what the subject is conscious of at the moment—what am I going to say now? of himself? no, not only of himself—of himself and of everything else, that is to say of the whole of his system. . . . It is less a matter of remembering than of rewriting history.[10]

To perform such a reading—or, indeed, to make any sense of the MOVE report at all—we will need to understand something of the "whole system" in which it was written, including the MOVE disaster and the political events that generated the report.

No neutral account of these events exists, but there are some facts, in each context, that are not disputed.[11] MOVE, an African American political organization under the leadership of John Africa, emerged in Philadelphia in the early seventies. MOVE members espoused a communal, vegetarian, naturalist lifestyle and a politics of confrontation.

10. Lacan, *Seminar I*, 13–14.
11. John Anderson and Hilary Hevenor's *Burning down the House: MOVE and the Tragedy of Philadelphia* (New York: Norton, 1987) gives a comprehensive account of the MOVE disaster, drawn from the MOVE hearings.

They established a number of collective houses, one of which, the Powelton Village house, was blockaded by the police for a number of weeks in 1978. The police eventually stormed the house; one patrolman died in the assault. Several MOVE members were beaten and a number of them were jailed after the Powelton Village attack.

In the late 1970s and early 1980s, MOVE continued to agitate for the release of its jailed members. By 1980, MOVE had settled into a central house at 6221 Osage Avenue, a street in an African American neighborhood sometimes described as middle class, sometimes as working class. Like many West Philadelphia streets, the 6200 block of Osage Avenue was a series of row houses, with stoops, small front yards, and back yards leading to an alley. Initial relations between MOVE and the neighbors were cordial, but conflicts emerged over MOVE's custom of feeding animals in the yard. They intensified when MOVE blocked the alley with a fence and became serious when MOVE began broadcasting denunciations of city officials into the neighborhood. The Osage neighbors complained to city officials, who were sympathetic but not helpful.

Early in 1985, the mayor asked various city officials to plan an action that would dissolve the MOVE house by arresting some of the adults, dispersing others, and moving the children to foster homes or other sites. On May 12, 1985, the police asked the Osage neighbors to evacuate their homes for twenty-four hours. The police then began an assault on 6221 Osage, spraying the house with a fire hose, injecting tear gas, firing tens of thousands of rounds of ammunition at it, and eventually attacking the structure on top of the house with a bomb. The bomb ignited stored gasoline, setting a fire which burned uncontrolled and destroyed the entire city block. All but two of the inhabitants of the house died. Many accounts show that they were trapped inside the burning house by police shooting into the alley behind the house.

Immediately after the MOVE disaster, the mayor appointed an eleven-member Special Investigation Commission to determine the causes of these events, to apportion responsibility for them, and to recommend steps that would prevent them from being repeated. The commission included five attorneys, three clergy, a businessman, a "community activist," and a former FBI agent.[12] Politically and racially, it was a diverse

12. The commission was chaired by William H. Brown III. Its members were Charles W. Bowser, the Reverend Audrey F. Bronson, Julia Chinn, M. Todd Cooke, The Reverend Monsignor Edward P. Cullen, Bruce W. Kauffman, Charisse R. Lillie, Henry S. Ruth Jr., the Reverend Paul Matthews Washington, and Neil J. Welch.

group. The commission had resources but few powers: it could hire investigators and call witnesses, but it could not indict, subpoena, or charge. Its main power was that of organizing its hearings, which were broadcast for five weeks in the fall of 1985, and of issuing a report, which was released the following spring.

It is impossible to discuss the effect of the report objectively, since the question of the report's efficacy is implicated with an evaluation of its goals and assumptions. The credibility of the MOVE commission was initially compromised, since it was appointed by the mayor whose actions it was investigating. But the commission did not, in fact, whitewash the city administration. The report found the mayor and a number of city officials guilty of gross negligence; the report is punctuated with expressions like "unconscionable," "failed in his responsibility," "reckless," and "doomed to fail." The commission's findings, however, had limited efficacy. Some public officials resigned, but the mayor was reelected, and no public official was indicted for his role in the disaster. The MOVE report was not sufficiently persuasive to hold the highest city officials accountable for their actions.

The MOVE commission had a second, more global task—to normalize the story of the MOVE catastrophe, framing it as an exceptional event caused by particular preventable errors that would never be repeated, or, in the words of the commission's charge, "to investigate the causes and provide means for the prevention of the events of May 13, 1985." Here, the commission's record is also ambiguous. Few of its structural recommendations have been implemented, but MOVE has been ideologically normalized in Philadelphia's civic discourse. When Ramona Africa, the only adult survivor of 6221 Osage, was released from prison in 1992, MOVE was declared to be a singular event, regrettable and closed. The related case of Mumia Abu-Jamal, an African American journalist facing the death penalty, is discussed without reference to the MOVE disaster.

But other impulses beyond those toward ideological normalization speak in the text of the MOVE report. Among its multiple voices, we can discern one which seeks in reflection on the MOVE crisis to shape a more inclusive and spacious public sphere. That voice continues to

---

The staff director was William B. Lytton; the deputy staff director was H. Graham McDonald. Carl E. Singley was special counsel. Emerson D. Moran Jr., the communications officer, drafted much of the final language of the report; Graham McDonald was responsible for designing its structure.

speak in public discourse about MOVE; the construction of such a voice is, in my view, the central achievement of the MOVE commission.

We can begin to hear that voice, and the accompanying echoes of official discourse, in an analysis of our three rhetorical terms—language, action, and narration—in the MOVE report.

Language in the MOVE Report

The writers of the MOVE report faced a number of problems typical of the production of public policy discourse: they were a diverse group operating under time pressure, budgetary constraints, and conflicting political and legal imperatives. The report was produced after several months of investigation; the commission and its staff orchestrated five weeks of hearings to support their provisional conclusion: the MOVE disaster had been neither a terrible accident nor the result of MOVE's intransigence. It was not even solely a failure of the police. Rather, the MOVE disaster demonstrated widespread inability, throughout city government, to contain or manage a crisis.

Beneath this consensus, serious differences in perspective among the commissioners remained. Commissioners had diverse views about MOVE, the Philadelphia police, the relative responsibility of the mayor and the police, and about what compensation should be offered the neighbors. Moreover, the central members of the commission wanted to issue an authoritative—and therefore unanimous—report. Not only was agreement difficult; it was also essential. Although in my interviews with commission staff I found no evidence that these writers constructed an audience outside Philadelphia, they sometimes considered very specific audiences within the city: the district attorney's office, which was deliberating about whether to indict city officials; the press, including specific reporters; and specific city officials whose resignations the writers hoped to encourage. Staff writers knew the inside jokes in the district attorney's office; commission members had years of experience with city officials. Not surprisingly, the authors represented both this collection of influential individuals and a generalized mass opinion under the rubric of "the public," invoking not Habermas's readers who put aside private interests to be persuaded by reason but a collection of individuals whose opinions were formed by competing interests. That collection was abstracted and generalized; readers who were seen as divergent from the "mainstream" were marginalized.

During the two-month recess between the end of the hearings and the commission's review of the first draft of the report, the commission staff experimented with various formats for the final report: a series of questions and answers addressed to major issues; an indexed summary of the commission's extensive investigation; a long report; a short report. But the commission's staff director, William Lytton, felt that the commission should quickly produce a "straightforward telling of what happened," a forty- or fifty-page narrative account, directed to the public rather than to city officials, and later augment it to produce a book-length report on the scale of the Attica report. As the commission's short report was prepared, it absorbed all the available resources and was accepted as its final report.[13] To write the short report, the commission staff adopted a format that organized both their work and the final text: they adopted a report form popular in public relations, the Minto pyramidal format.[14]

Commission Deputy Staff Director Graham McDonald was experimenting with drafts at home when his wife, Susan McDonald, suggested the Minto format, the house style of her employer.[15] The Minto pyramid format conventionally presents a series of conclusions, supported with specific examples and evidence arranged below the conclusion in an indented block. This format would present the commission's findings simultaneously with supporting evidence, so that facts seemed to speak for themselves.

The Minto format also suggested a procedure for composing the report. Each finding would be considered separately by the group: a working session would take up a series of related findings, which would be organized in narrative order in the final text. The commission could isolate its disagreements, increasing the chances of producing a unanimous report. The staff could segment and control the task of producing a written text from the commission's forty-three volumes of hearing transcripts and boxes of depositions. The final report would combine a journalistic urgency of narration—McDonald spoke of a "drumbeat of narrative"—with a structure that articulated findings closely with evidence.

The report, as it was eventually published, is in two parts. The "Find-

13. Personal interview, Graham McDonald, June 2, 1986.
14. Barbara Minto, *The Pyramid Principle: Logic in Writing and Thinking* (London: Minto International, 1982).
15. Personal interview, Graham McDonald, June 2, 1986.

ings" and "Conclusions" of the Philadelphia Special Investigation Commission include thirty-one points, each a relatively terse conclusion
about the operation of a city official or agency. To each finding is ap-
pended a series of indented "dot points" that illustrate it. The relations
between findings and dot points are quite complex and will repay study
later in this chapter. The findings are preceded by a "Chronology" of
the events of the MOVE disaster and followed by two "Additional
Comments," statements that the commission did not feel were supported directly by the evidence at hand but which take up issues seen
as political: the relation between race and the MOVE disaster and
the question of whether public officials responsible for MOVE should
remain in office. The second part of the report, the "Recommendations" of the Philadelphia Special Investigation Commission, was issued
separately. It consists of thirty-eight technical and procedural recommendations: for example, the police should maintain a list of experts in
explosives; emergency services should use a common radio frequency.
The "Recommendations" have not been controversial, inside or outside
the commission.

Unlike other commission reports—the Warren report on the Kennedy assassination, the Kerner commission report on the riots of the
sixties, or the Attica report—the MOVE report was not distributed
commercially. It was mailed to those who requested it, but its widest
dissemination was through the press. It was excerpted in the *Philadelphia Inquirer* (March 7, 1986) and quoted extensively in both print and
electronic media. The commission continued to function for six months
after the report was issued, distributing the document and organizing
its files. Then its papers were donated to the Temple University Urban
Archives, and it went out of existence. The MOVE report had a finite
material life as an artifact of language. Both formally, in its overall organization, and locally, in its specific choices of words, the MOVE report
responds to constraints of time. Its reception and influence were equally
local. Anyone wanting to find a copy of the MOVE report today would
have to retrieve it from archives or find it published in the *Temple Law
Quarterly*.[16] A document that strenuously tried to address and create a

16. Philadelphia Special Investigation Commission, "Findings, Conclusions, and
Recommendations," *Temple Law Quarterly* 59, no. 2 (1986). This issue also contains a foreword by William H. Brown III, the chair of the commission (267–302),
and C. E. Singley's "The MOVE Commission: The Use of Public Inquiry Commissions to Investigate Government Misconduct and Other Matters of Vital Public
Concern" (303–30).

public moved through the space of public discourse in a few months, ending as an article in a journal addressed to professional jurists.

The commissioners and their staff understood themselves as "the conscience of the community,"[17] but they were the conscience of a fragmented community, divided into groups that could discern no common interests or values. Those disagreements were phrased as issues of responsibility: Who did the commissioners answer to? Who was to blame for MOVE? One of the commissioners, Julia Chinn, who lived near the bombed-out neighborhood, refused to describe MOVE as a cult: "I have to live with whatever we take out of here."[18] Another commissioner, Bruce Kauffman, who would eventually dissent from the report's "Additional Comments," was reported to have said, "You can beat up on the [police] leadership all you want, but I won't go for beating up on the guy on the line."[19] Commissioner Charles Bowser, special counsel to the City Parking Authority, one of the first African Americans to compete for high political office in Philadelphia, argued that Mayor Goode could not be blamed for the MOVE disaster: because Goode had abdicated leadership, matters were beyond his control. In establishing the commission as a representative of the social forces that divided the city, the mayor also reproduced within it the failure of public rationality that generated the MOVE disaster. The commission's hours in the hearing room and its seven extended working sessions produced a text with only the most rudimentary common lexicon: the language of blame and responsibility condemns the killing of the five MOVE children who died in the attack on their house. Since the children were not political agents, they could be configured as innocent victims; the commissioners, individually and collectively, drew on a rich store of metaphors and figurative language to mourn them.[20] And the commission could agree on an underlying narrative schema, on a "drumbeat of narrative" that, the staff hoped, would "hammer home" the substantive point of the mayor's responsibility.[21]

17. Personal interview, Emerson Moran, May 19, 1986.
18. Emerson Moran, "Should the Mayor Resign?" *Philadelphia Magazine,* May 1987, 172.
19. Moran, "Should the Mayor Resign?" 166.
20. See Robin Wagner-Pacifici's *Discourse and Destruction: The City of Philadelphia versus MOVE* (Chicago: University of Chicago Press, 1994), 52–68. I am also grateful to Wagner-Pacifici for her early paper, "The Text of Transgression: The City of Philadelphia versus MOVE" (Philadelphia, 1987, typescript), presented at the Temple Women's Studies Forum.
21. Personal interview, Graham McDonald, June 2, 1986.

Within the gaps of the narrative—graphically represented as the punctuating dot points—other stories emerged. If the commission condemned the city for the deaths of the children, MOVE's transgression was subtler and more ideologically serious: MOVE appropriated language reserved to the state. The MOVE report begins by locating John Africa as a source of illegitimate discourse; MOVE members, we read in the support for the first finding, "believed that only the laws of John Africa need be obeyed." MOVE's transgression is configured, first, as a belief. After the declaration of a state of confrontation with the city, MOVE members used loudspeakers to broadcast into the Osage neighborhood their denunciations of city officials, appeals for the release of their jailed comrades, and finally their disgust with their weary and hostile neighbors. These broadcasts were generally described as obscene; at the border between free speech and public nuisance, they illustrated the impossibility of public discourse: Where else would MOVE have gone to ask for justice, if not to the streets of their own neighborhood? Where else could their neighbors have expected privacy, if not in their own homes?

This irony of audience and address, this fragility of public space, this uncertainty of the boundaries between the privacy of the home and the publicity of the street, was not lost on MOVE. Surviving MOVE members rejected the commission's claims to public credibility and refused to testify before it, but the two witnesses most closely associated with MOVE, Louise James and Laverne Sims, repeatedly questioned the legitimacy of the commission. They argued that although the broadcasts were obscene, they were not offensive. A listener who was scandalized by profanity must have known what it meant—must therefore have heard it before. Such a listener has no grounds for complaint. A listener who did not know what was being said, an innocent listener, would not have been offended. Osage neighbors did not concur with this defense; they held that although they might use profanity by choice, in their own homes, it was different to have profanity broadcast into the street so that they would overhear it in their bedrooms.[22] As Charles Bowser wrote in his concurring opinion: "Even though every other resident of the 6200 block of Osage Avenue may have indulged in obscenities and profanities more vile than anything forced upon them by the loud speakers blaring

22. Philadelphia Special Investigation Commission, *Hearings* (Philadelphia, 1985), 2 (Oct. 10, afternoon), 112–15, for James's testimony; and 1 (Oct. 9, morning), 16–18, for representative testimony by neighbors.

from 6221, their indulgence by choice does not empower others to impose the same material upon them involuntarily."[23]

Two transgressions are at issue: MOVE uses language that everyone agrees is common and that everyone but MOVE agrees is "out of place." What is acceptable in the privacy of the home is unacceptable broadcast on the street; what is acceptable on the street, "street talk," is unacceptable broadcast into the house. Quoting again from Bowser, "A family's home is not only its castle, it is also its haven, its safe harbor, its place for private contemplation."[24] The eroded public sphere has disrupted the domain of the private.

All of this is scandalous to the commissioners, who imagine a public sphere which does not include MOVE or its discourse, a public sphere which would resolve the MOVE catastrophe by making MOVE impossible. It is no wonder that Louise James, asked to explain what she means by "the system," responds by withdrawing from the commission and naming it as her adversary: "The system. The establishment. You." And later, Laverne Sims parodies the lexicon of public administration, observing, "I don't understand how people can use the word 'concern' while at the same time trying to kill you."[25]

Simultaneously, MOVE's characteristic lexicon emerges, as if by contagion, in the commission's report, particularly in the nomenclature for its central event. The order establishing the commission speaks laconically of "the events of May 13, 1985."[26] Press reports contemporaneous with those events usually refer to the "MOVE disaster" or the "MOVE catastrophe"; it is sometimes also called "the holocaust" or "the confrontation." The commission's favored term for these events was "confrontation," a very specific term, virtually a term of art, for MOVE. MOVE had formally declared itself to be in a state of confrontation with the city in the fall of 1983, and with the Osage neighbors at Christmas 1983. These declarations were motivated by a specific and quite moderate demand: MOVE wanted the district attorney to review the cases

23. Charles Bowser, *Opinion of Charles Bowser, Esq.*, typescript bound with *The Findings, Conclusions, and Recommendations of the Philadelphia Special Investigation Commission* (Philadelphia, Mar. 6, 1986), p. 7, Paley Library, Temple University, Philadelphia.

24. Bowser, *Opinion of Charles Bowser*, 5.

25. Philadelphia Special Investigation Commission, *Hearings*, 2 (Oct. 10), 105; 3 (Oct. 10), 15.

26. W. Wilson Goode, "Executive Order No. 5-85 Establishing the Philadelphia Special Investigation Commission," unnumbered first page of the Philadelphia Special Investigation Commission's report (Philadelphia, Mar. 6, 1986).

of its jailed members. *Confrontation* also meant an intensification of language: MOVE threatened the lives of police and city officials. As in scientific texts, this unacknowledged public quotation by the commission is a complex rhetorical tactic, marking contradictory relations to authority.

Confrontation, in MOVE's lexicon, was a conflict in which insurgent resolve provoked a revelatory display of repressive force. A confrontation is both an episode in a struggle and a performance. In using this term, quoting it from MOVE without acknowledgment, the commission accepts the assumption that this episode of death and destruction reveals the basic relations of power. The term *confrontation* positions the city and MOVE as equals, reciprocals: x cannot confront y without forcing y to confront x. Of all the available terms, *confrontation* most fully preserves MOVE's agency, and is least likely to figure its members as victims.

Such a commemorative quotation of MOVE is more remarkable for being, at least on the part of the main commission staff writer, unconscious. I asked Emerson Moran why he would not in this context have used such variants as "the crisis of May 13, 1985," or "the MOVE disaster," both terms used by other writers.[27] Moran's reply was interesting: "Because I would never use that word." The report as a whole, Moran said, did not sound like a bureaucratic document, but like a person, "a short guy with a bald head—me, because that's how I write."[28] Precisely at the point when the document is *not* an expression of a personal lexicon, when other voices speak in it, it is seen as deeply personal, a reinscription of the body of the writer. Further, that intimacy and privacy are seen as a negation of the text's disciplinary location: it is not a piece of bureaucratic prose, not an expert document, but a public text, "something people will read." What is spoken by a body is not "impersonal," not the fully differentiated discourse of bureaucracy. The public is configured, for the writer, as a space inhabited by bodies, marked by precisely the individuality erased in the Enlightenment public sphere. But behind the back of the speaker, bodies become inter-

27. I was adapting the procedures of Odell's discourse-centered interview, which elicits information about professional writers' composing choices. The technique is described in Lee Odell, Dixie Goswami, Anne Herrington, and Doris Quick, "Studying Writing in Non-academic Settings," in *New Essays in Technical and Scientific Communication,* ed. Anderson and others, 17–40.
28. Personal interview, Emerson Moran, May 19, 1986.

changeable. Through the short, bald body of Moran speak the dead bodies of MOVE members, in the words they would have chosen.

"Confrontation" is only one of many quotations, both acknowledged and tacit, in the MOVE report. In the report's "additional comment" on race, the commissioners, with Kauffman dissenting, agreed that the decisions that led to the MOVE disaster "would not likely have been made had the MOVE house and its occupants been situated in a comparable white neighborhood." This phrase was deeply contested within the commission—the wording was Commissioner Bowser's.[29] Arguments within the commission were so intense that the staff writers simply transcribed the wording that the commissioners finally agreed on, avoiding any revision or editing.[30] "Would not likely have been made had the MOVE house and its occupants been situated in a comparable white neighborhood" is an extremely interesting verb phrase, both syntactically and thematically. It is counterfactual; it refers to what would not have happened if things had been otherwise. It is also hedged: it refers to what is "likely" or probable rather than certain.

And this deeply marked syntax reflects a social truth about the MOVE catastrophe, although not necessarily in the way that the commissioners intended: there are no white neighborhoods "comparable" to the Osage neighborhood. The initial response of the city officials to MOVE was based on the unstable political alliances leading to the election of the first black mayor in Philadelphia. Those alliances, for which race was always salient, were played out among black elected officials, largely white city bureaucracies, the Osage neighbors, and a range of African American political organizations. In the African American community, where family relations have long been subject to public intrusion, crisis emerged at the disputed boundary between the public and the domestic.

The phrase "would not have happened in a white neighborhood" was an unconscious quotation of a very widespread figure in the popular discourse about MOVE. That discourse was recorded in *Voices from the Community,* a summary of forty-five extensive interviews with "average citizens" conducted by a group of journalists under the sponsorship of the American Friends Service Committee (AFSC) during the summer

29. Moran, "Should the Mayor Resign?" 171.
30. Personal interview, Emerson Moran, May 19, 1986.

before the MOVE hearings. *Voices from the Community* includes the following quotations:

> It may have been sparked by Black people in a Black neighborhood, trying to get the MOVE members, which were Black through the Black Mayor, but at the same time if it were white people trying to get white people out of the neighborhood it would not have happened.

> It would not have happened if MOVE had been in a white neighborhood. I don't think that the decisions to carry it out in that manner would have been so extreme. . . . I can't see them letting a house in the Northeast burn up with . . . white families in it.

> The handling of the entire situation, letting it go on as long as it did . . . is something that would not have happened in a white neighborhood.

> If something like MOVE moved into my neighborhood there would be more interest in what was going on. . . . I think that the people on Osage Avenue . . . let the situation . . . get out of hand. (This quotation was from a white interviewee.)[31]

A particularly florid example of the figure appears in Commissioner Bowser's concurring opinion. Speaking of the deaths of the MOVE children, Bowser writes:

> My personal feelings of guilt are made more burdensome by the conviction that other children in other neighborhoods would have received greater consideration. I believe that if the teen age child of the chief executive officer of a corporation had been in that house, the police would not have shot ten thousand bullets into the house, and they would not have dropped a bomb on the house.[32]

In the AFSC report, and vestigially in Bowser's opinion ("my personal feelings of guilt"), this counterfactual formula implies a complementary figure: Mayor Goode would survive the MOVE catastrophe politically because he was black. Just as a sonnet sequence juxtaposes the idealized courtly lady with the misogynist figure of the faithless woman, "would not have happened in a white neighborhood" joins "could not have

---

31. Linda Wright Avery, Burton Caine, William R. Meek, and Rev. Paul Matthews Washington, *Voices from the Community* (Philadelphia: American Friends Service Committee, 1986), 38, 39, 40.

32. Bowser, *Opinion of Charles Bowser*, 24.

been done by a white mayor." [33] The conjunction recurs in John Edgar Wideman's novel about MOVE:

> Leave the mayor alone, youall. Cat's doing his best. Hate to hear people bad-mouthing him. Specially black people. Finally voted in a black man, and now nothing he does good enough for you.
> Ain't about black.
> Bull-shit. You think they'd let him burn down white people's houses? Sheeit. He be hanging by his balls from some lamppost. [34]

The AFSC working group took as its task precisely the recovery of such "unofficial dialogue about fundamental questions going on across the city in living rooms, churches, and community gathering places." [35] They hurried to finish their work before the commission's official hearings; the introduction to the report notes that while the interviews were going on, the *Philadelphia Inquirer* was on strike. The journalists see themselves as salvage anthropologists, recording what would have otherwise been lost. [36] But this discourse, this "unofficial dialogue," is precisely the kind of discussion that Habermas described, in *The Structural Transformation of the Public Sphere*, as central to the emergence of publicity: serious talk among citizens, outside official responsibilities and channels, about matters of general importance. What was once public has been displaced, not into privacy, but into marginality; publicity is seen no longer as the dissemination of what has been developed in less public settings but as a contamination that irrevocably damages the popular. The public, then, floats free of any specific reference and is also understood in isolation from the broad currents of the popular, the "unofficial." We might even find in this elegiac labor a representation of Adorno's pessimism about the culture industry combined with Habermas's hopes for a democratic concert. [37] But the actual movement of discourses is far more fluid than this. Neither Adorno's fears nor Habermas's hopes are realized in this instance: the formula with colloquial

33. Joel Fineman, *The Subjectivity Effect in Western Literary Tradition: Essays toward the Release of Shakespeare's Will* (Cambridge: MIT Press, 1991).

34. John Edgar Wideman, *Philadelphia Fire* (New York: Vintage, 1991), 41.

35. Avery and others, *Voices from the Community*, 3.

36. For salvage anthropology, see Clifford, "On Ethnographic Allegory," 98–121, especially 111–12.

37. Horkheimer and Adorno, *Dialectic of Enlightenment*, 120–67.

currency is taken up into official discourse without attribution. Shorn from its context, uprooted, it no longer provokes a cynical indictment of Goode as a black-on-black criminal. The additional comment on racism is followed by a comment on elected officials in which citizens are encouraged to make up their own minds: the text will not organize public discourse but will refer it to some impossible other place.

The commission's unattributed quotation "would not have happened in a white neighborhood" addresses the difficulty of forming a public sphere under circumstances of racial division. The counterfactual "would not have happened" records an absence of commonality among the places of the city that might support a generalized and public understanding of its problems. Racism is reduced to an individual failure, defined by particular affiliations and memberships: an African American mayor cannot be responsible for a racist act. At the same time, the phrase organizes a figure of comparability, of failed reciprocity: it assumes the possibility of exchange which is not exploitative. The counterfactual traces out, in both colloquial discourse and the official language of the report, a gap in the fabric of ideology, a place where the conventional topics of race cannot account for either the divisions within the city or the common fate its citizens face. By using the phrase "would not have happened" in its sole comment on the racial significance of the catastrophe, the commission also appropriates an understanding of racial oppression as a failure of reciprocity, taking up this position from popular discourse and locating it within the syntax of blame and guilt. In expressing both the difficulty of thinking about race in the absence of a public and the difficulty of thinking the public into existence, the phrase "would not have happened in a white neighborhood" inscribes the report with a desire for such a space, where both comparability and difference could be sorted out.

In reading the public as an object of desire, expressed in absence and contradiction, I am diverging from the generally rationalist and cognitivist description of the public sphere associated with Habermas and his followers. Instead, I recall Žižek's treatment of the distinction between Lacanian "empty speech" and "full speech." Empty speech functions as a sign of recognition, a password: its propositional content is arbitrary. Such speech, according to Žižek, is the precondition for expressive full speech rather than its opposite. "Would not have happened in a white neighborhood" is at once empty of content and expressive of desire for "the space of articulation of the subject" which Habermas names as the public.[38]

At the same time, the attenuated public sphere, like material public spaces, becomes a poorly maintained point of transit, serving as a homeless shelter for intractable problems, problems which are more complex than the instrumental relation of means to ends. In this compromised space, complex languages like that of the MOVE report emerge: languages that form a dual system, inscribing both reason and desire, collaborating with both critical reflection and ideology, and operating both full and empty speech, both utopian aspirations and a blind search for closure.

Lacan, in his seventh seminar, confronts this doubleness of language, the difficulty of arriving, by means of language, at a sense of the real that permits the law to function as anything but a means of repression: "Reality is precarious. And it is precisely to the extent that access to it is so precarious that the commandments which trace its path are so tyrannical."[39] Nothing in the real renders it accessible to discourse; on the contrary, the real is that which we approach in error, controlled both by our own unconscious processes and by the impossibility of meeting the real on the "tyrannical" terms of law and sublimation. The discursive failure of the MOVE report to open these impossibilities to reflection repeats the MOVE catastrophe, in which the force of law operated without mediation, across the boundaries of public and private. A public space evacuated by reason was occupied by official violence and terror.

The MOVE report assigns error and impossibility to individual agents, who appear as its central characters. Only two individuals are referred to in the report by their proper names: Mayor Wilson Goode and John Africa, the leader of MOVE. (All of the MOVE members, beginning with John Africa, took the surname "Africa" as a substitute for their "slave names.") Although the commission's hearings establish that John Africa died in the attack on 6221 Osage, his death had not been acknowledged by MOVE at the time of the report. One of the functions of the document, then, was to account for a transgressive and wandering subject.

In its first finding, the report names John Africa; it returns to him in

38. Žižek, *Tarrying with the Negative*, 94–95.
39. Lacan, *Seminar VII*, 30–31.

the next to last finding, where his body is accounted for. John Africa is the initiator of MOVE's lawlessness ("They believed that only the laws of John Africa need be obeyed") and the prophetic instigator of the "catastrophic confrontation" between MOVE and the city. A producer of unauthorized discourse, he usurped the power to imagine his own history.

But while John Africa is named, even singled out, as a source of discourse, he is not individualized. In this report, he has no personal specificity; he functions rather as a place from which the report can begin, and on which it can close. His transgressive discourse is not reproduced or quoted. The report therefore constructs John Africa as an unauthorized speaker to whom we should not listen, and as a silenced victim. The creation of such a site is an ideological act; it reverses John Africa's initial discursive transgression. Both dreamlike and instrumental, the report's reversal is an example of the precariousness of the real, of its fragile border with the tyrannical. Having read the MOVE report, we need not read John Africa.

In its final pages, the logic of this project culminates. In accounting for the victims of May 13, the report lists "Vincent Leapheart (a/k/a John Africa)." The common law right of choosing a name is taken from John Africa and returned to official discourse, which names him in the style of an indictment. Such a construction of character is not simply a personal reflection on John Africa. We are dealing with discursive imperatives, as well as with the ritual need for a scapegoat or the ethical need for a villain. The disaster of May 13 took the life of a person named John Africa, and the MOVE report, unnaming him and renaming him, erases John Africa as a speaking, writing character and substitutes a victim, an object of violence. The report completes the act of violent expulsion that the MOVE catastrophe materially enacted.

Action in the MOVE Report

The text of the MOVE report understands and presents action in two ways: as an instrumental relation between means and ends and as a moral demonstration of individual character. Discursively, the report also models communicative and intersubjective action, oriented toward a public sphere. These notions of action coexist uneasily, in contradiction with each other.

The instrumental level of the MOVE report draws on a Weberian understanding of bureaucratic rationality in which the MOVE catastrophe is seen as a failure to adapt means to ends: too much force, used too late. In the hearings, the commission orchestrated a procession of city officials who apologetically explained that the official policy of avoiding a confrontation with MOVE prevented them from collecting overdue water bills, enforcing truancy laws, citing violations of animal hygiene, or inspecting the rooftop bunker for building code compliance. For that branch of public policy concerned with consistent bureaucratic procedure, the MOVE catastrophe is a crisis of enforcement, a failure to calculate the minimum of force and disruption that would contain a transgression of civic order. The "Recommendations" section of the report frames these questions quite explicitly within the norms of instrumental rationality: a good procedure would normalize future transgressions. The first recommendation suggests that city government form a "strategic plan" that can be adapted to "various threatening situations." That plan would "include guidelines for any operational plan"; it is a self-generating document. The inexorable temporality of transgression and the constituting nature of a crisis as a break in time are both to be contained within the plan. The plan is an instrumental text which will proliferate and replicate itself: it will be modified depending on the threat and will give rise to tactical and operational plans anticipating various acts of violence. A cross-reference leads the reader to a related recommendation, for Police Tactical Plans, which "should include contingency options" (recommendation 24). The writers of the report relocated their story counterfactually into the past as a projected narrative about a possible future. Such a narrative is now demanded as protection against future transgressions; the plan will contain MOVE in the past, as a singular event.[40] If the story of MOVE had been told before the fact, as a plan, with enough variation of outcome, the series of accidents, errors, and violent interventions would have been averted. The plan, a document of rationalization, takes on magical force. Its narrative of the future controls the past, rectifies errors, and establishes an agency which reduces the wanderings of language to a narrative path. The MOVE report advances instrumental rationality as a remedy for crisis and transgression. Instrumental reason is a calculation of means and ends which establishes the world as an object of control, circumscribing it, ex-

40. For a densely particular treatment of narrative in public policy discourse, see Emery Roe, *Narrative Policy Analysis: Theory and Practice* (Durham, N.C.: Duke University Press, 1994).

cluding from thought both mythical and mysterious discourses while drawing on their force. Instrumental reason also excludes self-reflection from public speech and writing; critique becomes an unacceptable risk. "Thinking objectifies itself to become an automatic, self-activating process; an impersonation of the machine that produces itself, so that ultimately the machine can replace it."[41] The logic of instrumental reason reduces the catastrophe to a singular event that could have been controlled, and therefore to an event that will not happen again. Had city officials acted rationally, MOVE would have been contained. Had they planned the confrontation, it would not have gotten out of control. If a planning body is instituted, such a disaster will never be repeated. Very strong readerly desires support such prudence: a desire to assign responsibility for death and destruction, to see it as a failure of the normal structures of the city, to place it securely in the past.

Such a normalization of crisis demonstrates the limits of instrumental rationality; it also demonstrates Habermas's disjunction between instrumental rationality and functionalist rationality. While agreeing with the Frankfurt School critique of instrumentalism, Habermas rejects their interpretation of modernity as marked by the subsumption of all cultural and ideological production to the functional needs of capital. Habermas asserts a disjunction between system rationality and the norms of the lifeworld, managed in only a limited way by bureaucratic structures.[42] Technical writing demonstrates the contradictory relation between the instrumental deployment of scientific knowledge and any project of Enlightenment. Similar tensions shape public discourse. System rationality adjusts itself through the nonlinguistic media of money and power, independently of the desires, motives, or explanations of individuals. There are limits to this process: a disenchanted culture has diminished ideological force.[43]

And indeed, the instrumental rationality that informs much of the MOVE report is pretty thin soup, ideologically speaking. The writers supplement their advocacy of good procedure with a meditation on agency, organized as a narrative of character about Mayor Wilson Goode. For the commission, the agency of the mayor is constructed as an instance of failed moral responsibility; its rhetoric for Mayor Goode is epideictic, a catalog of the terms of civic blame. But the report's blame is

41. Horkheimer and Adorno, *Dialectic of Enlightenment*, 25.
42. See *Theory of Communicative Action*, 2:350–51, and also Benhabib, *Critique, Norm, and Utopia*, chap. 7, "The Critique of Functionalist Reason."
43. Habermas, *Theory of Communicative Action*, 2:353.

incoherent, imperfectly realized. Moral blame implies moral agency, a realized subjective consciousness not ascribed to Goode. In the report, he is simultaneously worthy of blame and incomprehensible: both the failed leader and the ineffective CEO. And the MOVE report is not unique in this incoherent epideictic: the categories of blame and responsibility are deeply problematic in contemporary public discourse. The findings that name Mayor Goode identify him as a site of negation.

3. Mayor Goode's policy toward MOVE was one of appeasement, non-confrontation and avoidance.

Mayor Goode is first identified by his proper name; he will be designated as "the mayor" for the rest of the document. Goode and Africa are the only individuals named in the report; the conscious policy of the writers, designed to focus on systems rather than individuals, was to indicate characters by office, title, or affiliation: "the Managing Director," "a sergeant from the pistol range," "the Osage Neighbors." Goode and Africa were unconsciously exempted from this policy. Their names are, ironically, foregrounded by the general anonymity, so that the MOVE catastrophe becomes a combat between the two of them. The commission mobilizes the powerful explanatory categories of plot: Goode versus Africa, protagonist versus antagonist, agent versus counteragent. The findings continue:

6. In the first several months of his administration, the Mayor was presented with compelling evidence that his policy of appeasement, non-confrontation and avoidance was doomed to fail.
7. In the summer of 1984, the Mayor was told that the legal basis existed at that time to act against certain MOVE members. Yet, the Mayor held back, and continued to follow his policy of avoidance and non-confrontation.
9. More than any other factor, intensified pressure from the residents of Osage Avenue forced the Mayor to abandon his policy of non-confrontation and avoidance, and to devise a strategy for resolving the problem quickly.
10. The Mayor instructed the Police Commissioner to prepare and execute a tactical plan, under the supervision of the Managing Director. The Managing Director failed in that responsibility, and the Mayor allowed the Police Commissioner to proceed on his

own. [The findings are quoted here without their supporting points.]

After taking up the role of major officials, the report returns to the mayor in findings 15 and 17:

15. The Mayor's failure to call a halt to the operation on May 12th, when he knew that children were in the house, was grossly negligent and clearly risked the lives of those children.
17. The Mayor failed to perform his responsibility as the City's chief executive by not actively participating in the preparation, review, and oversight of the plan.

And after a summary of the police activities of the day, we read:

22. The Mayor abdicated his responsibilities as a leader when, after mid-day, he permitted a clearly failed operation to continue which posed great risk to life and property.
24. The plan to bomb the MOVE house was reckless, ill-conceived and hastily approved. Dropping a bomb on an occupied row house was unconscionable and should have been rejected out-of-hand by the Mayor, the Managing Director, the Police Commissioner, and the Fire Commissioner.

These findings are an anthology of negations. The mayor and his administration "failed to take any effective action," "discounted negotiations," and ignored the problem, even when presented with "compelling evidence that their policy had failed." When a legal strategy for limiting MOVE was suggested, the mayor failed to implement it. In the dot points supporting the ninth finding, these negations generate a global affirmative: MOVE was granted "the continued right to exist above the law." Agency is sustained as a refusal to act: the mayor is figured as a dead letter office, a nodal point at which information, complaints, and issues arrive, and from which nothing returns. His passivity is condemned in the strongest terms of moral and legal responsibility: "grossly negligent," "unconscionable."

In the instrumental world of the report, actions are related to each other as problems to solutions; every action not taken is a solution forfeited.[44] The counterfactuals that multiply in these findings generate a

---

44. See Richard Ohmann, *English in America: A Radical View of the Profession* (New York: Oxford University Press, 1976), for the ideology of problem and solution.

narrative series in which negation and inactivity characterize Mayor Goode. Even though other individuals were quite active during the period in question—John Africa was threatening confrontation; the police were collecting arms; the FBI was delivering explosives—the text locates agency in the single character who did nothing. Inactivity is figured as a provocation. From the mayor's appeasement proceed 10,000 rounds of ammunition.

Later, in finding 15, the mayor is reproached for failing to halt the MOVE operation. Having constructed for the mayor an agency of abstention, the commission generates from his character another failed instrumental solution: when action should have stopped, the mayor allowed it to continue. Instrumental reason takes precedence over narrative cohesion: the mayor's hesitation signifies his individual failure as a leader, whether he abstains from action or sponsors furious activity. Paradoxically, the mayor is both individually responsible for the catastrophe and depersonalized. His hesitation does not carry any emotional charge; it is unmotivated and contingent rather than expressive. Mayor Goode is to action, then, as John Africa is to language; he illegitimately engrosses a system of signification.

But the commission refused to draw the operational conclusions of its own terms of blame; they did not call for the mayor's resignation. When, in its final "additional comment," the commission took up the question of whether Mayor Goode should resign, they pointed out that voters choose public officials and declared: "After thoughtful discussion, the Commission concluded that the Report speaks for itself." One of the many instances of contagion in the discourse about MOVE, the commission's abstention recalls Goode's: the scenario of public irresponsibility will be repeated as Goode continues in office, serves a second term, and retires from public life with MOVE "behind him."

The characters John Africa and Wilson Goode are complementary. John Africa produces an unauthorized discourse that the report erases; Wilson Goode, who failed to articulate official discourse, functions as a site of blame. John Africa aspired to agency but is refunctioned as a victim; Wilson Goode, who urged restraint, is assigned responsibility for reckless, headlong action. Both characters disrupt an ideal economy of instrumental discourse, in which meaning moves without restraint from the centers of police power through the neighborhoods of the city, dispersing order and returning to the center as legitimation. Neither Goode nor Africa is an individualized, realistic "character"; they are places where the discourse of the report can be organized. The report uses these two proper names to argue the singularity of the catastrophe, its quality as a crime which is also a dreadful mistake, and therefore the unlikelihood that it will be repeated.

This difficulty is a rhetorical problem entailed in the corrosion of a public sphere. For the Enlightenment, public discourse permitted a relatively unproblematic transfer of praise and blame through topics such as courage and benignity, which named both individual dispositions and public virtues. Contemporary discourse, for which the boundaries of public and private are both fragile and opaque, is poor in terms that permit such easy transfers. Terms of praise and blame applied to individuals are likely to be drawn from a psychological or legal register, as if the actions of public leaders, which can cause or relieve suffering on inconceivable scales, are adequately explained by calling them "evil" or by pointing out that they violate federal laws.

The report establishes Goode as blameworthy by establishing his inability to act, or even to speak. In framing his silence, the report draws on testimony from Laverne Sims. Sims, asked what the mayor said in her meetings with him, replied, "The Mayor doesn't say too much. He listens but really he doesn't talk . . . [that] much."[45] In his own testimony, Goode accepted Ms. Sims's characterization. In the MOVE report, Goode's silence is generalized:

- All occasions on which the Mayor met with MOVE were instigated by MOVE members or sympathizers and were held for the sole purpose of airing MOVE's grievances. The Mayor's posture was to listen, but not to act. [Support for finding 5]

In Ms. Sims's account, the mayor's silence is a personal trait; her testimony is organized by the colloquial figure of someone who "doesn't talk much," generally a neutral characterization. Goode accedes to the characterization, perhaps because of its neutrality or perhaps because it resonated with the conventional wisdom that a good leader is a listener. In the report, the mayor's listening is a refusal of speech, a refusal to even choose the forum for speech; it is an abdication to MOVE. The mayor's silence thus circulates from MOVE to the city administration and the supporters of MOVE, substituting for the discourse of power—for the official, impossible words that would have restrained MOVE, contained its threat to the city, and eliminated the need for violence. Quotation here blames the mayor but also attempts to rectify

45. Philadelphia Special Investigation Commission, *Hearings*, 3 (Oct. 10), 121.

his shortcomings, to establish an economy of discourse within the bounds of the report that was missing in the public sphere of the city.

A final instance of quotation associated with Mayor Goode is especially poignant. In finding 22, which concerns the mayor's failure to cancel the operation at midday of May 13, the mayor is quoted as saying that he was prepared "to seize control of the house . . . by any means necessary." The report does not identify the mayor's unattributed quotation of Malcolm X. "By any means necessary," originally a rejection of nonviolence in the Civil Rights Movement, later a generalized call for militancy, has entered the common language as a wholesale expression for determination. But it is bitterly ironic to see this phrase, formed in a tradition to which MOVE was a distant and impoverished heir, used to justify their deaths.

Habermas has written on the contradictions between citizenship in a democracy and clientage to a welfare state:

> "Clients" are customers who enjoy the rewards of the welfare state; the client role is a companion piece that makes political participation that has been evaporated into an abstraction and robbed of its effectiveness acceptable. The negative side effects of institutionalizing an alienated mode of having a say in matters of public interest are passed off onto the client role in much the same way as the burdens of normalizing alienated labor are passed off onto the consumer role.[46]

Everything that Hegel has taught us suggests that the relation of clientage must also affect the bureaucrat. In the MOVE report, we read of a city bureaucracy, five years into the Reagan era, drained of its resources, deprived of effective agency, and reduced to an abstraction of governing. Regulations justify inaction. Raymond Tate, of Licensing and Inspections, overlooked the fence MOVE built to block the alley because his department "had no jurisdiction in a driveway" and determined that the rooftop bunker on 6221 Osage did not violate city regulations because it "was not structurally dangerous."[47] Tate considered that events vindicated his judgment—that bunker, after all, withstood intense rifle fire and was not dislodged even by fire hoses. Goode concentrates such parodic reduction of the power of government to its narrowest function; he becomes the bare act of listening, deprived of any intersubjective force: for Goode, to listen to someone is to ensure that their words will have no effect. The passivity and abstraction of clientage characterize

---

46. Habermas, *Theory of Communicative Action*, 2:350.
47. Philadelphia Special Investigation Commission, *Hearings,* 3 (Oct. 10), 235.

not MOVE or the Osage neighbors but city officials. The mayor is the chief client of the welfare state.

The report inscribes this passivity in its figure of the city as a body. The city administration decided that MOVE had become "too hot to handle," and they are "paralyzed"; the mayor wanted the managing director to act as his "eyes on things"; the city departments adopt a "hands off" attitude (finding 3). A contagion of the mayor's passivity reduces the city to a single catatonic body, hysterically refusing to touch or handle the matter of MOVE. In the last of the report's findings, the bodies of MOVE members are handled with cranes and buckets, "dismembered and commingled" (finding 31); the hysterical refusal to touch becomes grimly material. The city cannot survive contiguity with the transgressive bodies of MOVE; in order to restore the integrity of its official body, even the corpses of the MOVE members must be reduced to dust.

Such a text requires an analytic method at home with the irrational, a theory of the drive. The drive, we recall, organizes desire in relation to an object which always substitutes for—and deflects action from—desire's impossible and inconsequential origin. Within this text, we might notice that the drumbeat of narrative brings to bear on the MOVE catastrophe a desire for narrative closure. Since every possible reader of the report knows how these events end, we are implicated in the report's trajectory toward the death and destruction that resolve the MOVE crisis. We also desire to avert just that ending, to make it singular, to place it in the past.

The report also provokes a desire for a certain experience of reading. Kenneth Burke clarified how political discourse establishes boundaries of membership through correlative acts of identification and solidarity and of the expulsion of the outsider, the scapegoat:

> "Identification" is, by the same token, . . . to confront the implications of *division*. And so, in the end, men are brought to the most tragically ironic of all divisions, or conflicts, wherein millions of cooperative acts go into the preparation for one single destructive act. We refer to that ultimate *disease* of cooperation: *war*.[48]

We can fruitfully read this passage in conjunction with Habermas on the boundaries on the public and its silent exclusions and with Lacan on the dialectics of expulsion and identification in the vicissitudes of the drive.

48. Burke, *A Rhetoric of Motives*, 22.

As we have seen, for Lacan the drive is always deferred or, in error, deflected: it is at its center a structure of representation and substitution. In his later seminars, Lacan connected the drive and the possibility of its sublimation to the ethical—not in order to make any reassuring connection between "natural" desires and the good, but rather to argue for the fundamental contingency of all such connections and therefore to ground psychoanalysis in the body and its representations.

For the MOVE report, the figures of John Africa and of Mayor Goode are in many ways interchangeable, even though the text characterizes Africa as irredeemably other. The chain of events that led to the MOVE catastrophe can be initiated with either character: the segmented structure of the MOVE report allows for multiple, contradictory inceptions of action. Both characters are located in an undifferentiated milieu of "supporters" and "city officials" who surround them. They are locked in narrative complementarity, as if Africa caused Goode or Goode caused Africa. The report seeks to form from the two characters an object strong enough to support the drive. Lacan's term for desires associated with the drive was *dérive*, referring to the wake of a boat or the trail of an aircraft, suggesting that the subject addresses the intractable problem of satisfaction through wandering, under the sign of an absence.[49] "The satisfaction of the *Trieb* is, then, paradoxical, since it seems to occur elsewhere than where its aim is."[50] Neither Goode nor Africa functions as a satisfying image of civic leadership, or even of competent agency; in imagining them as complementary agents, the report disperses an image of power, of unlocalized and impossible agency.

The MOVE report multiplies scenarios for instinctual satisfaction—scapegoating, substitution, utopian rectification—and translates central characters and locations from one scenario to another. Goode appears as the object of Africa's attack, as a victim—and also as the vengeful attacker of Africa. The report is interested in defining the boundaries of membership in order to exclude Africa, but more fundamentally Goode, who is read out of the community that reprehends the reckless deaths of MOVE children. The dispersal of the bodies of MOVE members is repeated and mourned in the dispersal of the city officials who should have protected them, and the report imagines—although it does not dare suggest—that this dispersal will become complete, that the city administration will be dismantled. Within the boundaries of the report's

49. Ragland-Sullivan, *Jacques Lacan and the Philosophy of Psychoanalysis,* 75.
50. Lacan, *Seminar VII,* 111.

narrative, there is no membership without exclusion, no solidarity without the expulsion of an outsider—and no character who cannot be defined as the outsider to be expelled.

Classically, sublimation is the preferred alternative to scapegoating; the text of the report, however, follows the logic of symptom rather than sublimation. Lacan defined sublimation as finding substitute objects for the drive that did not eventuate in the formation of neurotic symptoms: "It is a paradoxical fact that the drive is able to find its aim elsewhere than in that which is its aim—without its being a question of the signifying substitution that constitutes the overdetermined structure, the ambiguity, and the double causality, of the symptom as compromise formation." [51] But precisely these overdeterminations, ambiguities, and doubled statements of causality mark the narrative of the report.

In any case, Lacan consistently dismissed as "pastoral" any notion that sublimation was necessarily connected to the "good," as misguided hope that what is natural could be accessible to consciousness without mediation, and that it might generate satisfaction without conflict. If we understand the narrative of the report as shaped by the vicissitudes of the drive, as implicated in errors and substitutions, we do not therefore project a rectified document free of error, which would distribute blame and praise without ambiguity and in which each agent is firmly located within the skin of a legally responsible public official. Such discursive good order is simply not available; the MOVE commission could not, by an act of the will, have created it. A rhetoric at home with the drive cannot advance pastoral hopes for a rectified, sublimated text.

I approach the MOVE report with my own desires: for an end to violence, for a work of memory that would recognize the victims, for a restoration of inclusive citizenship. My demand of rhetoric is that it do the work of displacement efficiently enough to avert violence, to open a space for reason and memory. The project of rhetorical analysis cannot exempt the report from the interrogation of such desires, an interrogation that will find it wanting.

But the MOVE report also imagines a public sphere which might have contained the transgression of MOVE, a form of communicative action that might have organized the dialectic of membership and division into talk rather than war. Habermas has observed: "It is primarily in these two channels [consumption and clientage] that new conflict

51. Lacan, *Seminar VII,* 110.

potentials of late capitalist society are growing."[52] In the case of MOVE, the relations of clientage created a network that linked MOVE to the neighborhood and its organizations, and to city government. Although both the city officials and the members of the commission were anxious to preserve a strong demarcation between MOVE and the city, the testimony before the commission reveals a pattern of connection and collaboration:

> Lieutenant Draper of the Philadelphia Police Department Public Affairs Office had contact almost daily with Nathan Foskey, a retired policeman who lived on the 6200 block of Osage Avenue. Draper grew up with Frank Africa, one of the central MOVE members.
>
> Gloria Sutton of the Philadelphia Commission on Human Relations had friendly relations with MOVE members, including Delbert Africa.
>
> Albert Meyers, a supporter of MOVE, was an old friend of Bennie Swans, of the Crisis Intervention Network, a quasi-public agency.
>
> Robert Owens, who worked with Swans, grew up with Conrad Africa.
>
> James Prior of the Crisis Intervention Network was embraced on the street by a neighbor who had been his schoolmate as a way of provoking MOVE members.
>
> Ralph Teti, the deputy city solicitor who heard many of the neighbors' complaints, went to church with Cassandra Carter, an Osage neighbor.

These personal ties are replicated in the treatment accorded both MOVE and the Osage neighbors by city agencies, treatment that scandalized the commission—not only did MOVE carry heavy weapons, but they were behind on their water bill! MOVE received housing rehabilitation money from the city and used it to build fortifications that the city would later violently destroy. The structures of ambiguity, double causality, and overdetermination that mark the report replicate the actions of the city, MOVE, and citizen organizations. This doubleness, an entwined structure of collaboration, made MOVE so intractable. Had MOVE really existed outside the social relations of the city, the organization would not have been scandalous; woven into the city's adminis-

---

52. Habermas, *Theory of Communicative Action*, 2:350.

trative structures and informal networks, it was an insoluble problem.

But just as the neurotic symptom expresses the subject's desire as a demand of the other, the collaboration between the city and MOVE expresses an impulse toward a different form of communication. If system colonizes lifeworld, the informal relations between MOVE and the city administration suggest the possibility of lifeworld colonizing system. While instrumental rationality demands that all citizens, without exception, pay their water bills, the city solicitor speaks to MOVE's next-door neighbor: "We belong to the same church and it's a common occurrence that people in the same church communicate; both the good and the bad."[53] In a city where the official monthly meetings of the central administration never discussed MOVE, we can only be grateful that there were some places where "both the good and the bad" would, from time to time, talk.[54]

This, of course, is not enough. The transfer of information from neighbor to city official is a very old event in the history of cities, and even the most highly developed conditions of modernity are not likely to stop it. But the text of the report represents, and unconsciously enacts, however unevenly and with whatever contradictions, the construction of a public sphere from such relations at the borders of the public and the private, where the good and the bad could talk together.

William Brown, chair of the commission, asserted the desire for such a public when he said, "You the people will be able to judge . . . you will be the jury."[55] Such a judgment would begin the "healing" that the city so urgently needed.[56] Brown stated that the "intricate testimony" before the commission would require the audience's full attention;[57] it had already been organized, orchestrated, and carefully planned to support the main burden of the report.[58] Under conditions of modernity,

53. Philadelphia Special Investigation Commission, *Hearings,* 3 (Oct. 10), 32.
54. These meetings included the police commissioner, head of Human Services, head of Mental Health, chair of the School Board, and directors of the Public Transportation System, the Licensing Bureau, and the Streets.
55. Philadelphia Special Investigation Commission, *Hearings,* 3 (Oct. 10), 7.
56. Philadelphia Special Investigation Commission, *Hearings,* 3 (Oct. 10), 5.
57. Philadelphia Special Investigation Commission, *Hearings,* 3 (Oct. 10), 13.
58. Both internal and external evidence points to the orchestration of testimony. The commission led a ballistics expert through a careful set of questions to justify calling the device that exploded on the MOVE house a "bomb" rather than, as the Police Department had been calling it, an "entry device." An hour or so of testimony supported a single noun in the report. Commission staff members confirmed, in interviews, that the testimony was carefully planned to tell the story whose outlines had become clear to the commission in its initial investigation.

all public discourse is mediated by extremely complex communicative practices, and no extended discussion could ever take place without careful planning—a planning which cannot, by its very nature, be neutral or disinterested.

The MOVE commission's hearings and its report are instances of a contemporary rhetoric in search of the public. Like all instances of civic rhetoric, the report and the hearings seem less authentic for being the object of discursive labor. The same impulse that led Enlightenment theorists to distrust figure and ornament in political oratory makes us suspect the techniques used by the commission: attention to credibility and to voice, exploitation of the resources of time, of duration, and of delay. But there can be no reconstruction of the public without rhetoric, and such a reconstruction will necessarily use the distinct arts, ornaments, and figures of contemporary discourse.

We read in the MOVE report multiple configurations of social action. The text explicitly investigates agency in its reflections on explanation and blame, in connecting events to individuals. And issues of agency shape the text unconsciously, in the way individuals and events are named and in silent quotations, incoherence, and error. An impulse to exclude coexists with, and motivates, an impulse to broaden the boundaries of the public.

It is that last impulse that we turn to now, tracing out the desire for a public sphere in this document so deeply implicated with the decay and corrosion of the public. Syntactically, the text includes multiple voices in its many quotations, including quotations of MOVE's nomenclature for the central event, the "MOVE confrontation," and of colloquial explanations for the racial character of that event. The text imagines forms of activity that support a public sphere and forms of discourse that might reconstruct it. Not all these invocations are successful, or even coherent. If the public sphere is attenuated, its realization is likely to be contradictory.

Within the nascent discourses of the public sphere, language functions as a dual system in which both desire and rationality are deployed and used to represent one another. What makes sense instrumentally becomes a figure for averted disaster, for a repeated miraculous escape. The objects of fear and reprehension are taken into the project of talk, urged to speak, and their discourse is simultaneously remembered and forgotten. The text distributes actions and reactions with judicious impartiality over the surface of its plot, and also elaborates a discourse of nightmarish punnings and punishments.

Nothing in the structure of political discourse, nothing external to it in the social world, nothing in the relations of speakers to one another, guarantees that in public discourse the better reason will prevail over the worse. Nothing in any of those arenas, nor anywhere else, guarantees that in the domain of the public, any speaker will distinguish the better from the worse reason. If the starry skies above us no longer proclaim what is true about the natural world, there is no moral law which speaks reliably within us about how we ought to act in the domain of the social. Hence, the difficulty of organizing—or even inhabiting—society. What distinguishes public policy writing, along with scientific discourse, as a discourse of modernity is its availability as a relay, a place where the topics and figures appropriate for expressing desire and rationality are converted into one another—hence also the need for rhetoric, for some art of persuasion which can use both the better and the worse reasons to coordinate activity.

A rhetoric for modernity cannot promise historical deliverance, totalized understanding of the social, or any guarantee of the efficacy of a historical subject's political interventions. Admitting all that, I also raise the possibility that while rationality is not reliably discernable, while it is fundamentally entangled with desire, it is also not a meaningless concept. Since the texts of public administrative and political discourse are produced intersubjectively, and since there is no position within intersubjective relations that stably—or even provisionally—guarantees the truth of its discourse, these texts are always provisional. But provisionality, multiplicity of positions, contests over what counts as an adequate description or as a good reason—none of these disputes over the landmarks or borders of rationality makes sense unless there is some territory to fight over. We can understand rationality as an emerging array of practices of language, about which speakers and writers can disagree but also about which they can come to agreement. We can isolate some of the relations that support or block such an agreement: to exclude a speaker or to prescribe what the speaker will say or what kinds of questions he or she will raise or address is to block the possibility of assent from that speaker, and indeed from any participant in dialogue who understands the speaker's interest as legitimate. We can specify some of the constraints on reaching such agreement, particularly constraints of time: public policy discourse must work with a temporality that is exigently structured by other discourses; the social text is always *in time* and *on time*, whereas the scientific text can choose to be simply *about time*.

Narration in the MOVE Report

It is through narrative that the text manages its articulation in time and orchestrates the relations of its writers and readers, composing a story told by someone to someone else. The MOVE report's drumbeat of narrative is a common figure in public policy discourse and is especially central to commission reports on civic disasters. Like reports written after the Chicago and Detroit riots, the MOVE report must explain and normalize a story of racial violence. Even within this difficult universe, the MOVE commission's task is especially hard: it deals with official violence, leading to substantial losses of life and property, occurring during the administration of Philadelphia's first black mayor.

Writers for the MOVE commission, having studied some exemplary commission reports, would have seen their usual pattern. Narrative is followed by commentary; a focused account of disaster is followed by an explanation of its causes.[59] The Detroit report, for example, traces the riot from the initial outbreak of violence on Belle Isle through episodes of violence in African American neighborhoods, ending with the race riots in the Cass Corridor. The Detroit commission's conjectures on the causes of violence—agitation by African American newspapers, restiveness among African American veterans—are raised in a final discussion, after the narrative, much as the interesting speculation in a scientific paper might be confined to the final discussion section. The MOVE report, however, uses narrative as its sole structuring principle, disperses the commentary among the episodes of the narration, and segments the narrative into numbered, sequential, but discontinuous "findings." Narrative is both a principle of arrangement and a mode of reasoning.

The MOVE commission report is also exceptional in its choice of an opening moment. Unlike the Chicago and Detroit reports, the MOVE report begins with a description of the preconditions of the MOVE catastrophe rather than with its first violent episode. In the MOVE report, narrative does not follow a sequential temporal logic but is repeatedly interrupted by subordinated analyses, reflections, and assignments of blame. Like other civic reports, the MOVE report reasons instrumentally, treating complex social issues as problems of adapting means to

59. Anthony Platt, *The Politics of Riot Commissions, 1917–1970: A Collection of Official Reports and Critical Essays* (New York: Macmillan, 1971). See also Frank Burton and Pat Carlen, *Official Discourse: On Discourse Analysis, Government Publications, Ideology and the State* (London: Routledge and Kegan Paul, 1979).

ends. However, this project is continually undercut and exceeded by a project of reconstituting the public sphere within which the report will be received and understood.

The narrative logic of the MOVE report organizes its figures of temporality and causality. Within the discrete episodes, or "findings," of the report causality is regularly figured as sequence, and a similar metonymic formula prompts several important divagations from the report's temporal arc. The MOVE catastrophe is also refigured in a series of puns, metaphors, and figures of repetition. Together, these violations of normal temporality—and of normal instrumental causality—suggest a remarkably discontinuous and contradictory narrating persona for the MOVE report. That narrator is engaged in a work of deferral and displacement which is also a labor of memory.

A typical episode in the report includes a finding supported by indented dot points; the graphic and formatting devices of the text suggest that the material following each finding is evidence for it. That structure, however, is often adapted to other ends: subordinated material provides background, continues the narrative, or amplifies a subsidiary point.[60] Finding 15, which addresses the fate of the MOVE children, combines narrative and argument, ending with an account of the MOVE children returning to the house:

15. THE MAYOR'S FAILURE TO CALL A HALT TO THE OPERATION ON MAY 12TH, WHEN HE KNEW THAT CHILDREN WERE IN THE HOUSE, WAS GROSSLY NEGLIGENT AND CLEARLY RISKED THE LIVES OF THOSE CHILDREN.
   • On Saturday, May 11, and Sunday, May 12, the Mayor was briefed on the plan by the Police Commissioner and was aware that children were known to be inside the MOVE residence. Nevertheless, he authorized the commencement of the operation.
   • No children were taken into protective custody. At least two children, who were passengers in a car, were allowed to pass through a police barricade on the day before the evacuation of the neighborhood, with no attempt made to detain them.

The point of finding 15, its contribution to the advancing argument of the report, is to characterize the mayor's policy as "gross negligence."

60. Susan Wells, "Narrative Figures and Subtle Persuasions," in *The Rhetorical Turn*, ed. Simons, 208–38.

This term resonates in multiple registers: it is a legal term specifying criminal behavior by a public official; it is also in common use for serious dereliction of duty. We might expect, then, that the subordinated material might specify how the mayor's decision to continue the assault on the MOVE house qualified as negligence: when did the mayor have an opportunity to call off the attack, and what were his legal obligations to the children? The pyramidal format was designed for just such a presentation of segmented points and their support. Barbara Minto imagined the pyramid as a representation of the dialogue between reader and writer:

> Making a statement to a reader that tells him something he does not know will automatically raise a logical question in his mind—for example, Why? or How? or Why do you say that? The writer is now obliged to answer that question horizontally on the line below. In his answer, however, he will still be telling the reader things he does not know, so he will raise further questions that must again be answered on the line below. The writer will continue to write, raising and answering questions until he reaches a point at which he judges the reader will have no more logical questions.[61]

Finding 15, however, entangles the commission's writers in the contradictions of agency: they are at pains to elaborate something that Mayor Goode did not do, a failure that is not only an abstention from action but an abstention from ending the actions of others. In showing that the mayor knew—or, more precisely, that he knew that it was known—that the children were in the house, the report establishes his culpability. He did not blindly continue the assault; it was not a mistake; he should have known better. This sentence also creates a complex temporal location for the report. The finding is phrased in the simple past, collocating with its immediate context: an action *was grossly negligent*. But the diegetic force of the finding is not carried by its verb tense: the mayor's action *was* not negligent in the past but *is* in the present. The sentence frames, not a proposition about past action, but a present evaluation. The finding also takes up a precise past moment, "on May 12th," accounting for the mayor's actions while preparations were being made for an attack on the house scheduled for May 13. The mayor's negligence is constructed as a discrete action, as a past state, and as a present judgment. At the same time, narrative traction is kept in play. The first support point moves the frame of the action from the time of

---

61. Minto, *The Pyramid Principle*, 14.

the operation to the days and hours before it; the final verb, "authorized," marks the discrete moment when the mayor allowed the attack to begin.[62]

While grammatically the finding has moved back from the day before the attack to more remote preparations for it, its topical focus has moved from preparations for the operation to the question of how it began. The second supporting point returns to the issue of removing the children from the house, already discussed at length in the previous finding: "Directives to remove the children from 6221 Osage Ave. were unclear, poorly communicated and were not carried out" (finding 14). Logically, the incident of the children being driven through a police barricade belongs in the support for finding 14, but the narrative structure of the report takes precedence over its argument. Having moved back to May 11, the report takes up its narrative thread there, with the preparations for the assault. The movement of the children on "the day before the evacuation of the neighborhood" was carried out—that is, May 11—shifts the topical focus of the text from "protection of children" to "preparing for the operation." The evacuation of the neighborhood, not otherwise mentioned in the findings, here aligns the events of the report with the reader's existing schema of the Osage Avenue catastrophe. Part of the common civic knowledge about the MOVE catastrophe is the tableau of police going from house to house, collecting house keys and warning residents to leave, to pack an overnight bag, and to leave a day's food and water for their pets, and of the residents leaving, many of them never to return. Against this action of orderly retreat, the commission ironically places an image of children being taken for a ride, moving through a police barricade, and returning to the house where they would die. The commission constructs a counterfactual: if x had not happened, then y would never have happened, or would have been safe, or would have been alive. Other instances of this figure include:

- The misuse of the explosives in the morning virtually destroyed the front of four row houses. Once the MOVE house was laid open by this blasting, tear gas could have been introduced into the house without blowing a hole in the roof. [Support for finding 19]

62. For a helpful discussion of tense formations and narrative discourse, see Suzanne Fleischman, *Tense and Narrativity: From Medieval Performance to Modern Fiction* (Austin: University of Texas Press, 1990).

- The Mayor paused only 30 seconds before approving the dropping of explosives. Had he taken more time before making such a critical decision, he may have considered the presence of the children, the possibility that gas was on the roof, and the possibility that explosives were stored in the MOVE house. [Support for finding 24]

26. Even after the bomb exploded and ignited the fire, life and property could have been saved without endangering any of the police officers or firefighters by using the "squirts" to extinguish the fire on the roof while the fire was in its incipient stage. [finding 26]

28. Police gunfire prevented some occupants of 6221 Osage Ave. from escaping from the burning house to the rear alley. [finding 28]

- Police observed the man [who had attempted to escape] climb a fence in the alleyway, and then "he fell back down" and was lost to view. One officer said he saw the child [whom the man had been carrying] crawling back toward the MOVE house. [Support for finding 28]

The repeated invocations of contingency, of the possibility of disaster averted, of at least of some lives being saved, cohere with the instrumental register of the report: if the proper means had been matched to the appropriate ends, then tragedy might have been averted.

Such counterfactuals also resonate with the report's invocation of an (equally counterfactual) public sphere; they imagine a context within which the terrible events of May 13 would have been opened to reflection as they happened, as if such reflection would necessarily have turned rational agents away from disaster. In the hearings, and for similar reasons, observers focused on the actions of Officer James Berghaier, the patrolman stationed behind 6221 Osage Avenue who rescued the young boy Birdie Africa, now known as Michael Ward, from the flooded alley. Charles Bowser observes:

> Had not Officer James Berghaier demonstrated the compassion, and accepted the duty every adult owes to every child, Birdie would have escaped the flames only to drown in a pool of water. It was a profound moment in the tragic drama of May 13 on Osage Avenue. With the fire raging around them, and gun men lurking in the shadows of the black alley scene that framed them, they were thrown together by policies, procedures, positions, and ideologies neither of them fully understood.[63]

63. Bowser, *Opinion of Charles Bowser*, 62.

The meeting of Berghaier and Birdie Africa reverses the report's terrifying image of a man leaving 6221 Osage "clutching a child and carrying a .22 caliber rifle" only to be driven back into the burning building (finding 28).

, The language of the MOVE report organizes at once a normalizing ideological discourse and an imagined, emergent public discourse that practices reason and utters desire. In the case of its counterfactuals, the report rectifies the MOVE tragedy as a mistake, something that need not have happened, and also configures it as an inexorable event, fated to happen, even though at many junctures it could have been averted. Simultaneously, we can discern in these counterfactuals a sketch of a discursive situation in which all possible futures are untangled, laid out as possible chains of actions and consequences, and subjected to a public process of planning that did not exclude those most affected. Finally, we can read in them, at the level of rhetorical figuration, an inscription of MOVE as a narrative of repetition, associated with strong desires to complete and to derail repetition.

If Berghaier's rescue of Birdie Africa repeats and rectifies the appearance of the unnamed gunman carrying a child, it also repeats and reverses earlier images of a man carrying a child and escaping attack drawn from the earlier siege of an earlier MOVE house in Powelton Village. Former Police Commissioner O'Neil testified that when MOVE members left the Powelton Village house in 1978, "in their cowardly fashion each of them had a child in front of them, probably with the exception of Delbert Africa [who was] clobbered and subdued." [64] The image of a man carrying a child out of a house under attack is repeated three times in the MOVE crisis and read alternately as a rescue of the child or an attempt to shield oneself with the child, as cowardice or courage.

Within the MOVE report and its supporting testimony, we read multiple repetitions of the Powelton Village confrontation. Osage is a prolonged pun on Powelton: armed MOVE members, barricaded in a house, are surrounded by police, firemen, and neighbors. Rhetorically, the Osage catastrophe repeats Powelton with minimal difference. Such a repetition is deeply threatening, especially since it is a figure without limits: since there are still MOVE houses in Philadelphia, another confrontation is possible. Even remote events, like the Branch Davidian Waco disaster, in June 1993, can be read as one more repetition of the

64. Philadelphia Special Investigation Commission, *Hearings,* 1 (Oct. 8), 67.

central elements of this story: charismatic leader, endangered children, a siege, fire, and death.

Such dangerous repetition is marked in the report on the level of language: puns and repetitions continually entangle witnesses before the commission. The multiple senses of *move* are especially troublesome to the transcriber of the hearings. We read "I would like to MOVE up in time," and "Your advice to them . . . was to MOVE," both written in capitals in the official transcript. Elsewhere, we encounter an "armed urban gorilla group," and in a rare moment of self-consciousness, "MOVE literally moved the entire city government to a standstill." Even the public utilities pun: Water Commissioner William Marrazzo claimed that MOVE's unpaid bills "did not float to the top" of the Water Department's management.[65]

The pun holds the idea of repetition on the surface of the text, as a verbal figure, or even as a mistake, so that it passes without criticism; a deeply threatening repetition in time is reduced to a more manageable coincidence in space.[66] Within the relentless forward trajectory of the narrative, the pun holds the text's sense of its repetition of others.

That repetition is an object of fear and of desire. It is clear from the early testimony before the commission that, for the police, the death of Officer Ramp in the Powelton Village confrontation was entirely salient to their planning at Osage Avenue. Consider Commissioner O'Neil's statement about his failure to discipline the police who beat Delbert Africa: "I think if you had seen those men immediately before that when they had the blood of Policeman Ramp on their arms and on their clothing you too, sir, would have understood."[67] Police who had taken part in the Powelton Village operation were barred from Osage Avenue, but the order was widely ignored. The very tempo of the attack on Osage Avenue, the headlong rush to enter the house on May 13, was an attempt to correct and reverse the prolonged siege of Powelton Village, as if it were the length of the blockade that had caused the bloodshed.

The hearings and the text of the report display the congruences between the two events. The term "hostage," for example, echoes

65. Philadelphia Special Investigation Commission, *Hearings,* 1 (Oct. 9, afternoon), 55; 3 (Oct.10, afternoon), 44; 3 (Oct. 10, afternoon), 229; 3 (Oct. 10, afternoon), 146; 3 (Oct. 10, afternoon), 147.

66. For the role of puns in the official discourse of the Meese report, see Stewart, *Crimes of Writing,* 253–84.

67. Philadelphia Special Investigation Commission, *Hearings,* 1 (Oct. 8), 106.

between the narratives of Powelton and Osage: women and children were considered hostages in Powelton Village; in 1985, the neighbors claimed to be hostages;[68] various witnesses identify the MOVE children, women, and men (except for Frank Africa) as hostages. On the other hand, the police refused to use tear gas during Powelton Village for fear of injuring children, but they used it without hesitation on Osage Avenue. The MOVE report itself refers to the Powelton Village confrontation as an unused repository of administrative experience:

• A critique of the 1978 confrontation, which had been prepared by the Police Department's highest ranking officers, was never reviewed by the 1985 planners. [Support for finding 12]

But the repetition of Powelton Village also demonstrates that the destruction of MOVE and the Osage neighborhood was fated. To see Osage Avenue as fated itself repeats, in a different key, the sense that the events were contingent mistakes: in both narratives, events elude agency or intention. If it was fated, a deadly repetition, then it had to happen: if it was all necessary, it was not so sad. The tragic, in this register, becomes a way of avoiding difficult questions.

For Freud and Lacan, the tragic is a less tractable representation of our commerce with the death instinct. J. B. Lefebvre-Pontalis, participating in Lacan's second seminar, insisted on the dual orientation of the repeated action: in translating from the past, it is also oriented toward a future state of satisfaction, a sort of remembered future, an object of anticipatory nostalgia. Pontalis links this future function of repetition to progress, to "broader and broader integrations," to an almost Habermasian "purveyor of human progress."[69] Tacitly responding to Pontalis in a later seminar, Lacan found in *Antigone*'s tragic celebration of the death instinct and of the repetition implied by blood relations a rejection of law, something outside the limits of progress, of any integration, something that brought us face to face with the disturbing beauty of desire and the loss implied in its psychoanalytic recognition.

We are very close to both understandings of the tragic in the story that we are reading out of the MOVE commission report. The story of the terrible deaths, of the catastrophic destruction of a whole neighborhood, is presented by the commission as a story of nobody having

68. Philadelphia Special Investigation Commission, *Hearings*, 1 (Oct. 8), 57; 1 (Oct. 9), 15.
69. Lacan, *Seminar II*, 23.

learned anything, a story of stupid repetition. We cannot hold together the secular, ordinary, and quotidian nature of the possible "broader integrations"—better police training?—with the images of violent death that the report repeatedly invokes but never presents to us. And perhaps it is wise that the report that narrates so many actions and abstentions from action by city officials on May 13 does not narrate the deaths of MOVE members or of the MOVE children, the desperate escapes of Ramona Africa and Michael Ward, or the destruction of so many homes. What can be learned from this violence, even with the fullest reflection, does not justify all that pain.

Like *Oedipus Rex* in Lacan's reading, the MOVE catastrophe is a tragedy that turns upon temporality, upon knowledge that is only accessible at certain times, and upon the possibility of those times being too late to do anyone any good. Like other tragedies, it invokes the limit of law and intelligibility, not in its findings or in any of its artfully arranged structures of irony or suspense. Rather, the limit demarcates the boundaries of the political, specifically of the public sphere.

The testimony of the Osage neighbors details the attrition and corrosion of communication, the collapse of the lifeworld in the face of instrumentalized politics. When MOVE first came to the block, it was possible to talk: "their children would play with our children." [70] Then, as MOVE's project of freeing its jailed members was blocked, talk ended; neighbor after neighbor testified to the commission that "you couldn't talk to them." [71] Lloyd Wilson, who felt that he and Frank Africa once "had the same philosophy of life, where we had to co-exist," reported that after Christmas 1983, he could no longer talk to Frank Africa and only heard his voice at night, in his bedroom, through a loudspeaker. For many, MOVE's failure to acknowledge neighbors on the street, an almost obligatory custom in African American communities, signaled not only the end of talk but the end of the possibility of talk. If the lifeworld was not able to sustain dialogue, there was all the more need for a public sphere into which problems could be transposed. Ms. Sims, rejecting the role of the witness and taking on the role of the questioner, insisted on the disjuncture between the private grievances that coalesced around MOVE and the political response to them: "Be-

70. Philadelphia Special Investigation Commission, *Hearings*, 1 (Oct. 8), 110.
71. See in Philadelphia Special Investigation Commission, *Hearings*, 1, testimony by Lloyd and Lucretia Wilson (Oct. 8, morning), 85; and by Clifford Bond (Oct. 9, afternoon), 17.

fore you recess, I just want to make it clear in my mind so that I understand. . . . Am I to assume that the bomb was dropped on the MOVE people because Frank beat his mother?"[72]

A bomb was dropped on the MOVE people, and on scores of homes. No boundaries contained MOVE's transgressions; no one learned how to reopen the dialogue, to make talk possible again. So opaque to learning was the moment of the MOVE catastrophe that it is rendered virtually transparent by a group of eleven people, assembled through normal channels, meeting over a few months. The MOVE commission did better, learned more about what MOVE was about and what might have been expected to happen, than the responsible agents of the city during the eighteen months of confrontation. In that act of learning, they came to imagine, in contradictory and unsatisfactory ways, a public space and a public voice. Without themselves articulating a solution, they found forms of textuality that took up and included MOVE, the Osage neighbors, the "community," the "public." They wrote at the limit of civic knowledge: that limit marks the MOVE report as a tragic document. Among the multiplied counterfactuals of the report, the most sobering is the existence of a text that so many writers could agree upon, a text that outlined a more rational method of dealing with MOVE than any that had been followed.

Although the report approaches the limits of the civic, it does not transgress them; although it deals with issues of inclusion and containment, it does not contest those terms. The logic of the MOVE report is relentlessly instrumental; it enacts a desire for a more inclusive public sphere, but it is scandalized that not everyone feels at home in the public as now constituted. The report sponsors reflection but does not itself carry out the labor of understanding, the work of constructing language that can open the public sphere to disparate discourses, transparent to reason.

The balance sheet of this attempt is mixed. Before the report, some Philadelphians believed the mayor's explanation that the whole disaster had been a terrible mistake, or the police commissioner's claim that it had been caused by MOVE's intransigence. Neither explanation was publicly credible after the report. But no public official was indicted for his part in the MOVE catastrophe; no official faced charges under federal law. Two of the four main public officials resigned before the report

72. Philadelphia Special Investigation Commission, *Hearings,* 1 (Oct. 9), 139.

was released; the fire commissioner resigned soon after; but Mayor Goode, battered by the report, was renominated, reelected, and served a second full term.

In this text, then, we read public policy discourse as a discourse of modernity, with its irreducible temporal location, its contradictory promise to open the domain of the social to reflection, and its inability to organize such reflection. Such contradictions, as we have read them in this chapter, open the domain of the tragic, but they are not necessarily closed by that encounter.

CHAPTER SIX

Giving an Ordered History: Narrative in the Discourse of the Classroom

•　　•　　•　　•

The discourses of modernity are not outside us, external objects for analysis, originating in an academic elsewhere—engineering or cosmology, or one of the more instrumental social sciences. The discourses of modernity are ours: we write them; we speak them, even in the humane space of the classroom.

Which means that I also speak them. This complicity is not easy to talk about: it is one thing to say that all realizations of the public are necessarily fragmentary, and another to say that the discourse of my own classroom operates through exclusion, transgressive desire, and contradictory aspirations to rationality. Usually, academic work seems more mundane. Small victories, episodes of cynicism, or moments of reciprocity are the stuff of my teaching, as they probably are of yours. It was the work of my most intransigent student, Andrea Gibson, to refuse those consolations, to question the discursive relations of the class, and to demonstrate the impossibilities that supported it.[1] I tell her story, not for its pathos, and certainly not as a model of teaching practice, but to honor the demand Andrea made by taking up her unsparing reflection on education. As a teacher, I approach this as a story of error, just as the MOVE commission read a story of failed discourse as a narrative of personal failure. And there is certainly enough blame here to go around.

---

1. "Andrea Gibson" is a pseudonym; "Andrea" has seen and commented on this chapter, and I am grateful to her for discussing it with me.

Every student in the class and every teacher to whom I have told this story has a distinct judgment about Andrea's intervention and my response. Such judgments and responses are part of the useful lore of teaching, but this essay will think about Andrea's intervention as a demonstration of the ordinary relations of production in the classroom.

In the spring of 1985, Andrea Gibson was one of fifteen students in "Sex, Rhetoric, and Language," my women's studies class. We met once a week, in a long session, downtown. Andrea was a doctoral student in religion; other students were studying linguistics, sociology, English, and women's studies, at various levels. In the first weeks of the class, we had read Robin Lakoff's early essay *Language and Women's Place*.[2] We had also begun Dale Spender's *Man Made Language*.[3] Work on women and language was just then moving from Spender's muted group theory to more complex ethnographic and psychoanalytic theories of gender variation; I projected a common journey from muted group theory toward more sophisticated feminisms.

At the end of the third session, when I asked Andrea to do a report, she replied that, as a pass/fail student, she did not expect to do written work. I had forgotten that she was not taking the course for a grade, and I also expected to see some of her writing, however informal; it seemed like a good idea to clarify the situation, although it was well after ten o'clock, and everyone was anxious to get home. I asked Andrea to bring a plan for her work to class next week. It would help me to remember her status and would let me know how she was handling the material and what I could reasonably expect her to do. I expected a half-page list of assignments and dates. Instead, Andrea left in my mailbox a densely handwritten three-page narrative, beginning with an account of the circumstances in her life that had brought her to the course. There, I read the story of two marriages, four difficult children, fifteen years of abusive relationships, and life in poverty, sometimes on welfare, never on an income higher than $15,000. During this time, Andrea had completed high school and her bachelor's degree, entered the doctoral program in religion, and been awarded a fellowship. Andrea's note ended with various proposals for course work, one of which, she reminded me, we had previously agreed on. Andrea came late to the next class. During the break, I saw her briefly, confirmed her sense of our previous agreement, and did not mention the rest of her note.

2. Robin Lakoff, *Language and Women's Place* (New York: HarperCollins, 1975).
3. Dale Spender, *Man Made Language* (London: Routledge and Kegan Paul, 1985).

A week later, the class was discussing gender and language acquisition. The discussion was led by Yvonne, the only African American member of the class; she argued that the culture of her Muslim cousins showed how minority discourse communities could effectively support their children's language development. It was the kind of intense and friendly discussion that usually goes somewhere: Yvonne knew a lot about the African American Muslim community, and students had many questions about the role of Muslim women, the forms of speech they developed, and the relations between domestic and public life. But Andrea became more and more upset during the report. Finally, she stood at the end of the seminar table and spoke angrily. Yvonne, she said, was romanticizing poverty. If Yvonne's nephews were doing well, what did that say about Andrea's children, who had not survived poverty and deprivation without scars. Andrea felt that the report and discussion insulted her and that they denied her experience of motherhood at the margins of society and told her that her pain and the problems of her children were her own fault. In fact, according to Andrea, all the discussions in the class had systematically ignored the fierceness of oppression among the very poorest, including especially her experience. Andrea's denunciation went on for ten minutes, which is a long time. Two students were having trouble controlling their tears. I remember that my hands shook.

Andrea's intervention implied a demand that Yvonne deny her experience in order to affirm Andrea's. Repeatedly, members of the class told Andrea that such a demand was unacceptable. I told Andrea that she could not shout at Yvonne or attack her personally. Other members of the class, many of whom were experienced in the dynamics of small groups, also responded to Andrea, attempting to contain her outburst or to find a common ground or to establish some dialogic relation. None of our remarks had much effect. It looked to me as if the class could not take much more of this: I moved to control the damage and asked for a break.

After a break, Andrea left, and by way of a rest, I gave the lecture on language acquisition that I had planned for the second half of the class. At the end of the period, I looked at the drawn faces of the students and realized that I could not postpone discussion of what had happened until the next week. Yvonne, in particular, was shaky and ashen. As I opened the topic, Andrea came back into the room—she had been listening at the door—and accused me of betraying her by discussing her in her absence. I would have to call the security guards to get rid of her, she said. I dismissed the other students, who were edgy now and worried about leaving the empty building after ten, and went with Andrea to the lounge. Soon, I was yelling at her, as if ours were a very bad domestic row. I was more angry at Andrea than I had been at the student I found stealing his classmates' wallets; more angry than I would be at the functionary who checked me off his list every week when I taught under injunction. Andrea suggested that we calm down and lower our voices.

Eventually, we came to an understanding, which is not the same as coming to an agreement. I told Andrea that everyone in my classes, including me, had to be willing to question their statements. Andrea replied that if all her teachers could call all of her beliefs into question, there would soon be little left of her experience. Since she was not an academic, and since the university was a strange territory for her, she had to exempt her perceptions from question if she wanted to remember why she had come to academic life in the first place. We agreed that it would be impossible to proceed under such different assumptions; we tacitly recognized that I had the institutional power to make my assumptions stick. Andrea left. She stopped attending class and took a grade of incomplete.

Yvonne also left; although we spoke on the phone several times, and she told me that she intended to return, she never came back to class and eventually handed in a sketchy project. Eight of the other students in the class took incompletes, some of which still stand. Discussions in the class were shell-shocked and tentative for weeks.

This event is not a happy one; it speaks of a general difficulty in insurgent cultural institutions and ideologies—the working-class urban university, women's studies programs, collaborative classrooms—and a failure of my own practice as a feminist teacher concerned with issues of language. Like the case of Dora, that high modernist ironic narrative, it is a story that proffers and hides its secret, its key—desire in unexpected places.[4]

I do not want my readers to see Andrea's as a happy story, in which everything works out in the end. (Years later, though, I sat in a seminar on the rhetoric of science with Andrea. We said very little, until a day when I was asking polite questions and she looked at me obliquely and asked, "Why don't you just go after him?") I do not want to romanti-

4. Freud, *Dora*.

cize my own role in this event, which was certainly not heroic. But the serious reflections that Andrea's intervention sponsors are derailed if the event is read as a mistake or as an individual failure of either teacher or student. I also recognize that such an impulse is ungovernable: just as every reader of the Dora case can think of a strategy that would have cured her—or at least kept her in analysis—no discussion of pedagogy can avoid the reader's hope that skillful management could have averted crisis, that properly handled, this class would have continued its orderly dilation of the narrative of progress until the appointed end of the semester. But perhaps this incident can also be used to continue, without any triumphant gesture, the work of the Dora case: to use an extreme situation, in which normal methods were not only frustrated but resolutely counterproductive, as a way of describing what is assumed by those methods, what it is that they do not see.

Andrea's intervention could have been staged in any course—and, it turned out, several teachers had stories to tell about Andrea's insisting that the police would have to throw her out. But it is probably not accidental that Andrea wrote her story in a class that had been reading muted group theory and had been thinking about silence and misdirection.

Andrea used a narrative of difference and disability to bid for a relation of solidarity with me, a solidarity confirmed by the differences between us. On the basis of that solidarity, she could renegotiate the exchanges of classroom discourse on more advantageous terms. I was a woman, and so I should be sympathetic: presumably, I did not have four children or a difficult past or an uncertain income, and so my sympathy would be expressed as a difference between my expectations of Andrea and my expectations of other students, as a softening of my teacherly demand. Andrea's text described her as under pressure: she was the mother of four troubled children, getting by without much money, taking graduate courses and making up incompletes, studying for her language exam, and taking my undergraduate course even though it met no institutional requirement. More, Andrea described her difficulties as the effect of a lifetime of injustice against her as a working-class woman. Andrea's letter invoked me as both a colleague, someone on her side, and as a representative of the institution, someone enforcing onerous requirements. The "pressure" on Andrea comes both from people and from institutions and their requirements. Andrea's narrative enters the institutional world of the university and asks for a renegotiation of its terms, a reorientation in the direction of the personal. She bids to be understood, not as a bearer of obligations, but as the object of pressures that the reader would do well to mitigate. This strategic use of narrative on Andrea's part is not at all unusual. "I'm feeling a lot of pressure right now" is a conventional opening for student narratives that explain transgression or failure: it invokes a relation of intimacy which might abolish all such debts. It is customary for a student to present a teacher with a story of pressure, and we call these stories excuses.

But written student narrative has, in academic communities, a generic status that both Andrea and I ignored in our interaction. It is an exceptionally rich and well-developed genre, deeply situated in the institutions of the university: students normally begin college writing courses, regardless of their method or content, with some sort of narrative writing. The first assignment may be an autobiography or a comment, usually in narrative form, on someone else's autobiography. In freshman anthologies, the privileged opening texts are often literacy narratives, stories of the subject's accession into written language: Malcolm X in prison, copying the dictionary; Helen Keller spelling out "water." After reading these texts, students may be assigned to recount their histories as writers. In "writing-intensive courses"—and my course on women and language was designated as writing intensive—students may be asked to begin their work by writing about their own experience with the course material; similar narratives may be requested as the semester continues.

Narrative occupies this strategic position in composition pedagogy for an array of theoretical and practical reasons. Students generally write good stories; their essays show us what they want us to know about them. Having learned the elements of narrative, students can adapt them to a surprising range of academic subjects and assignments. Expressivist pedagogy, an important branch of composition theory, uses narrative as a point of initiation for all student writing; feminist teachers are likely to value it for its association with consciousness-raising.[5] Students' stories about their lives, written out and given to teachers, are currency in the exchange of texts that structures the classroom. Unlike

5. For expressivism, see the works of Peter Elbow, including *Embracing Contraries: Explorations in Learning and Teaching* (New York: Oxford University Press, 1986), *Writing with Power* (New York: Oxford University Press, 1981), and *Writing without Teachers* (New York: Oxford University Press, 1973), and also the critical account in James Berlin, "Rhetoric and Ideology in the Writing Class," *College English* 50 (1988): 477–94, and a challenging current adaptation in Stephen

other narratives in this culture, they do not prompt an answering disclosure, they are not appreciated as performances that display the self, and they are not expected to either celebrate the speaker or affirm values shared with the reader. Whatever point student narratives might have is not usually applied by the teacher to herself, generalized, or taken as a cue for other stories, although these are the culturally appropriate forms for responding or replying to a story.[6]

Usually, in fact, the teacher's reply to the student's narrative includes no affective response to its content. A teacher instead evaluates it as a performance of academic discourse and comments on its coherence—its tenacity in building to a point and its fluency in amplifying that point with details. These features, of course, are likely to be the focus of the teacher's instruction; by commenting on them at the opening of the semester, the teacher is constructing his or her own narrative of development, in which a student learns to do something new or to do something in a different way.

Andrea's narrative, far from disrupting the exchanges of the classroom, simply presents an anomaly within them: there is a disjunction between the text as illocution and its generic status. She writes a transgressive narrative—a discourse by the student that does not promise docile improvement. Such narratives are well known within what Stephen North has called the lore of teaching.[7] A beginning teaching as-

---

Fishman and Lucille McCarthy, "Is Expressivism Dead? Reconsidering Its Romantic Roots and Its Relation to Social Constructionism," *College English* 54 (1992): 647–61.

Feminist pedagogies have been heavily influenced by the work of Carol Gilligan, including *In a Different Voice* (Cambridge: Harvard University Press, 1982). The central application of Gilligan to pedagogy has been Mary Filed Belenky, Blythe McVicker Clinchy, Nancy Rule Goldberger, and Jill Mattuck Tarule, *Women's Ways of Knowing* (New York: Basic Books, 1986). For pedagogical work directly related to issues of narrative and gender, see Linda Peterson, "Gender and the Autobiographical Essay: Research Perspectives, Pedagogical Practices," *College Composition and Communication* 42 (May 1991): 170–83; and Don Kraemer, "Gender and the Autobiographical Essay: A Critical Extension of the Research," *College Composition and Communication* 43 (Oct. 1992): 32–39. For Lacanian pedagogical feminism addressed to the teaching of writing, see Constance Penley, "Teaching in Your Sleep: Feminism and Psychoanalysis," in *Theory in the Classroom,* ed. Cary Nelson (Urbana: University of Illinois Press, 1986), 129–48; and its application in Laurie Finke, "Knowledge as Bait: Feminism, Voice, and the Pedagogical Unconscious," *College English* 55 (Jan. 1993): 7–27.

6. See Labov, "The Transformation of Experience in Narrative Syntax," 354–96.

7. See North, *The Making of Knowledge in Composition,* 19–56, for a discussion of lore.

sistant is likely to hear about students who write about dismembering their English teachers or who produce unintentionally hilarious accounts of their parents' deaths or stories of an ectopic pregnancy told from the point of view of the fetus. They will also learn the available rubric for these performances, the lore's tactics for containing them: acknowledge and distance the personal content, do not evaluate the essay, request another performance.[8] Composition pedagogy here becomes postmodern: it assumes a radical division in the writing subject, responds to only those elements of the subject that it can interrogate, and believes that the other elements can carry out their discourse unheard. (It is a distinguishing mark of lore that it uses multiple and contradictory models of the writer and the language.)

Andrea's misrecognition was to seek out in a writing teacher a correspondent and an interlocutor, to assume that my request for writing was an invitation to dialogue rather than a cue for performance. My misrecognition was a failure to see that I had been given, not an idiosyncratic personal note, but a transgressive narrative. Rather than containing and distancing it, I had responded to Andrea's answer to my question and postponed—forever, as it happened, or at least until this essay—my reply to the rest.

Andrea saw her narrative as an argument for muted group theory. She began with a reference to Lynn Bloom's essay "Anxious Writers in Context," which she read as an application of muted group theory to the problem of writer's block.[9] She ended her narrative by stating that sex and class, together, affect powerlessness and that powerlessness leads to muteness. Her proposed paper would be on powerlessness and muted group theory. The narrative is presented as a performance in aid of a theory about language. It might be appropriate, then, to examine that theory.

Muted group theory was among the first feminist theoretical formulations about women's relation to language. Countering notions that women are deviant or deprived speakers, muted group theorists located the deprivation in the system of language. Thus, as Cheris Kramarae said:

8. Richard Miller, "Fault Lines in the Contact Zone," *College English* 65, no. 4 (Apr. 1994): 389–408, presents a careful analysis of an equally resistant case of transgressive narrative.

9. Lynn Bloom, "Anxious Writers in Context," in *When a Writer Can't Write,* ed. Michael Rose (New York: Guilford, 1985).

The language of a particular culture does not serve all its speakers equally, for not all speakers contribute in an equal fashion to its formulation. Women (and members of other subordinate groups) are not as free or as able as men are to say what they wish, when and where they wish, because the words and the norms for their use have been formulated by the dominant group, men.[10]

And Dale Spender described her thesis in *Man Made Language:* "I was arguing that men controlled the language and that it worked in their favor."[11] Muted group theory shaped both scholarly work in language and popular feminist fiction.[12] Before Deborah Tannen's wildly popular books, it was the most accessible feminist theory of gender variation in language.

Although muted group theory proved durable, it has long been superseded in linguistic circles by psychoanalytic, deconstructivist, and ethnographically grounded theories.[13] Muted group theory understands language as a tool or implement: something that serves, something that works, something that can be grasped, something that can be stolen. Like other insurgent theories of language, beginning with Rous-

10. Cheris Kramarae, *Women and Men Speaking* (Rowley, Mass: Newbury House, 1981), 10.

11. Spender, *Man Made Language,* 5.

12. See, for example, Mary Daly's work, particularly *Websters' First New Intergalactic Wikedary of the English Language,* in cahoots with Jane Caputi (Boston: Beacon, 1987). A version of muted group theory can be found in Eve Kosofsky Sedgwick's *Epistemology of the Closet* (Berkeley and Los Angeles: University of California Press, 1990), which suggests that since men are less likely to refer to perspectives other than their own, they are more likely to shape the "common semantic stock" than are women (4). There is even science fiction about muted group theory: Suzette Hayden Elgin's *Native Tongue* (New York: DAW, 1984) and *The Judas Rose* (New York, DAW, 1987).

13. See, for example, J. Coates and D. Cameron, eds., *Women in Their Speech Communities: New Perspectives on Language and Sex* (London: Longman, 1989); Deborah Cameron, ed., *The Feminist Critique of Language: A Reader* (London: Routledge, 1990); and Dede Brouwer and D. de Haan, eds., *Women's Language, Socialization, and Self-Image* (Providence, R.I.: Foris, 1987). For a selection of sociolinguistic essays, see S. McConnell-Ginet, R. Borker, and N. Furman, *Woman and Language in Literature amd Society* (New York: Praeger, 1980). For a critique of theories that conflate "women's language" with perceived gender, see Dennis Baron, *Grammar and Gender* (New Haven: Yale University Press, 1986). For psychoanalytic treatments of women and language, see Helene Cixous, *La jeune née* (Paris: Union Générale d'Éditions, 1975); Luce Irigaray, *Speculum of the Other Woman,* trans. Gillian Gill (Ithaca: Cornell University Press, 1985); and Luce Irigaray, *This Sex Which Is Not One,* trans. Catherine Porter (Ithaca: Cornell University Press, 1985).

seau's, muted group theory operates as a narrative about the origin of language. If speakers "contributed" differentially to the development of language, or if language was formulated by a group, then language was initiated as an act of domination within a society. Derrida's critique of such theories of origin obtains here.[14] Like Rousseau, muted group theorists propose a double origin of language: Rousseau opposes the calculating language of the north to the expressive language of the south; muted group theorists posit a dominant, muting, masculine language and the future origin of an expressive and adequate women's lexicon and syntax that will "invest the language with our own authentic meanings."[15] All of these moves assume an authentic and accessible female self prior to language, a self which is female before it speaks, which speaks, in some sense, before it is muted. This self is already differentiated by gender without the agency of an Other constituted in language. It possesses, if only potentially, meanings which will be available for deployment when a language capable of carrying them is invented. This self is essentially female: it can be described as silenced, because it has been imagined as univocal.

For these and other reasons, I was critical of muted group theory, and it had been one of my goals in the course to contest it. Andrea had heard my critique of muted group theory and had agreed with elements of it. Why did she choose to argue this theory with her life story? Alternatively, why did she choose to phrase her argument as a narrative of her life?

We might turn first to Gramsci for guidance. Discussing the relation between the "man of the people" and the intellectual who approaches him with an extended and, in fact, unanswerable argument, Gramsci notes:

> But should the man of the people change his opinions just because of this? Just because he cannot impose himself in a bout

14. Jacques Derrida, *Of Grammatology*, trans. Gayatri Spivack (Baltimore: Johns Hopkins University Press, 1974), 165–268 ("Genesis and Structure of the *Essay on the Origin of Languages*").

15. Spender, *Man Made Language*, 5. A critique of this aspect of muted group theory can be found in Maria Black and Rosalind Coward, "Linguistic, Social, and Sexual Relations: A Review of Dale Spender's *Man Made Language*," in *The Feminist Critique of Language*, ed. Cameron, 111–33. As Black and Coward put it: "One wonders how, without already having a language, the patriarchs around the linguistic conference table managed to communicate to each other their plans about such a complex and sophisticated system. Did they draw pictures, or did they have a syntax-free language?" (118).

of argument? In that case he might find himself having to change every day, or every time he meets an ideological adversary who is his intellectual superior.[16]

If we can separate this statement from its elitist phrasing, it is an apt description of Andrea's dilemma. I was more used to arguing theories of language than she was. If she changed her mind about language every time I presented an argument that she could not answer, she would come to think much more like me than any sensible person would want to. Muted group theory functioned—for Andrea and for other members of the class—as a powerful explanatory framework that could support their explorations of ideas about language and help them connect such ideas with concrete social experiences. Gramsci projected a similar path in the development of philosophical ideas by the man of the people.

For the members of this class, including Andrea, muted group theory warranted the cohesion and inclusive membership of the speakers in the class and placed within a broad framework their immediate experiences of language. Muted group theory, with its strong narrative traction, could—and did—tell the story of an upper-class eighteen-year-old bolting up from her fiance's family table in tears because she had nothing to say. It could also explain the difficulty of a twenty-year-old who had some things to learn about writing academic papers, of a middle-aged returning student hesitant to speak in class, and of a lesbian who searched for the language to analyze the pictures of female bodybuilders that compelled and moved her. All these experiences of being at a loss— and in this classroom, as in every other classroom, the most common experience of language was that of being at a loss—were managed and contained by muted group theory, which displaced loss and deprivation from the speaker to the system of language. Like most writers, these students felt the resistance that language offers to the project of expressing and creating meaning. Meaning always seems to be deferred, never to arrive within the intersubjective space that ties writer to reader. The words that will make one's experience or understanding accessible, that will satisfy all the desires and demands implicit in the relationship between reader and writer—those words are always not here yet, in a very concrete sense. They always seem possible—and hence the fury of revision—but they never arrive. Muted group theory formed a framing nar-

16. Antonio Gramsci, *Selections from the Prison Notebooks of Antonio Gramsci*, ed. and trans. Quintin Hoare and G. N. Smith (New York: International, 1971), x.

rative, a metanarrative, with strong explanatory power: it was a home for Andrea's story of victimization, with which it joined seamlessly.

By telling me this story, Andrea repeats Dora's narration to Freud, a story that he too recognized as an argument, albeit an embarrassing one, with its assertion that she is a victim, that she has been silenced. Andrea posed Dora's question, one before which pedagogy is nearly as helpless as psychoanalysis: "This is all perfectly correct and true, isn't it? What do you want to change in it now I've told you?" Dora's story replied to Freud's demand that she "give an ordered history" of her symptoms by producing instead a transgressive narrative, a history from which her own desire had been excluded.[17]

I am no analyst; following the contingencies of the classroom, I neglected and ignored Andrea's story; she responded with a transgression that was both more and less than a story. And that transgression—Andrea's attack on Yvonne—did not assure everyone in the class that they were all alike. It was heard as an injunction to remember and to think about the circuitous paths that brought these students to this class. At the class session after Andrea's intervention, an older student said, "Those days that she was talking about were so hard. I hate to remember them." As she spoke, I saw on her face, for the first time, the marks of social class, including especially a deep fatigue. This student's past might have been harder, but her present was quite hard enough. Muted group theory and the stories it framed had permitted this student's amnesia, my blindness, and their assumption of homogeneity; something in Andrea's intervention dissolved the amnesia and permitted difference to emerge, although in a form resistant to discourse.

If Andrea's text told the life story of a victim under the sponsorship of muted group theory, her intervention ruptured both that narrative and the assumption of homogeneity that supports muted group theory. Andrea asserted an irreducibly individual, almost ineffable, understanding of oppression, launching it as a demand to the class and as an assault against Yvonne, whose marginal status was most like her own, but whose understanding of oppression was historical and social, and whose defense against it was communal. It was precisely those historical and social relations that Andrea's narrative text had foreclosed.

In her text, the events of difficulty, suffering, and pressure had also

17. Freud, *Dora*, 51. "The patients' inability to give an ordered history of their life in so far as it coincides with the history of their illness is not merely characteristic of the neurosis. It also possesses great theoretical significance" (Freud, *Dora*, 31).

marginalized the intellectual interest that brought her to the university. We never learn what, substantially, Andrea was interested in, so that her text both tells and repeats a story about the silencing of women. It is a story about her inability to speak, but the story never permits speech to emerge, never breaks into its own topic. Instead, the narrative invokes muted group theory as a trope, as a supplement, which inserts the individual experience of resistance and deferral into a more general narrative that makes no demands on the subject but regulates the subject's demand by institutionalizing deferral. The language does not yet express your thought, and it was never intended to. But it will, later, when it has been reinvented by women.

Nothing in this discourse allows dialogic rejoinder. If, as a female teacher, I reply, my speech is displaced; if I do not, I collude in the silencing of women. The narrative text postpones Andrea's claim to reason; it substitutes for a discourse shaped by figures of analysis and implication. Such a discourse would have allowed her interest in women and language to actually blossom rather than specifying how unlikely and difficult such a blossoming would be. For us to denominate this writing as "reason" would be to collude with the most naive myth of Enlightenment. But I myself desire, a desire that is not merely pedagogical, a discourse of Andrea's that would have done justice to her experience, that might have found in the structures of differentiation and reflection a passage into language rather than a threat to be averted or deflected onto others.

In some field where discourse replies to discourse, someone might have read in Andrea's text its insistence upon deferral and its discontinuity and internal contradiction, and found there the accents of desire, a desire for a particular experience of and access to language. My reading of Andrea's text postponed again her desire for an interlocutor, for that moment when the student is willingly or unwillingly moved from the station of a subaltern speaker and heard as a colleague. I read Andrea's narrative as an informative note rather than a transgression. She raised the stakes and moved beyond the containing structures of muted group theory to use the classroom as a space for the performance of difference: by insisting on a language that would reflect her experiences, she demonstrated the limits of a theory that assumed that all women share a similar experience of language.

I met Andrea's demand by invoking the rules of the institution in which it was staged. She should set aside her perception of social difference so that we could have a discussion—about social difference. I repeated, in pedagogical language, the figure of deferral and delay. I sponsored delay in the name of solidarity, which I specified with a rule that every member of the class had to be willing to call their beliefs into question.

That concept, too, should now be called into question. My response to Andrea's narrative (more properly, to her transgressive outburst) was spoken from within the project of appropriating and critiquing Jürgen Habermas's thought, the project which, for better or worse, has emerged in this book. It is odd, but not surprising, that my treatment of Andrea reflected a position of Habermas that I find quite problematic: the distinction between mythical and modern ways of understanding the world. I was identifying Andrea's use of muted group theory with that mythical interpretation of the world which Habermas says, "makes possible not only a theory that explains the world narratively and renders it plausible, but also a practice through which the world can be controlled in an imaginary way."[18] This worldview, Habermas says, does not realize its own differentiation from the world as language but presents a totalized conflation of word and object, a confounding of the actions of speaking about a thing and operating on it, so that the mythical worldview, conflated with the experience that it reflects, becomes reified. Against the hermeneutically charitable bracketing of such a worldview as meaningful or coherent or complete, Habermas proposes a graceless and inconvenient criterion: "The adequacy of a linguistically articulated worldview is a function of the true statements that are possible in this language system."[19]

And there are a number of "true statements" that cannot be articulated within muted group theory, such as:

> Gendered human beings do not exist outside language. Both sexes use language strategically, but differently. The conventions of exchange between teacher and student can supervene the conventions of exchange within gender groups.

To make an inventory of these statements is to describe the limits of the theory. Habermas would suggest a more open system, one characterized by "readiness to learn and openness to criticism."[20] Andrea's narrative and muted group theory appear, by this light, to be closed

18. Habermas, *Theory of Communicative Action*, 1:48.
19. Habermas, *Theory of Communicative Action*, 1:51.
20. Habermas, *Theory of Communicative Action*, 1:62.

and fragmented, unfalsifiable, unverifiable, unchangeable, invitations to stagnation.

We might want to rescue from this analysis a sense of alternatives. To the questions posed by Dora—Isn't this all true? What do you want to change?—more than one reply is possible. The answer I gave, the one that I have recounted, advances a formal and methodological, but quite demanding, claim: I want you to reflect. What I wanted changed was the speaker's relation both to her narrative and to her own intervention in the class. Both speech acts must submit to questioning, become open, and subject themselves to the cost of doing business with incompatible ideas, with inconveniently different people. In enforcing that rule, I was assuming that truth escapes the determining force of social relations, of institutional constraints, and of historical practices.

But, against this universalist and rationalist reading of Andrea's narrative, another reply is possible, one based not on any notion of hermeneutic charity but on an understanding of discourse as discontinuous and differentiated. Andrea had presented me with a narrative that argued a point, a point that she knew I would take issue with. Like the most dunderheaded naive reader, I responded to the narrative by contesting her point rather than by reading her story. And finally, when this contest was refused, I enforced my demand for reason with a magical act of exclusion; if you will not subject your thought to criticism, I told her, you have no place in this conversation called reason.

I could also have met Andrea's story with a version of the reply that Lacan reconstructs for Freud in the Dora case: "What is your desire in this story? When does it become your own, and not an account of the victimage of the beautiful soul?"[21] Another graceless question, another inconvenient question, another efficacious question.

After Dora told her story, she dreamed it. Andrea wrote her story and then, in her intervention in the class, performed it, moving from the deepest textual privacy to a full publicity. Like Dora's dream, Andrea's intervention is a translation, a rather full translation, of the implicit story of desire beneath the written text. In Andrea's intervention, she performed what she had written: sociological themes of privilege and its denunciation; the assertion of the speaker's autonomy (she stood at the table, took the role of teacher); an assumption that she would be cast

---

21. Jacques Lacan, "Intervention on Transference," in *Feminine Sexuality: Jacques Lacan and the École Freudienne,* ed. Juliet Mitchell and Jacqueline Rose (New York: Norton, 1985), 65–66.

out (you'll have to call the campus police on me). As in the written narrative, these quite discontinuous selves are connected by the assertion of marginality: she was excluded; she was in control; she would be expelled. What is writ larger and plainer in Andrea's intervention, however, is the imperial force of this marginality; it will tolerate no other form of difference, no racial minorities, no religious communities. Marginality is, here, always mobile, never assumed, never relinquished, and unanswerable. The norms of seminar talk, which seeks through a prolonged apprenticeship to make all hearers adequate to all speakers, were profoundly disrupted. If Andrea's narrative text sought to disrupt the special exchanges between teacher and student, her interruption sought, more sharply, to disrupt the exchanges among students, the commerce in discourse of the classroom.

Such an intervention confirms and repeats the isolation of the speaker: Andrea enacted the story that her narrative laconically transmitted. By claiming difference, the speaker exempted herself from the system of exchanges that she sued to enter. But that system has always required difference for its operation, producing difference in those rare instances where it did not come to the classroom already marked. And Andrea's story, as we have seen, restored to the class their own memories of difference.

Andrea's bid was impossible, then, but not unrealistic. There is, after all, a position in the classroom that is both inside and outside the classroom's system of exchange, a position from which the speaker demands response but which is exempted from questioning. This position is the teacher's. In the classroom, the teacher asks questions, receives answers, and replies with more questions. The teacher determines when she will be questioned and whether she will reply. She weaves question and answer into a cohesive chain, rejecting without justification those answers which do not fit the coherent structure of discussion she projects, and connecting the chain of any one discussion to the serial narrative of the course as a whole. More or less skillfully, more or less overtly, the teacher elaborates a narrative in the classroom, usually a happy story. Thus: you students used to be unable to write; now you are confident writers. Or: you used to take language for granted; now you see how complex and important it is. The students' written narratives, taken in early in the semester, are the raw material for the teacher's extended and elaborated narrative of growth and transformation. The teacher's narrative is more powerful for not being marked as her story but for emerging from dialogue among speakers. I had been elaborating just such a narrative in my critique of muted group theory, although my story was quite unsatisfactory in its sobriety: you students used to think that your difficulties with language were all a result of gender differences, but now you see that both gender and difficulty are irreducibly and necessarily implicated in and by language.

Nobody in the class liked this story. Andrea contested it in her written narrative and, more seriously, when she disrupted my monopoly on the elaborated narrative of the class. She did what only a teacher can do with decorum: she stood, she ruled another student out of order, she declared herself unsatisfied with the level of class discussion, and she proposed herself as arbiter of well-formed utterances. In her intervention, she interrupted the story of muted group theory and its critique and imposed a new story on the class: it would now be organized into events before and after her intervention. That event could only be discussed in her presence, but she would always be absent. The story of the class became—and for me remains—a scandal in which reason could only be produced in a magical act of rejection and repudiation.

It may be that my narrative for the class had produced a discursive situation so asymmetrical and impossible that it necessarily evoked an extreme and transgressive response. Andrea's intervention repeated my sad news to the class—that gender identity cannot be recovered or rendered authentic because it is already and only formed in language. It is one thing to announce the common subjection to language; it is another thing to hear about it. The teacher's act of enunciation gave me a place to stand over against the social and academic discourses that have spoken me and been spoken through me; students had much less access to these multiple positions. We might see muted group theory as a shaky and hastily constructed place to stand, with its narrativization of silence, its proposition of silence as a theme for discourse. Andrea bypassed that shaky place for speech and awkwardly took up mine, announcing that the right to elaborate such extended narratives is not a matter of age or education or custom. It is established in relations of power that must every minute be renewed and renegotiated in the classroom. Indeed, it took only two hours for Andrea to become the soft-spoken professional, for me to become the crazy woman yelling abuse, ineffectually denouncing what she will not permit.

Our speaking positions were exchanged and renegotiated, but within limits that ensured that one and only one of us had to be crazy. They also ensured that my assumption of that role would be temporary: I would not stay crazy for long. I reinvoked the fundamental rule of the classroom, a rule that all statements can be called into question, a rule that is stated universally but operates differentially. Andrea's statements would be questioned more often and more seriously than mine; I would retain the power to shape the classroom narrative. I invoked reason as a ritual practice, one that expels what is divergent. Andrea agreed, complied—and came no more. We mutually enacted one identification, a splitting, several acts of possession, reaffirmed our prior boundaries, and withdrew.

I constituted Andrea as a speaker who was my match and my equal, one who could play by the most strenuous rules, who no longer needed instruction, whom it was appropriate to engage rather than to correct. I colluded with her bid to take, not just my place, but rather the impossible place of the idealized interlocutor of the teacher, the pedagogical Other of my Other.

Pedagogy normally locates narrative outside reason, as its raw material: a story should have a point, it should be coherent, but it need not be reasonable. Narrative, which shapes and enables so much of pedagogy, becomes a kind of artificial negativity, a national park of oral discourse within the industrial landscape of academic language. When Andrea presented me with her narrative and her intervention, I temporarily revoked that exemption, which had been pushed past its limits. I demanded that she make sense of her story. If that demand bears any fruit, and sadly enough, it was barren for these students, for this class, it is in demonstrating (again) that the classroom is inhabited by desire—our own desire for our students' happiness, for their unproblematic initiation into our schemes of discourse, and, most ungovernably, for their emergence as our equals, as people with whom it is appropriate to have an equal fight. This desire led me into forms of magic that are not entirely benign. Unless we elaborate a form of reason that does not operate through a blind exclusion—even clear-sighted exclusion would be an improvement—the students most likely to fulfill this desire are also those most likely to thank us cordially and come no more.

Andrea's intervention and the work of writing about it, reflecting on it, and reading about it also raise the issue of relating pedagogical practice with critical theory. Although it is possible to imagine a happy taking up of Andrea's discourse outside pedagogy—a therapeutic rectification of her speech in psychoanalysis or a framing of her experience within the analytic terms of a political movement—the discourse of the classroom did not support the conversation that her speech opened. Andrea's claim was impossible for pedagogy: in asserting the irreducible singularity of her oppression, she was right beyond question. In claiming that her ideas should be exempt from questioning, Andrea made a demand for privileged, unquestioned speech that the classroom cannot support. Her claim demonstrates the contradictory structure of the classroom, which accepts all students but nothing that they believe. The most routine classroom questions—How do you know that? Have you considered all the implications of what you are saying?—are somewhat rude in social settings; the prolonged mutual scrutiny of positions that characterizes classroom talk at its best would, in a social situation, constitute "fighting words." Andrea's final demand was a scandalous opening of this contradiction; it shows why teaching is an impossible profession, and also why being a student is an impossible activity.

Nothing in either Lacan or Habermas softens this impossibility. A Lacanian reading of Andrea's intervention would see it as a deflected expression of desire, immobilized by the construction of a stable self, which mistakes the discourse of the other for its own speech. And we repeat that error analytically in speaking of a stabilized and deluded self as if some other self, mobile and clear-eyed, were ready to hand, capable of escaping such entanglements. Nor is Habermas much help to us, identifying failures to reflect, measuring the distance between rationality and classroom discourse. Andrea might well have agreed, and gone on to declare that, as far as she was concerned, rational critique could wait for a while, and that a stable self, however delusory, was just what she needed.

Differentiation, here, becomes fragmentation. Not only are critical theory, psychoanalysis, and pedagogy distinct, but they have no possible bearing on one another. A similar position is argued by Stanley Fish in *Doing What Comes Naturally: Change, Rhetoric, and the Practice of Theory in Literary and Legal Studies.* Fish argues that there is no necessary connection between critical theory and various interpretive practices, including the reading of literature, the practice of law, and teaching. His claim is presented under the sponsorship of rhetoric. "We live," says Fish, "in a rhetorical world." [22]

22. Stanley Fish, *Doing What Comes Naturally: Change, Rhetoric, and the Practice of Theory in Literary and Legal Studies* (Durham, N.C.: Duke University Press, 1989), 25.

The rhetoricism of that world is enforced in the practices of interpretive communities. For Fish, interpretive communities are not so much groups of people who agree with each other as ways of organizing experience which, when shared by individuals, achieve density and elaboration.[23] The interpretive community is not a concrete social grouping but a formal structure—a series of rules of interpretation and implication—that generates a social grouping, a "consciousness of community members." Not all shared passions and methods form communities: we could not speak properly of the interpretive community of Japanese ski wear designers. Interpretive communities, rather, are exemplified most clearly by professions and disciplines. By extension, they include communities of belief that support professional and disciplinary practices: for *Doing What Comes Naturally,* the central cases are law and literary study, and the defining marginal case is academic feminism.

The practices of professions as interpretive communities are necessarily informed by judgments of value that are secured through persuasive practices rather than transcendentally grounded. These judgments are directed toward the survival and development of the profession as a social institution, a self-interested project based on the profession's production of knowledge. *Doing What Comes Naturally* is an extended discussion of what follows if we hold open the aporia that Andrea's intervention presents to us: classroom discourse (in fact, all concrete and socially situated discourses) presents its own exigencies; those exigencies rule out the possibility of change in the conduct of business. Such a position has serious implications. If there is no bridge between critical theory and various concrete discursive practices, if there is no possible purchase of theoretical reflection on institutional practices, then approximations of rationality are anchored in the practices of professions rather than in universal assumptions of language. Using such a framework, Fish elaborates readings of contemporary theory in which Habermas becomes a naive utopian and Freud is a particularly brutal reductive interpreter.

But in thinking about the relation between critical theory and pedagogical practice, we encounter two institutions rather than one undifferentiated "interpretive community." Pedagogy is an intersubjective and institutionally located practice, but it is not an interpretive com-

23. Fish, *Doing What Comes Naturally,* 140.

munity in Fish's sense. Teaching is the largest, most inchoate, and most complex of the contemporary professions.[24] But pedagogy is also located within the discourses of academic disciplines: in my case, at the borders of literary study and women's studies. These multiple discourse communities provide a means, however provisional and unsatisfying, to negotiate the aporia that Andrea's intervention reveals.

Pedagogy is a professional practice that necessarily unfolds in time. I have spoken of how narrative unfolds the structure of lived time and opens to reflection the experience of temporality. Those operations occur unevenly and resistantly in pedagogy. Pedagogical time is articulated, indeed overarticulated, by institutional structures. Universities classify individuals by their places on institutional "clocks": undergraduate/postgraduate, tenured/untenured, upper division/lower division. The academic year articulates shorter passages of time, establishing between an individual teacher and her students a circumscribed relation unique among the professions. You "have" or "take" a teacher for a course; someone "is" your teacher when they work with you through a final project; you do not hire a teacher or keep one on retainer. Time is articulated in both the broad pattern of the term and the lapidary rituals of each class period, as the teacher and class determine what counts as the class opening and closing, negotiate the balance of speakers, determine topics and modes, and set the tempo of work. Although these structures support the work of teaching and help to articulate it for both teacher and student, the time of teaching itself is ungoverned and incalculable. The structures of institutional time, ubiquitous in academic life, appear over against the time in which reading and writing are undertaken, a time without clear boundaries, discontinuous and inchoate. Teaching is impossibly shaped by the doubled temporality analyzed by Ricouer—distension of the soul moves independently of relations of causality. A teacher might, in some authoritarian fury, plan every moment of classroom discourse, designing a series of lectures and exercises that would lead students through an idealized sequence of instruction, and make use of every instant of what is called "class time." But nothing could happen in that class: no response to puzzled looks,

24. See Barbara Ehrenreich and John Ehrenreich, "The Professional-Managerial Class," in *Between Labor and Capital: The Professional-Managerial Class,* ed. Pat Walker (Boston: South End Press, 1979); and Barbara Ehrenreich, *Fear of Falling: The Inner Life of the Middle Class* (New York: Pantheon, 1989), 17–56.

no unplanned call for questions, no general pause for thought. Without such interruptions and recursive moments, teaching is impossible. But in both the authoritarian classroom and more relaxed pedagogies, all of the conversation in the classroom is constrained by time. Just as discussion in the public sphere is shaped by the need to arrive at timely decisions, conversations in the classroom are constrained by the end of the period, the week, the semester. The lion that Freud used to provoke the Wolf Man, the forcible limitation of discourse, springs not "only once" in the classroom but at the end of every term.[25]

Indeed, my direct interactions with Andrea were compressed and often hurried. The period had ended, and it was not safe to linger in the empty building; the break was over, and the class was ready to resume work; someone came late or left early or just decided not to come at all. Such articulations of time are a kind of discourse between teacher and students, ending (for now) in the students' general choice of "incomplete" as their last utterance to me. Psychoanalysis is familiar with such discursive deployments of time; issues of time and temporality are also prominent in the lore of teaching. But critical theory, as a disciplinary practice, has an uneven relation to the temporality of the classroom. If the discursive forms of critical theory are the extended lecture, the conference talk (think of the influence of the 1966 Johns Hopkins conference on structuralism), the long essay, and the seminar talk, these forms of work are changed, however subtly, when they become classroom lectures, passages of questions and answers, or scraps of notes about what to do next. We might remember Lacan's pedagogical interview with M. Primeau, a talk that shows us something about his analytic practice but is not at all psychoanalysis.

Fish is right, then, to point out that the time of theory and the time of practice, the time of critical reflection and the time of classroom exigency, are distinct, and to connect that disjunction to distinctions among practices of knowledge. He is wrong, however, to claim that neither the forms of knowledge nor their pedagogical realizations ever intersect. That disjunction becomes critical in Fish's treatment of composition: "practice has nothing to do with theory, at least in the sense of being enabled and justified by theory. This leaves me and you only

25. Sigmund Freud, "Analysis Terminable and Interminable," in *The Standard Edition of the Complete Psychological Works of Sigmund Freud*, ed. James Strachey (London: Hogarth Press, 1975), 23:219.

with a few worn and familiar bromides: practice makes perfect, you learn to write by writing, you must build on what you already know."[26]

If, as Fish argues, there is no link at all between the interpretation of experience and theory, then subjects can come to theoretical reflection only by a disciplinary formation that denies them access to the sources of their own interests in reflection. For Fish, to do what comes naturally is not to theorize at all; disciplines grow, as it were, by ideologically kidnapping students and socializing them into alien modes of thought. By arguing for the rupture between theoretical propositions and the interpretation of experience, Fish has also ironically leveled the professional distinctions that he is otherwise at pains to argue. If no discipline within the academic professions has specific purchase on any element in the social, then all disciplines—and all of their allied professions—are alike textual and rhetorical practices. If all are alike, all can be analyzed by the same rhetorical armamentarium. Indeed, in one of the final chapters of *Doing What Comes Naturally,* "Rhetoric," Fish presents a version of the antifoundationalist rhetorical pantheon (Gorgias to Burke) that is stunningly ahistorical.

The pressing problem of the discourses of modernity is not their lack of consequence but the difficulty of opening the intersubjective links between them, of conducting a broad discourse on the boundaries of knowledge and the conduct of the social. Such opening requires a renegotiation of discursive hierarchies, a project that Fish's disjunction between theory and practice does not support. Although for Fish, philosophy is distinct from social life, literary theory is distinct from literary criticism, and antifoundationalist rhetoric is distinct from composition theory, they are not all distinct in the same way.[27] Philosophy and literary theory are distinct because they are defined professional activities, with their own density, their own business to transact. And what they are distinct *from*—social life, textual interpretation—is equally dense, historically situated, and serious. But antifoundationalist rhetorical theory is not distinct from a professional discipline of composition pedagogy. It is distinct from a body of unchanging lore ("You learn to write by writing"), which has nothing to offer sustained reflection and nothing to counsel but the mutual drudgery of teacher and student.

26. Fish, *Doing What Comes Naturally,* 355.
27. For the disjunctions between philosophy and social life, see Fish, *Doing What Comes Naturally,* 28; for those between literary theory and criticism, see 335.

Pedagogy, for Fish, is arrayed in a timeless time: it is time spent, immune from professional progress, the opposite of contentious, agonistic literary criticism, that paradigm of a healthy profession. It is a good thing for literary studies to be marked by "an army of active researchers, exploring new territories, sharing their discoveries and projects with one another, meeting regularly to explain, debate, and proselytize";[28] for an analogous army to arise among the ranks of compositionists would be a waste of resources, an expenditure of intelligence without effect. What needs to be known about the teaching of writing is already codified; it is, in Fish's terms, not really a profession at all, since it can claim no body of knowledge worth passing down but simply operates through the sheer application of raw, undifferentiated, pedagogical force: you learn to write by writing.

At this point, three contradictory pairs of concepts have been put into play by my analysis of Andrea's intervention: the disjunction between the profession of teaching and academic disciplines; between the institutionally structured time of the university and the multiply articulated time of the written text; and finally a disjunction internal to pedagogy, which alternatively privileges the learning subject and the critical discourse through which learning advances. These disjunctions are analogous. In all of them, the institution of education, concerned with reproducing specific competencies in specific subjects, is set against the ungovernable critical force of differentiated investigations, raids on the territory of the unknown, attacks against the stability of what is already known.

In the case of Andrea these lines are crossed once: in Andrea's initial narrative, she presents a text. She undertakes the temporal reconstruction of her lived time, deploys that reconstruction in place of an argument, and attempts—unsuccessfully, as it happened—to use narrative to subvert the institutional structures that assigned her a fixed place (in this case, pass/fail student). Andrea's narrative was recuperable: it belonged to a subgenre of student narratives well understood within the lore of teachers. But in crossing the boundaries between the articulated time of the class and the ungoverned time of learning, Andrea's text suggested the possibility of forms of writing that might take up the institutional structures of the university without being exhausted by them.

28. Fish, *Doing What Comes Naturally*, 203.

I am thinking here not of any utopian development of a pedagogical sublime but only of the self-conscious application and careful development of current practices such as collaborative journals, computer-linked classes, or Berthoff's dialectical notebook.[29]

Such forms of writing render visible, to both reader and writer, the intersubjective negotiation of meaning that they undertake. Rather than metaphorically representing the articulated time of the institution, such texts map over the institutional time a metonymical reference to the ungoverned time of teaching and learning. Teacher and student write to each other; students write to students; the written text is prolonged through the weeks of the semester and perhaps beyond, so that "class time" is textualized, opened out into the space of writing.

Such forms of writing make the intersubjectivity of disciplinary discourse, occluded by the conventions of objectivity and impersonality, available to students. No classroom genre resolves the aporia of Andrea's impossible and justified demand. But such forms can open the subject of knowledge to reflection and soften the bitterness of reflection by giving students and teachers more than one position within the discourses that they produce. When discourses become textual, they are available outside relentless structures of "class time," and therefore also outside the narrative structures of progress and amelioration elaborated by the teacher.

What students write provides us with a way to think about the knowledge that we are creating with them, and about how knowledge is deployed within the social. Such thought is not an exotic activity over against social production; it is a practice of language among the others available in universities: it can itself be taught, extended, reflected upon. When student writing is studied as a serious form of textual production, then the discourses of the disciplines become available for study as concrete rhetorical negotiations, socially situated practices of rationality. As teachers, we may continue to approach our students with impossible

29. For useful work in theory, politics, and pedagogy, see Richard Bullock and John Trimbur, *The Politics of Writing Instruction: Postsecondary* (Portsmouth: Boynton/Cook, 1990); Marilyn Cooper and Michael Holzman, *Writing as Social Action* (Portsmouth: Boynton/Cook, 1989); Patricia Harkin and John Schilb, eds., *Contending with Words: Composition and Rhetoric in a Postmodern Age* (New York: MLA, 1991). For the dialectical notebook, see Ann Berthoff, *Forming/Thinking/Writing: The Composing Imagination* (Upper Montclair, N.J.: Boynton/Cook, 1978).

demands and ungovernable desires; in seeking to change the state of its object, pedagogy may be at best a benign sadism. But to understand peledagogy as the production of particular texts does help us to see that, if the classroom is a place where rationality and desire must meet, they have never been confined to opposite sides of the desk.

CHAPTER SEVEN

Montaigne and
the Discourses
of Modernity

• • • • T he *Essais* of Michel de Montaigne demonstrate the limits and structures of the discourses we have been analyzing.[1] They explore issues of rationality and desire; they confront the differentiation of discourses in early modernity; they deploy and resist narrative as a device for normalization. I will not read the *Essais* as a study of the origins of the discourses of modernity, an issue too complex to be taken up here. Rather, I will read the essays as demonstrating the limits of modernity. Montaigne works with tropes central to the discourses of science and of public policy. He reflects on those tropes, and on the larger discursive forms that support them, in aid of his investigations of subjectivity in language and time. His text, then, meditates on themes central to this study; the *Essais* appear

1. Michel de Montaigne, *Les essais,* 3 vols., ed. Pierre Villey (Paris: Presses Universitaires de France, 1965). Unless otherwise noted, quotations from Montaigne in English are from Donald Frame's translation, *The Complete Essays of Montaigne* (Stanford: Stanford University Press, 1943). I have generally provided both Villey's and Frame's readings; where quotations are short, I have sometimes given only the English version. I have also used, from time to time, *The Essays of Montaigne, Done into English by John Florio,* 3 vols. (New York: AMS Press, 1967). For a contemporary treatment of the issues of Montaigne translation, see Tom Conley, "Institutionalizing Translation: On Florio's Montaigne," in *Demarcating the Disciplines: Philosophy, Literature, Art,* ed. Samuel Weber, Glyph Textual Studies 1 (Minneapolis: University of Minnesota Press, 1986). Quotations in English not ascribed to Frame or to Florio are my translations. Subsequent references will be given parenthetically in the text.

here not as an "early version" of themes more fully explored elsewhere but as a particularly demanding investigation of their connections and possibilities.

The *Essais* demonstrate the relations among language, action, and narration. Montaigne's writings about science (specifically, medicine) and public discourse (specifically, the question of cannibals) test the limits of emergent disciplinary discourses.

Language, Action, and Narration in Montaigne

Montaigne's investigation of writing, his "essais," is an extended vernacular prose text written for publication that exemplifies a distinct textual practice of modernity. The prose of the *Essais* is very precisely described in Jeffrey Kittay and Wlad Godzich's account of early modern prose, *The Emergence of Prose.*[2] Kittay and Godzich note that, from its inception, prose was associated with nonfiction and with a mode of performance outside the conventions of communal occasions. Prose is marked by a sustained multiplicity of deictic structures, including not only those pronominal forms and demonstrative adjectives that shift with the speaker but also the linguistic markers of the text's reference to itself. The deictic system therefore simultaneously indicates what is external to the text and organizes the situation of the writer and reader in relation to the text and its referent. The developed prose of modernity manages deixis by imputing the text to a constructed neutral subject whose authority is guaranteed by cohesion—the writing subject that organizes scientific writing and that the MOVE report approximates but does not achieve. Prose organizes multiple forms of deixis, so that the literate reader passes from one discursive frame to another, modifying his or her sense of the referential force and temporal location of the text according to its shifting deictic structure.

Quotation is central to those structures. As Kittay and Godzich put it:

> To disjoin the known from the knower is to limit the knower, put the knower in a kind of quotes, that is, always a product of prose's deictic ground, not a source thereof. What is said in prose, whether attributed speech (*parole*) or not, is to be taken as grounded locally, as if in quotes, not finally.[3]

2. Jeffrey Kittay and Wlad Godzich, *The Emergence of Prose: An Essay in Prosaics* (Minneapolis: University of Minnesota Press, 1987).
3. Kittay and Godzich, *The Emergence of Prose,* 133.

Montaigne's prose approximates no neutral subject; the authority of his text is not secured through cohesion. However, the *Essais* articulate multiple systems of deixis, and the reader is assisted in moving among them through quotation; for Montaigne, quotation keeps in play his claims to truth and his purchase on the reader's desire. Writing in the tradition of the early Renaissance miscellany, Montaigne renounces precisely those claims to reference that he will later make in favor of a project of giving pleasure, coupling his renunciation with assertions of absolute fidelity of quotation and full self-disclosure. In the essay "Des livres" (2, essay 10), Montaigne discusses both the accuracy of the essays and his use of quotations, although, as usual in Montaigne, the connection is paratactic:

> C'est icy purement l'essay de mes facultez naturelles, et nullement des acquises; et qui me surprendra d'ignorance, il ne fera rien contre moy, car à peine respondroy-je à autruy de mes discours, qui ne m'en responds point à moy; ny n'en suis satisfaict. Qui sera en cherche de science, si la pesche où elle se loge: il n'est rien dequoy je face moins de profession. Ce sont icy mes fantasies, par lesquelles je ne tasche point à donner à connoistre les choses, mais moy. . . . Ez raisons et inventions que je transplante en mon solage et confons aux miennes, j'ay à escient ommis parfois d'en marquer l'autheur, pour tenir en bride la temerité de ces sentences hastives qui se jettent sur toute sorte d'escrits, notamment jeunes escrits d'hommes encore vivants, et en vulgaire, qui reçoit tout le monde à en parler et qui semble convaincre la conception et le dessein, vulgaire de mesmes. (407–8)

> This is purely the essay of my natural faculties, and not at all of the acquired ones; and whoever shall catch me in ignorance will do nothing against me, for I should hardly be answerable for my ideas to others, I who am not answerable for them to myself, or satisfied with them. Whoever is in search of knowledge, let him fish for it where it dwells; there is nothing I profess less. These are my fancies, by which I try to give knowledge not of things, but of myself. . . . In the reasonings and inventions that I transplant into my soil and confound with my own, I have sometimes deliberately not indicated the author, in order to hold in check the temerity of those hasty condemnations that are tossed at all sorts of writings, notably recent writings of men still living, and in the vulgar tongue, which invites everyone to talk about them and seems to convict the conception and design of being likewise vulgar. (296)

Montaigne's initial demonstrative, "C'est icy purement l'essay," one of his many punning references to the title of his book, is deeply paradoxical in its deixis: if *this* is the essay, then what is the statement that indicates the essay? The demonstrative establishes an undefined discursive space; it is itself not a test, or at least not a simple test, of Montaigne's natural faculties. The bracketing demonstrative organizes the rest of the text as a quotation; although Montaigne is here invoking the humility *topos* common to Renaissance prefaces,[4] he uses it not to foreground the writer's submission to the reader but to renounce any claim to knowledge, locating his renunciation within the very boundaries of the text rather than in the customary preface or *envoi*. The distinction between text and frame blurs.

The prose text is doubled: there are *essais* and there are the *Essais*. And the writing subject is also doubled. Montaigne is not answerable to himself for these ideas; he stands outside himself and judges himself. We are presented with two Montaignes: the Montaigne we know through his fancies and the Montaigne who knows himself through his fancies—and the singular deictic carries them both.

This doubling of the deictic framework that articulates the text to the represented world operates throughout the *Essais*. The essay explicitly performs and makes available the relation of the subject to knowledge that other prose forms elide and assume. The conventions of scientific discourse that prompted Latour's scientist, injecting a rat, to invoke his distrust of the researcher are here explicit, on the table. Because Montaigne stands outside this text (although also in it), recording the best understanding of Montaigne the knower of the world, we are to take the text as an accurate representation of this knowing subject, located in time: "Thus I guarantee no certainty, unless it be to make known to what point, at this moment, extends the knowledge that I have of myself" (296).

Temporality, in the *Essais*, is closely linked with language, and indeed with Montaigne's choice of the vernacular. Within the hierarchy of printed texts, Montaigne understands the place of the vernacular text as temporary and provisional:

> J'escris mon livre à peu d'hommes et à peu d'années. Si ç'eust esté une matiere de durée, il l'eust fallu commettre à un langage

4. Terence Cave, "Problems of Reading in the *Essais*," in *Montaigne: Essays in Honor of Richard Sayce*, ed. I. D. McFarlane and Ian Maclean (Oxford: Clarendon, 1982), 133.

> plus ferme. Selon la variation continuelle qui a suivy le nostre jusques à cette heure, qui peut esperer que sa forme presente soit en usage, d'icy à cinquante ans? Il escoule tous les jours de nos mains et depuis que je vis s'est alteré de moitié. (982)

Or, as Florio has it:

> I write my booke to few men, and to few yeares. Had it beene a matter of lasting continuance, it should have beene compiled in a better and more polished language: According to the continuall variation, that hitherto hath followed our French tongue, who may hope, that it's present forme shall be in use fifty yeares hence? It dayly changeth and slips our hands: and since I could speake the same, it is much altred and wellnigh halfe varied. (3:229)

And of course, that "since I could speake the same" has its own story to tell, the story of Montaigne's singular accession to language. According to the *Essais,* Montaigne's father undertook to bring him up in Latin—interrupting, as it were, the succession of the mother tongue (1:xxvi, 129; Villey, 173). Therefore, if Montaigne is to be believed, he was put under the charge of a German doctor who was fluent in Latin and ignorant of French. (Although biographers have doubted that Latin was Montaigne's first language, oddly enough no Montaigne scholar seems to have doubted that Montaigne's father did undertake such an experiment.) Montaigne's father made an inviolable rule that his son would only be addressed in Latin, so the whole household was Latinized.[5] Montaigne claimed that he lost his pure and ready Latin only later, when he was sent to school—his father allowed himself, like a sick man greedy for a cure, to be swayed by common opinion and abandoned his experiment. For Montaigne, then, inheritance from the father is particularly—though not necessarily successfully—the inheritance of discourse, of a particular practice of language.

Language, specifically the text of the *Essais,* forms an alternate body for Montaigne, or, as he puts it, a *corps solide* (783; Frame, 595). It

5. Donald Frame, while accepting the story of the Latinized household, conjectures that if Montaigne's account of his infancy is correct—that his father had him brought up by neighboring peasants—his first language would have been the Gasçon dialect (Frame, *Montaigne: A Biography* [New York: Harcourt, Brace, and World, 1965], chap. 1). Whether we accept Montaigne's account of Latin as his first language or follow Frame, we have good reason to locate him in a multilingual setting, a milieu in which standard French is only one of the available languages, and not the most prestigious, stable, or widely understood. It complicates matters that Montaigne's mother's family were Spanish Jews.

moves the writer into a more mobile and extensive intersubjective space. But day-to-day and face-to-face, Montaigne's inheritance of language, like his corporeal inheritance, is fragile, intractable, and located in time and mutability:

> Le langage latin m'est comme naturel, je l'entens mieux que le François, mais il y a quarante ans que je ne m'en suis du tout poinct servy à parler, n'y à escrire: si est-ce que à des extremes et soudaines esmotions où je suis tombé deux ou trois fois en ma vie, et l'une, voyent mon pere tout sain se renverser sur moy, pasmé, j'ay tousjours eslancé du fond des entrailles les premieres paroles Latines: nature se sourdant et s'exprimant à force, à l'encontre d'un long usage. (810–11)

As Florio has it, preserving Montaigne's dizzying tense structure:

> The Latine tongue is to me in a manner naturall; I understand it better then French; but it is now fortie yeares, I have not made use of it to speake, nor much to write: yet in some extreame emotions and suddaine passions, wherein I have twice or thrice falne, since my years of discretion; and namely once, when my father being in perfect health, fell all along upon me in a swoune, I have ever, even from my very hart uttered my first words in latine: Nature rushing and by force expressing it selfe, against so long a custome. (3:30)

The idiosyncratic experiment which interrupted, for Montaigne, the succession of vernacular from mother to child constructed for him a connection to the tongue of the ancients; his patrimony assured him a place in an unchanging language. (Indeed, Montaigne the native speaker of Latin is an emblem of patrimony, of a resemblance of sons to fathers which secures paternity against the passage of time.) The father tongue forces from the interior of the body a forgotten speech that is the voice of nature itself. For the living Montaigne, that language proclaimed the death of the father; for the Montaigne of the *Essais,* that language is prose, the chosen medium of the discourses of modernity, in the form of the published book, the exemplary modern text.

Such work with language supports, for Montaigne, a complex understanding of action in relation to desire and rationality. If we understand action as causal intervention in events in the world, then the *Essais* are a social action, formed by negation and revision. The *Essais* are explicitly presented as a substitute for the public activity Montaigne had renounced: he writes them in retreat, after years of public work. Although Montaigne continued his public labors, culminating in two terms as mayor of Bordeaux, during the composition of the *Essais,* they are presented as the work of retirement, of *l'oisiveté.* In the preface, Montaigne declares that "je ne m'y suis proposé aucune fin, que domestique et privée" (3) (that he has set himself "no goal but a domestic and private one," 2). Throughout the essays, Montaigne insists that this text is not to be understood as an intervention in the social: it is too casually written; its matter is too ordinary; it was written in haste. He himself is not good at public affairs, too slow, too lazy, too ethical and old-fashioned.

But of course, the *Essais* reflect on public life, on the order of society, on the nature of public and specialized discourses. They are not casual scribblings but seriously and painstakingly prepared for publication. Montaigne published the *Essais* in 1580 and then carefully annotated and amplified the text, publishing a new edition, with additional essays, in 1588. That text was again annotated and amplified and was published by Montaigne's adopted daughter, Marie De Journay, in 1595.[6] The text as we have it records fifteen years of labor with language, marked in the editorial practice of differentiating the three "strata" of the text as A, B, and C.[7] The *Essais,* every word saturated with intentionality, were offered as an alternative to the discourse of public life, in which the efficacy of words is uncertain, in which the lie is often necessary, sometimes unconscious, and sometimes even virtuous.

Montaigne's essay "De la force de l'imagination" (1:xxi) offers a model of action articulated in time. Montaigne asserts that imagination can make people take on forms that they study or desire, even to the extent of changing their sex. He relates how he cured a friend of impotence on his wedding night through a *"singerie"* with an enchanted coin. He discourses on the unreliability of the penis, taking the role of its paid advocate, and finds it no more wayward than any of the other organs, even the will: "Veut-elle tousjours ce que nous voudrions qu'elle voulsist? Ne veut-elle pas souvent ce que nous luy prohibons de

6. Pierre Villey, *Les sources et l'évolution des "Essais" de Montaigne,* 2d ed., 2 vols. (Paris: Hachette, 1933; reprint, 1938). See also Villey, ed., *Les essais,* 1:viii.

7. For representative work on the evolution of the *Essais,* see David Maskell, "Evolution of the *Essais,*" in *Montaigne,* ed. McFarlane and Maclean, 13–34; and François Rigolot, "Montaigne's Purloined Letters," in *Montaigne: Essays in Reading,* ed. Gerard Defaux, *YFS* 64 (1983): 145–67. For a recent study showing that the *Essais,* like many other Renaissance texts, were revised and expanded to make them eligible for new licenses, see George Hoffman, "The Montaigne Monopoly: Revising the *Essais* under the French Privilege System," *PMLA* 108, no. 2 (Mar. 1993): 308–19.

vouloir: et à nostre evident dommage?" (103) ("Does it always will what we will it to will? Doesn't it often will what we forbid it to will, to our evident disadvantage?" 73). We read of imaginary cures and of imaginary harms: a swallowed pin, the evil eye, birthmarks. Montaigne ends by conceding that the essays are discourses on what is possible, not necessarily on what has happened. Although Montaigne does not allow himself to change details in the stories he has heard, he cannot vouch for the truth of what he writes, and he especially renounces any project of writing true and contemporary history.

The uncertain boundaries of the self, its subjection to an uncontrollable desire, the blurred division between mind and body, and the uncontainable replication and splitting of the self—which will not will what we will it to—are paratactically connected to the impossibility of discourse guaranteeing its own truth. Writing this text is a practice of finding representations in social discourse capable of sustaining desire and then searching for some logic of entitlement to connect them with an available system of rationality. Such a practice of signification is explicitly placed over against the composition of extended, coherent discourses on political and historical topics, texts that will form "extended narratives."

Montaigne experienced the waywardness of one such text, Étienne de la Boétie's essay "De la servitude voluntaire," which he had planned to set at the center of the first volume of the *Essais*. La Boétie's essay was posthumously published by radical Protestants as "Le Contr'Un," as an argument for resistance to Catholic princes, a position both La Boétie and Montaigne considered pernicious.[8] Donald Frame locates the impetus for the composition of the *Essais* in Montaigne's horror at the use to which his friend's text had been put: if a man's most treasured beliefs can be so easily distorted, then it is worthwhile to leave a very full and accurate self-portrait, so that you will be secure from slander after your death.[9] Whether or not the unauthorized publication of La Boétie's essay is responsible for the *Essais,* we do know that it is responsible for his decision not to include "De la servitude voluntaire" in the first volume after the essay "De l'amité."

Montaigne acknowledges that the variety of accidents makes all sto-

8. Étienne de la Boétie, *Oeuvres completes,* ed. Paul Bonnefon (Geneva: Slatkine Reprints, 1967).
9. Donald Frame, "Considerations on the Genesis of Montaigne's *Essais,*" in *Montaigne,* ed. McFarlane and Maclean, 1–13.

ries plausible, so readers can augment the text with their own examples; Protestants can find support in a text by an enthusiastic, even rigid, Catholic. Derrida has taught us that such uses of the text cannot be policed; "De la servitude voluntaire" is still published and distributed by anarchists.[10] Throughout the *Essais,* and particularly in "De la force de l'imagination," rationality is seen as a system of multiple ungovernable connections.

"De la force de l'imagination," then, argues for the ungovernability of discourse. Talk can cause impotence and cure it—and cure it by either frank therapeutic disclosure or by a *"singerie"* with a gold coin and a bathrobe. The essay presents a series of anecdotes in which a signifier is as good or better than the signified: the gaze—of a pregnant woman, of a falconer—can mark a child, bring birds from the air. The eye links a system of signification to the body, a collection of unruly organs, each of them following its own law: Montaigne's interest is in "l'estoite cousture de l'esprit et du corps s'entre-communiquants leurs fortunes" (104) (the "narrow seam between the soul and body, through which the experience of the one is communicated to the other," 74). What inhabits that narrow seam is language, whether organized as charm, spectacle, or discourse, and Montaigne insists that language, uncontrollably and unpredictably, transforms bodies, carries people through time and space, and determines beauty, gender, even sanity.

Central to this economy is the penis, which becomes in "De la force de l'imagination" a Lacanian phallus: as the signifier of the desire of the Other, it sustains a whole system of signification. In castration (figured, in this essay, as impotence), the phallus organizes the subject's relation to sexual difference, history, and the law. Montaigne suggests two ways in which that relation can be played out. The subject can impute desire and the lack of desire to the other and find in the other the object, alternatively, for punishment and worship:

> Amasis, king of Egypt, married Laodice, a very beautiful Greek girl; and he, who showed himself a gay companion everywhere else, fell short when it came to enjoying her, and threatened to kill her, thinking it was some sort of sorcery. As is usual in matters of fancy, she referred him to religion; and having made his vows and promises to Venus, he found himself divinely re-

10. See, for example, Étienne de la Boétie, *The Politics of Obedience: The Discourse of Voluntary Servitude,* introduction by Murray Rothbard (New York: Free Life Editions, 1975).

stored from the first night after his oblations and sacrifices. (71; Villey, 101)

Or we can parodically place the phallus within the system of law, as Montaigne does when he imagines that he has been paid to defend the penis. In this court of the imagination, the phallic power of signification is no longer localized: every organ of the body speaks, signifies, follows its own will. Our hair stands on end; our voice speaks or is paralyzed; farts emerge in tune with verses (72–73; Villey, 102–3). If the body is traversed by signs, and the will forms itself in those travels rather than being governed from some inviolable center, then Montaigne suggests that the best we can do is to bring our discourse into this play, to place the law at the service of eroticism rather than bringing eroticism under the sway of the law. Or, as Lacan would have it:

> This passion of the signifier then becomes the new dimension of the human condition, in that it is not only man who speaks, but in man and through man that it [ça] speaks, that his nature is woven by effects in which we can find the structure of language, whose material he becomes, and that consequently there resounds in him, beyond anything ever conceived of by the psychology of ideas, the relation of speech.[11]

The alternative, for Montaigne, is to operate the law as a system of domination—like Amasis, we can find a scapegoat for our frustrations in the other—or to come under the sway of the law, to find ourselves entangled by the relations of speech in the drama of another's punishment. For Montaigne, law identifies representational accuracy with truth: Montaigne insists, against any such claim, that the *Essais* do not represent anything beyond speech. He will accurately repeat what is told him; he makes no further claim to truth:

> Car les Histoires que j'emprunte, je les renvoye sur la conscience de ceux de qui je les prens.
>   Les discours sont à moy, et se tiennent par la preuve de la raison, non de l'expérience: chacun y peut joindre ses examples: et qui n'en a point, qu'il ne laisse pas de croire qu'il en est, veu le nombre et varieté des accidens.
>   Si je ne comme bien, qu'un autre comme pour moy. (105)

> . . . I refer the stories that I borrow to the conscience of those from whom I take them. The reflections are my own, and de-

---

11. Jacques Lacan, "The Meaning of the Phallus," in *Feminine Sexuality,* ed. Juliet Mitchell and Jacqueline Rose (New York: Norton, 1982), 78.

pend on the proofs of reason, not of experience; everyone can add his own examples to them; and he who has none, let him not fail to believe that there are plenty, in view of the number and variety of occurrences. If I do not apply them well, let another apply them for me. (75)

Montaigne leaves to the reader the task of evaluating and placing the stories. He includes the talk of others on the thinnest of credentials: one tale comes from a Swiss servant, who is "of a nation little addicted to lying" (74). Stories are attached to subjects, but any subject will do: Montaigne is not systematic about acknowledging or concealing which stories reflect his own experience. Intersubjectivity, normalized as an ethical interest in useful and efficacious (rather than narrowly accurate) discourse, motivates Montaigne's renunciation of any historical claim to truth. Instead, he subjects himself to "la preuve de la raison," a test replicable only in that it is available to any reader. What does not make sense in the discourse of medicine might make sense historically, or in the register of customary knowledge, or in that of some specialized art: "those who like falconry have heard the story of the falconer . . ." (75; Villey, 105).

The renunciation of representation is couched in the technical language of rhetoric, a discipline that Montaigne never names without contempt: he claims for his essays the proof of the possible. The "possible" designates a *stasis*, or genre of question, which classical rhetoricians saw as their particular territory, distinguishing it from the true, which was the domain of the philosopher.[12] But Montaigne repeatedly rejects both the project of rhetorical demonstration and the rhetorical devices he uses so deftly; he writes, he says, without arrangement or amplitude,

12. Central accounts of *stasis* begin with book III of Aristotle's *Rhetoric,* which poses four central questions for an orator: fact, harm, degree of harm, and justification (Aristotle, *On Rhetoric: A Theory of Civic Discourse,* trans. George A. Kennedy [New York: Oxford University Press, 1991], 258–59). These questions were elaborated by the Greek rhetorician Hermagoras, whose lost work on stasis was widely influential. Cicero takes up stasis in *De oratore, Books I and II,* trans. E. W. Sutton and H. Rackham, Loeb Classical Library (Cambridge: Harvard Univ Press, 1959), book II, chaps. 24–27. For the Renaissance, central treatments of stasis were that by the unknown author of the *Rhetorica ad Herennium,* published as *Ad C. Herennium de ratione dicendi* (*Rhetorica ad Herennium*), trans. Harry Caplan, Loeb Classical Library (Cambridge: Harvard University Press, 1954), book 2; and Hermogenes, *On Stasis* (Ray Nadeau, "Hermogenes's *On Stasis:* A Translation with an Introduction and Notes," *Speech Monographs* 31 [Nov. 1964]: 361–424). These texts are surveyed in Ray Nadeau, "Classical Systems of Stases," *Greek, Roman, and Byzantine Studies* 2 (1959): 51–71.

in ignorance of phrases and terms, even of the commonplaces. The rejection of public life becomes a generic rejection of rhetoricized discourse and of the figures of language most associated with it.

In "De la force de l'imagination," the probable, Montaigne's chosen terrain, stands over against connected historical narrative. A plot rooted in history, a plot with the power to carry along the weak and uncertain speaking subject, might lead him to mis-speak:

> ennemy juré d'obligation, d'assiduité, de constance; qu'il n'est rien si contraire à mon stile qu'une narration estendue: je me recouppe si souvent à faute d'haleine, je n'ay ny composition, ny explication qui vaille, ignorant au-delà d'un enfant des frases et vocables qui servent aux choses plus communes; pourtant ay-je prins à dire ce que je sçay dire, accomodant la matiere à ma force; si j'en prenois qui me guidast, ma mesure pourroit faillir à la sienne; que ma liberté, estant si libre, j'eusse publié des jugemens, à mon gré mesme et selon raison, illegitimes et punissables. (106)

> being a sworn enemy of obligation, assiduity, perseverance; . . . there is nothing so contrary to my style as extended narration. I cut myself off so often for lack of breath; I have neither composition nor development that is worth anything; I am more ignorant than a child of the phrases and terms that serve for the commonest things. And so I have chosen to say what I know how to say, accommodating the matter to my power. If I took up a subject that would lead me along, I might not be able to measure up to it; and with my freedom being so very free, I might publish judgments which, even according to my own opinion and reason, would be illegitimate and punishable. (76)

Or as Florio would have it, he might "haply publish judgements, agreeing with me, and consonant to reason, yet unlawfull and punishable" (1:102). Historical discourse is beyond Montaigne's capacity to control the rationality of his own text, and it is dangerous, because rationality is punishable. For historical discourse, legitimacy and punishment are the topics of praise and blame.

It is not a simple matter, or even a good idea, to reduce one of the *Essais* to a thesis: to chart his contradictory movement through topics and texts is the central figure of the best contemporary criticism of Montaigne.[13] But we might look at the chain of connections established in "De la force de l'imagination": the imagination shapes desire, causes

13. Patricia Parker, "Gender, Ideology, and Gender Change: The Case of Marie Germaine," *Critical Inquiry* 19, no. 2 (winter 1993): 337–64.

and cures illness, and generates the multiple accidents of life. Like Lacan's discourse, the imagination is efficacious rather than pleasant. Related in stories that have happened or were possible, these events are the
pretext for the discourse that Montaigne collates or arranges, proceed-
ing according to his sense of what is reasonable and probable; his text is
therefore located in a world of readers and writers who act upon one
another. Over against this world, Montaigne projects the world of
historical entrainment, of a body subjected, not to the changing signi-
fications of discourse, but to the relentless force of a narrative which
represents the world rather than someone's speech. Such a narrative implicates its author in the actions of history and renders him subject to
the law. Montaigne renounces such narratives, incorporating history
and the law in his text as quotation or exemplum. The emptiness and
mobility of the imagination make discourse possible.

The speaking subject who circles about those limits so regularly and
so insistently is formed in the very attempt to compose a text about
them; it is the absence of La Boétie that prompts Montaigne to write,
that organizes the first volume of the *Essais*.[14] The uncontrollable proliferation of La Boétie's text constrains its absence in the *Essais*. All that
is represented in the *Essais* is language, language and its limits—pain,
death, absence, love.

That representation and those limits are organized in Montaigne's
performance of narrative, as well as in his refusal of it. Despite Montaigne's renunciation of extended narrative, the *Essais* include any number of stories small and large. Every page is marked by miniature narratives, stories that display a seductive range of toils and devices. In the
first essays, for example, we read of the dialectician who dies of shame
after losing a public argument, of Emperor Maximilian, "aussi religieux
qu'un pucelle" (18), who ordered that whoever dressed him for burial
be blindfolded, of deathbed revelations and deceptive ambassadors. But
the *Essais* refuse narrative normalization. Montaigne repeatedly insists
that he writes whatever comes into his head, that his essays are digres-
sive, as unstructured as the wind that is his metaphor for consciousness.
Very few readers have felt comfortable taking these statements at face

14. For the subject in Montaigne, see the essays by Anthony Wilden: "Montaigne on the Paradoxes of Individualism," in *System and Structure: Essays in Communication and Exchange* (London: Routledge, 1980), 88–109; "Montaigne's *Essays* in the Context of Communication," *MLN* 85 (1970): 454–70; and "Pars
divers moyens . . . ," *MLN* 83 (1968): 577–97. For the absence of La Boétie, see
Michel Butor, *Essais sur "Les Essais"* (Paris: Gallimard, 1968).

value; it is quite usual for readers of the *Essais* to fabricate a plot for them. The traditional division is tripartite: there are early Stoic essays, middle skeptical or Pyrrhonist essays, and late "balanced" essays.[15] The *Essais* later came to be read as *"mobiliste"*;[16] in this reading, Montaigne progresses from an unachievable ideal of constancy to an acceptance of the mutable self. Current readings are likely to find other tripartite divisions: Starobinski's *Montaigne in Motion* reads the *Essais* as a meditation on the limits of doubt, moving from the rejection of outward appearances to a reacceptance of the limited integrity of the surface.[17] Those who resist a thematic narration of the *Essais* sometimes tell a story of its text. A central figure in the scholarship on Montaigne is a comparison among the various strata of the text, although their organization into three levels, corresponding roughly to 1580, 1588, and 1595, is itself a simplification of the text's multiple and continuous revisions.[18]

The *Essais* begin with a set of exemplary stories about the conduct of war and the affairs of princes. They end with a list of Montaigne's preferences in clothing, fruit, and daily habits, and include along the way discussions of medicine, the supernatural, the worthy men of antiquity, and the joys of friendship. Although no reader who has been socialized by Dickens or prime-time television can avoid generating a narrative from this series, the *Essais* are arranged to frustrate narrative connections. The *Essais* favor topics that resist narration—the moment of death, the choice of a friend: "La mort ne se sent que par le discours, d'autant que c'est le mouvement d'un instant" (56) (death is not felt except by discourse, because it is the movement of an instant). Montaigne's friendship with La Boétie is not a story to be told; it happens because "c'estoit luy, par ce que c'estoit moy" (188).

Montaigne argues instead for reflexivity, for a project of self-knowledge. Such self-knowledge would be anything but schematic or moralizing; it constructs reflexivity over against the discourses of knowledge and power. Reflexivity is proposed as mediating desire and language:

> La carriere de nos desirs doit estre circonscripte et restrainte à
> un court limite des commoditez les plus proches et contigues;

15. This is the thesis of Villey's *Les sources et l'evolution des "Essais" de Montaigne.*

16. Albert Thibaudet, *Montaigne* (Paris: Gallimard, 1963).

17. Jean Starobinski, *Montaigne in Motion* (Chicago: University of Chicago Press, 1985).

18. Maskell, "Evolution of the *Essais*," 32.

et doit en outre leur course se manier, non en ligne droite qui
face bout ailleurs, mais en rond, duquel les deux pointes se tien-
nent et terminent en nous par un brief contour. Les actions qui
se conduisent sans cette reflexion, s'entend voisine reflexion et
essentielle, comme sont celles des avaritieux, des ambitieux et
tant d'autres qui courent de pointe, desquels la course les em-
porte tousjours devant eux, ce sont actions erronées et mala-
dives. (1011)

The range of our desires should be circumscribed and restrained to a narrow limit of the nearest and most contiguous
good things; and moreover their course should be directed not
in a straight line that ends up elsewhere, but in a circle whose
two extremities by a short sweep meet and terminate in ourselves. Actions that are performed without this reflexive movement—the actions, for example, of the avaricious, the ambi-
tious, and so many others who run in a straight line, whose
course carries them ever forward—are erroneous and diseased
actions. (773)

Reflexivity implies a renunciation of the narratives of accumulation and
progress, whether optimistic and ameliorative or pessimistic and nihilist.
The objects of desire are not necessarily to be found at the end of the
narrative train; they are proximate goods, formed in relation to the self
which is traced out in the short sweep and termination of desire. If we
renounce the grand narratives of ambition and avarice, however, we
have not therefore placed ourselves beyond their scope: Montaigne is
mayor of Bordeaux, intervenes in the religious wars, and acts as magis-
trate, even if "the mayor and Montaigne have always been two" (774).

This doubling of the self and the social role, an analogue to the doubling of the text in prose deixis, can be read as a tactic for avoiding
narrative entrainment rather than as a modern celebration of interior
subjectivity; as Timothy Reiss has pointed out, the private Montaigne is
an uncertain bundle of impulses rather than any stable interiority.[19] The
doubled subject efficaciously forestalls narrative: it provides a juncture
that allows the text to switch tracks without derailing. Exploiting these
possibilities, Montaigne enacts ever more insistently and explicitly a
practice which is necessarily reflexive, which is intersubjective in its most
intimate texture, which is also public, open, and expansive: the writing,
extended revision, and publication of the *Essais* themselves. In the *Essais*, writing and reading become forms of action, and the story of the

19. Timothy Reiss, "Montaigne and the Subject of Polity," in *Literary Theory
and Renaissance Texts*, ed. P. Parker and D. Quint (Baltimore: Johns Hopkins University Press, 1986), 115–49.

written text, recursive, doubled, and irrecoverable, becomes the only story worth telling.[20]

Montaigne's investigation of reason, desire, and intersubjectivity encounters the discourses of modernity in his discussion of science, specifically the nascent science of medicine, and in his discussion of conquest and colonization, which raises issues central to public discourse. The early modern context recognized only primordial forms of differentiation: the special status of theology, the terms of art of the traditional professions, the emergent language of statecraft. Against these forms of differentiation, Montaigne poses a profound distrust of innovation, the humanist's aesthetic distaste for specialized terms of art, and a neutral's wariness of the language of religious wars. In the *Essais,* we can see how specialized truth claims and gestures of reference were read outside the institutional settings that had begun to foster them. Whether or not Montaigne's text marks the beginning of an early modern differentiation of reason, he certainly wrote outside it.

Montaigne and the Discourse of Science

Montaigne was an interested spectator of science and the discourse of science, taking up medical discourse in two essays, "De la ressemblance des enfans aux pères," which closes book 2, and "De l'experience," which closes book 3. In "De la ressemblance des enfans aux pères," the discourse and practice of medicine are read as a project of domination. Medicine is described in political terms: we encounter "confusion d'ordonnances" (767), "la jurisdiction de la medicine" (766), and "cette authorité tyrannique qu'ils usurpent" (769). Over against this authority, Montaigne poses his own inherited distrust of doctors and their remedies, a kind of prolonged natural experiment.

Montaigne distrusts medicine by inheritance, because of his family's good health and, "with doctors, fortune is much more valuable than reason" (579). If, elsewhere in the *Essais,* Montaigne argued for the superiority of reason, of judgments about the probable, over experience, here he has privileged above reason a specific kind of experience, almost against his own better judgment: "for all those predispositions that are born in us without reason are bad" (580). If the distrust of medicine is inherited, so, for Montaigne, is disease—he inherits kidney

20. See Struever's *Theory as Practice,*182–209, for a treatment of Montaigne as heir of a Renaissance practice of ethical reflection located within friendship, originating with Petrarch's letters.

stones from his father. Inheritance brings both health and sickness and locates us relentlessly and irrationally within the time of mortality.

Montaigne offers a long and circumstantial account of his sufferings with the stone, contrasting its syncopated attacks and remissions with the occult latency of the disease transmitted from a father who had yet not shown any symptoms of the stone to a son who lived to be forty-five before his first attack. Inheritance, on its face the simplest of patrimonial relations, becomes a mystery:

> quel monstre est-ce, que cette goute de semence dequoy nous sommes produits, porte en soy les impressions, non de la forme corporelle seulement, mais des pensemens et des inclinations de nos peres? Cette goute d'eau, où loge elle ce nombre infiny de formes? (763)

> What a prodigy it is that the drop of seed from which we are produced bears in itself the impressions not only of the bodily form but of the thoughts and inclinations of our fathers! And how does that drop of fluid lodge this infinite number of forms? (578)

Over against this mysterious correspondence of bodies and minds, Montaigne finds in medicine a singular and contradictory practice of language. The doctor's description of the world is a command; it denies its intersubjective grounding even as it interpellates the patient as an object of therapy. Medicine, for Montaigne, is "leur art," but also "leur doctrine" (764), "leur regles" (765), and most tellingly, "leurs ordonnances" (766). Montaigne's critique of medicine is also organized as an account of the orders, customs, and *habitus* of doctors. Medicine had not, by Montaigne's day, developed either the disciplinary status of a mature science or the institutional status of a profession.[21] His understanding of it, as merely the sum of the experiences of its practitioners, is as accurate as it is relentless. But doctors also speak within his text. Montaigne borrows a recipe for curing the stone with goat's blood from a popular medical text, Laurent Joubert's *Erreurs populaires au fait de la medicine et regime de sante* (1579); he quotes Joubert silently and redisposes the time and circumstances through which the recipe came to him.[22] The shifting frameworks of the text's deixis include both Montaigne as medical speaker and Montaigne as patient, concealing and revealing his longstanding absorption in the art he satirizes.

21. For medicine and professionalization, see Larson, *The Rise of Professionalism*.
22. Robert Cottrell, *Sexuality/Textuality: A Study of the Fabric of Montaigne's "Essais"* (Columbus: Ohio State University Press, 1981), 73.

The essay doubles medicine: there is medicine, a noble science, and then there are doctors. Or, in Montaigne's most succinct formulation: the Romans enjoyed good health, "non pas sans medicine, mais ouy bien sans medicin" (767), "not without medicine, but indeed without a doctor." We are reminded of Montaigne's reflections on his own name: "There is a family in Paris and one in Montpellier named Montaigne, another in Brittany and in Saintonge, called de la Montaigne. The change of a single syllable will tangle our threads so that I will share in their glory, and they, perhaps, in my shame" (475). The name, rather than guaranteeing propriety, indicates in its contingency the instability of deixis; a syllable transforms *mine* to *theirs;* from the addition of an *e* springs the calamity of doctors.

For Montaigne, medicine is not simply the administration of drugs or other treatments. He does not doubt that there are natural substances that preserve health; he himself has used medicinal baths, sometimes with profit. But medicine is also a practice of language that articulates the time of the subjected patient, imposing on the multiple and heterogeneous episodes of individual life a single and continuous narrative, that of illness, with its crises and remissions: "The doctors are not content with having control over the sickness; they make health itself sick, in order to prevent people from being able at any time to escape their authority. From a constant and perfect health, do they not derive an argument for a great illness to come?" (581). Theirs is a narrative that cannot fail: the doctor is vindicated by success, but his failures are silent. Within this narrative, roles are assigned asymmetrically: patients voice symptoms and suffer; doctors give orders but do not suffer. Montaigne quotes Aesop's story of the doctor who has only one reply to all his patient's complaints, "That's good." Every symptom denotes the power and efficacy of treatment; the doctor need not respond to the specificity of the patient's suffering but only reinscribe it within the system of the science.

Into the narrative of treatment, the doctor inserts timeless and universalizing discourses about the causes of illness—humors, atoms, bodily powers, air, nourishment, or spirits (585)—and the powers of drugs—operating to heat or cool, dry or moisten, different organs, at different times (587). Into the contingent individual narrative of suffering, the doctor inserts the universal discourse of diagnosis and cure, a discourse that emerges, finally, in the *"ordonnance,"* the specification on the body of the patient, and at a particular time, of the operative universal: "You take parsley broth for the next five days." This order promises to close the narrative of suffering, a promise that Montaigne, sustaining repeated attacks from the stone, knew would go unredeemed.

Montaigne refuses to allow medicine to articulate his time and refuses medicine's claim to universal and timeless truths about his body. He parodies and ridicules the technical language of medicine, "un langage à part, une escriture à part" (770). For Montaigne, the arguments of physicians share all the weakness of his own discussions of the probable: contradictory propositions can easily be true, and they proliferate endlessly. Aperients can be dangerous to those suffering from the stone, or useful purgatives. It is better to urinate often, or to contain the urine. Intercourse is salutary, or dangerous, or salutary when well regulated: "Voilà comment ils vont bastelant et baguenaudant à nos despens en tous leurs discours. Et ne me sçauroient fournir proposition à laquelle je n'en rebatisse une contraire de pareille force" (776) ("That is how they go juggling and trifling at our expense in all their reasonings. And they could not provide me with one proposition to which I could not construct a contrary one of equal force," 589). We remember the remark from the essay "De la coustume" ("On Custom"): "I think that there falls into man's imagination no fantasy so wild that it does not match the example of some public practice, and for which, consequently, our reason [*nostre discours*] does not find a stay and foundation" (79; Villey, 111).

The proliferation of reasons, of probabilities, makes meaningless any distinction we might want to make among rationality, imagination, fantasy, and practice. Since so many doctors enjoin so many means of treatment, giving plausible reasons for them all, it is prudent to follow doctors only in indifferent matters, or where they can do no harm. The generalized reason of the humanist sage, invoked by Montaigne as *"jugement,"* stands against the specialized practice of medicine. Montaigne does not simply take as given the doctor's individual injunction to him, but collates the contradictory injunctions of all doctors to all patients. He textualizes the discourse of medicine, opening it to reflection and critique and locating its judgments in time—no longer the time of the patient's narrative of suffering but that of the history of medicine from Galen and Paracelsus, a history in which contradictions are syntagmatically arrayed beyond the normalizing power of any Truth Will Out Device. Since each generation of medical writers has reversed the prescriptions of their predecessors, medicine presents no story of amelioration but simply one contradictory episode after another.

Against the reason of specialized medicine, Montaigne offers the gen-

eral corrosive of doubt prompted by good judgment. The issue for
Montaigne is the doctors' claim to certainty about the effects of drugs,
based on "l'experience qu'ils ont faite" (781) (the experiments they
have done). But drugs work, Montaigne asserts, mainly because of their
"quinte essence," an occult or hidden property. Only *usage* can give us
instruction about it, since "par nostre raison nous ne sçavons trouver la
cause" (782) (we do not know how to find the cause of their efficacy by
reason). Unlike the acts of reading and writing, operations of reason,
Montaigne here assigns experimental medicine to the problematic
sphere of *experience,* a term which included "experience" and "experiment." Montaigne accepts nondeductive evidence or *instruction* about
drugs (for example, inspiration from a daemon or common reputation);
he distrusts deliberate trials of specific medicines for specific illnesses.
Montaigne's preference for reputation recalls Aristotle's distinction between "artistic" and "inartistic" rhetorical proofs. Artistic proofs are
drawn from reason and probability and are more reliable than inartistic
proofs, such as physical evidence, oaths, and testimony exacted by tor-
ture (*On Rhetoric,* I, 2). Since reason is useless at determining the
"quint essence" of a drug, the only sensible course is to rely on prolonged and extended experience, codified as tradition. Experiments
with treatment, like inartistic proofs, are therefore held to be contingent. Just as the legal practice of antiquity distrusted inartistic proofs as
open to forgery and valued the argument from probability, Montaigne
argues for medical proofs based on probability rather than on empirical
demonstration. Montaigne is particularly skeptical of unmotivated experiments: the number of possible drugs is infinite, as are the maladies
they can treat and the ways of administering them. The experimenting
doctor would be guided in his researches "neither by theory [*argument*], nor by conjecture, nor by example, nor by divine inspiration, but
by the sole movement of fortune" (595; Villey, 782). And since fortune
is contingent and unrationalized, any experiment based on fortune cannot warrant belief. Even if a cure was demonstrated, how could a doctor
know that the treatment caused it? How could an experiment based on
contingencies be repeated? Who records the progress of a cure? How do
we know that contrary experiences do not exist? "But that three witnesses and they three physicians should lay down the law to mankind is
not reasonable [*n'est pas la raison*], unless human nature had deputed
them and chosen them, and declared them to be our arbiters [*syndics*]
by express power of attorney" (595; Villey, 783).

The discourse of medicine is a closed system, organized by universalizing and rationalizing narratives; it is also necessarily arbitrary and contingent. Montaigne's objections here—let me join now the chorus of those who find him "modern"—anticipate the issues that biology, as it developed into a differentiated discipline, would take up in regulation of experimental design. The last pages of "La ressemblance des enfans aux peres" are a catalog of topics in experimental method: hypothesis formation, isolation of variables, controls, causality versus association, sample size, replicability—even the issues of observation effects and uncertainty are raised. Paradoxically, Montaigne's critique of medicine's *experience* specifies precisely what medicine most needed to develop as a science: a sense of method, of the possibility of mapping the natural order inductively, giving over the philosophic question of "quint essence" in favor of the accumulation of verifiable experiments. The causes and properties, however occult, that can explain the actions of drugs and that can make medicine rational cannot be understood by our reason. Irrationality, evaded and disguised, is associated with the authority of doctors, their concealment of their craft in mystery.

Montaigne counterposes to the experiment suggested by chance his own patrimonial experiment. Three generations of fathers have distrusted medicine: "Medicine is based on examples and experience; so is my opinion. Isn't that a very clear-cut and advantageous experience [*experience*]? . . . My ancestors had an aversion to medicine by some occult natural inclination" (579; Villey, 764). If drugs can operate through occult properties, then other equally occult properties can prompt us to avoid drugs. If doctors can draw conclusions from their experiments, we can draw conclusions from our experiences. Against the timeless and universal assertions of doctors, Montaigne locates his own experiment very precisely: we read proper names, ages, and a particular duration—eighteen years short of two hundred. The experiments of doctors, by contrast, suffer from abstraction, projecting a generalized patient, unlocated in time or space and also divorced from contingency, relying on chance, unmotivated by any reliable understanding of the body.

Montaigne with Foucault

These issues—control of the patient, authority of the doctor, the articulation on the body of the patient of a system of medical discourse—

recall the central themes of the work of Michel Foucault, from his early *The Birth of the Clinic: An Archeology of Medical Perception* to the discussions recorded in *Technologies of the Self: A Seminar with Michel Foucault*.[23] And Montaigne's perspective on medicine does eerily anticipate Foucault's, not least in his usage of *la police* to refer to the order of the state, the organization of medicine, and the care of the body.[24]

Like Habermas and Lacan, Foucault provides a distinct pathway through the texts we have been reading. All these theorists have addressed the problem of modernity, and their usefulness depends on preserving their distinction rather than canceling out all the interesting moments in each's thought. But Foucault can help us read Habermas, and Montaigne, more reflectively.

For Foucault, the reliability of reason is essentially implicated in the knowing subject, ideologically constituted as transcendent to warrant the reliability of knowledge, but always also entangled in a social network of domination and subordination. That network, Foucault called power. Power is not a means of repression but rather productive of knowledge, and it operates by exclusion, by silencing and marginalizing. It is by silencing certain subjects—madmen, criminals—that forms of knowledge—psychology, criminology—are inaugurated. "Every society has its regime of truth, its 'general politics' of truth: that is, the types of discourse which it accepts and makes function as true."[25]

For Habermas, the disciplines, particularly the social sciences, emerge through an irreversible differentiation of reason. Disciplines emerge through the evolution of discourse rather than through the exclusion of speakers. Disciplines establish local norms for communication which instantiate, with greater or less fidelity, the noncoercive and egalitarian relations of the ideal speech situation.

Both of these frameworks are ambivalent toward positive knowledge. Both locate a critique of positive knowledge in a deep sense of the difficulties and possibilities of the present. In spite of the widespread readings of Foucault as a nihilist critic of reason in all its contemporary

23. Michel Foucault, *The Birth of the Clinic: An Archeology of Medical Perception*, trans. A. M. Sheridan-Smith (New York: Vintage, 1973); Michel Foucault, *Technologies of the Self: A Seminar with Michel Foucault*, ed. Luther Martin, Huck Gutman, and Patrick Hutton (Amherst: University of Massachusetts Press, 1988).

24. But see Foucault's commentary on this Renaissance usage in *Power/Knowledge*, quoted in Paul Rabinow, ed., *Foucault Reader* (New York: Pantheon, 1984), 277.

25. Michel Foucault, *Power/Knowledge* (New York: Vintage, 1980), 132.

manifestations, and of Habermas as a believer in progress and perfectibility, neither Habermas nor Foucault dismisses the texts of modernity or reads them without suspicion. Habermas recognized that the ideal speech situation, that most modest of utopias, exists only as the critical force generated by its absence, and Foucault repeatedly located himself within the structures of disciplinary knowledge.

But Foucault saw power as the unspoken, extradiscursive subject of all the discourses of knowledge. Discourse always proceeds in darkness, ignorant of its own subject, so that its manifest content is to be understood as a symptomatic gesture toward the reticulation of a network of power relations. Discourse may not tell us anything about the structure of the natural world or of social life; critical theory indicates its silence and the sedimentation of the relations of power within specific texts. Habermas, on the other hand, reads the discourses of the disciplines as referring, silently, to the structure of the transcendent knowing subject; it is the role of critical theory to correct this orientation and to point out that the disciplines are supported, not by the transcendent subject, but by the structures, norms, and implications of communication itself.

For Foucault, critical discourse points out what is unavoidably unknown to the disciplines, so that criticism is necessarily indifferent to their claims; for Habermas, critical discourse corrects the self-understanding of the disciplines, including their claim to unmediated representation of the world. Both prize the reflexive moment of critique, locating there the possibility of a discourse that may not produce positive knowledge but does not produce deception or illusion.

For Foucault, the discipline of reflexivity is a negative practice,[26] as represented in his discussion of *Las Meninas*. Although the painting is organized through the gaze of the king and the labor of the painter, precisely those elements are excluded from the domain of the representation.[27] Analogously, the disciplines are dependent on practices of language that they cannot recognize. The critic who points out this absence cannot supply what is missing, just as we who view *Las Meninas*,

26. Negativity is of course a theme associated with both celebrations and critiques of the Frankfurt School. For Adorno on negativity, see *Negative Dialectics*, trans. E. B. Ashton (New York: Seabury Press, 1973). Habermas has been at pains to separate Foucault's sense of negativity from Adorno's; see Habermas, "The Entwinement of Myth and Enlightenment: Rereading *The Dialectic of Enlightenment*," *New German Critique* 26 (spring–summer 1982): 13–20.

27. Foucault, *The Order of Things*, 3–16. See also Habermas's discussion of this passage in *The Philosophical Discourse of Modernity*, 259–60.

standing in the place of the royal couple, can experience them as absent but do not for all that make them present in the representation. For Habermas, alternatively, reflexivity is inherent in the structure of the communicative act: the very fact of illocution is a peremptory call to accountability.[28] For both Foucault and Habermas, reified procedures ordering the self according to a predetermined schema are the enemies of reflexivity. Foucault traces these "technologies of the self" to Greek and Roman practices of self-knowledge; Habermas speaks of the limits of those practices and of the systematic violence of system.[29]

Foucault's and Habermas's are two distinct and contradictory methods of grounding critique and of connecting it to its objects. Although Foucault recognized, in his final interviews, the importance that the Frankfurt School might have had in his work, his treatment of discourse is grounded in quite different assumptions.[30] We cannot be simultaneously concerned with, and indifferent to, the question of truth in representation in the social sciences; we cannot simultaneously hold that all representations operate power and that the truth of representations reflects their adequacy as speech situations. Therefore, whereas a Foucauldian reading of Montaigne would turn on Montaigne's anticipation of the development of medicine as a regime of control, a Habermasian reading would develop a distinct understanding of Montaigne's critique of medicine. Montaigne's essays on medicine can be read as ambivalent responses to differentiation, simultaneously anticipating the development of a more highly differentiated medical discourse and critically counterposing that discourse to the inexpert, but balanced, judgment of the sage.[31] These readings operate in complementary ways, a Foucauldian reading foregrounding the text as representation and a Habermasian reading foregrounding the text as discourse.

28. Habermas, *Theory of Communicative Action*, 2:73–76.

29. For Foucault on sexuality, see his *The History of Sexuality*, 3 vols. (New York: Pantheon, 1978–86). For Habermas on structural violence, see *The Theory of Communicative Action*, 2:186–87; for the limits of the subject-centered paradigm, see Habermas, *Philosophical Discourse of Modernity*, 185–294.

30. But see Grady, *The Modernist Shakespeare*, for an account of Foucault's response to Habermas and for an argument that sees Habermas and Foucault as compatible.

31. See, for example, "De la phisionomie": "Socrates makes his soul move with a natural and common motion. . . . His are inductions and similes drawn from the commonest and best-known actions of men; everyone understands him. Under so mean a form we could never have picked out the nobility and splendor of his admirable ideas, we who consider flat and low all ideas that are not raised up by learning, and who perceive richness only in pomp and show" (793).

Since both readings are grounded in reflexivity, Montaigne's text becomes relevant to both Foucault and Habermas, not simply as an object of analysis, but as a compelling voice in the discourse. Both readings—and for that matter, Lacan's critique of the subject as irreparably divided—are in their distinct moments convincing. Neither Habermas nor Lacan addresses the issue of how we are to understand the forms of language and thought characteristic of a divided subject, a subject constituted in intersubjective discourse. We can read the *Essais* as one version of a mobile and reflexive subjectivity that supports and locates the work of critique. Such a subject does not serve as a guarantee of truth or as a location of value. Rather, the subject is a narrative armature supporting the interrupted trajectory of desire, a deictic frame within which the text's babble of quotation can be organized, a hopelessly mixed metaphor. The subject's life marks the text's location in time and its quality as a labor of language.

Montaigne repeatedly asserts the time of writing in the *Essais* against the unitary time of the medical experiment. The fluid and multiple temporality of Montaigne's *essai,* a time interior to the subject but discursively available, at once sponsors a critique of experimental science and suggests its matured discursive forms. The medical experiment, a "preuve de raison," is undertaken conjuncturally, once, but asserts its unitary truth for all time. How, Montaigne asks, can the physician locate his experiment in the subject's time of life, the time of year, astrological time, and the course of the illness? The impossibility of sorting through these frameworks is described as a matter of losing Latin: "le sens humain y perd son latin" (782). The patrimonial language that locates the subject outside time fails; there is no safe time inside or outside this text.

Immediately after mounting this critique of the discourse of science, Montaigne inserts a letter to Madame de Duras into the essay, marking it with the time of its composition, just as the opening of the essay was marked with the time that had elapsed since he began the project. The letter serves as a quotation of the moment of Mme. Duras's entrance, a textual equivalent to the moment of *Las Meninas.* But as readers, we stand within the frame: we see Montaigne and the manuscript he was writing (and what he wrote over it, in subsequent editions); we see Duras's entrance and his surprise: "Madame, you found me at this point when you recently came to see me" (595). The work of language permits, supports, even encourages a multiplication of temporal frames that move us freely among the available subject positions. The text holds together the time of the experiment, the time of Montaigne's critique, the moment of Mme. Duras's entry into the room, the moment when, after Montaigne's death, she reads the essay, and also the moment when he turns from her to "resume the thread" of his argument (597), "vous me donnez bien congé de reprendre le fil de mon propos, duquel je m'estoy destourné pour vous entretenir" (785) ("Surely you give me leave to resume the thread of my argument, from which I had turned aside to talk to you," 597).

Montaigne's address to Mme. Duras is the context for his denomination of the *Essais* as his alternate body, his *corps solide*. It is subject to time; the vernacular text is not permanent, or even especially long-lasting. Montaigne's practice seeks to multiply the subject rather than preserve it, to establish it in difference rather than identity. In the very early essay "De l'oisiveté," Montaigne admitted that, since retirement, his mind had become unsettled, divided, and fanciful and that he wrote down these thoughts so that *they*—not he, mind you—would become ashamed of themselves. His is no project of Stoic integrity, but the reluctant and tentative working out of a textual practice that opens a divided and multiple subject to reflection. The practice of writing becomes a model or metaphor for other multiplications of the subject: "The mayor [of Bordeaux] and Montaigne have always been two" (774).[32]

Within the *Essais*, issues of politics, government, and history are closely associated with the vicissitudes of the subject, particularly in relation to patrimony. Since the time of history is not one context among many but an inescapable and exigent framework for both experience and reason, the intervention of the subject in history and the pressure of history on the subject are both crucial to the *Essais*.

Public Discourse: The Path of the Cannibal

We can read in Montaigne's treatment of cannibalism a limiting instance both of intersubjectivity and of patrimonial inheritance. "Des cannibales" constructs a discursive practice that contains the cannibal in language, suggests that speech and writing are less absolute forms of incorporation of the other, and articulates patrimony as a narrative organized in time rather than as consumption of fathers by sons.

32. For a full treatment of the plural subject in Montaigne, see Tzvetan Todorov, "L'Être et L'Autre: Montaigne," *YFS* 64 (1983): 113–44.

"Des cannibales" is not Montaigne's only treatment of cannibalism. The *Essais* include two other images of cannibalism, both meditations on the social and intersubjective. In "Couardise mère de la cruauté" ("Cowardice, Mother of Cruelty") (2, essay 27), Montaigne describes the execution of George Sechel, leader of a Polish peasant rebellion. He was bound to a wooden horse and tortured for three days, during which his followers were given no food or water:

> In the end, while he still lived and could see, they gave his blood to drink to his dear brother Lucat, for whose safety he kept praying, drawing upon himself all the hatred for their misdeeds. And they had twenty of his most favored captains feed on him, tearing his flesh with their teeth and swallowing the morsels [*deschirans à belles dents sa chair et en engloutissants les morceaux*]. The rest of his body and his inner parts, when he was dead, were boiled and given to the others of his followers to eat. (530; Villey, 701)

Montaigne's second treatment of cannibalism occurs in his description of meeting his friend La Boétie:

> Our friendship has not other model than itself, and can be compared only with itself. It is not one special consideration, nor two, nor three, nor four, nor a thousand: it is I know not what quintessence of all this mixture, which, having seized my whole will, led it to plunge and lose itself in his; which, having seized his whole will, led it to plunge and lose itself in mine, with equal hunger, equal rivalry [*d'une faim, d'une concurrence pareille*]. (139; Villey, 189)

Against these two passages, we read in "Des cannibales" Montaigne's account of the Tupis, an American tribe who sent a delegation to Rouen in 1562.[33] Montaigne describes the Indians' society, kinship, warfare, and religion in ethnographic detail. He recounts their good treatment of war prisoners, their courage, and their ritual murder, but comments that it is no more cruel than the torments inflicted during the religious wars.

In these three passages, we read, dispersed, the syllables that together will form the nightmare anagram of the MOVE disaster: dreams of the other as desiring, of the possibility of a harmonious, indeed erotic, resolution of the tensions of the social; of the other as the object of a bloody

---

33. For an account of this visit, see Eric Cheyfitz, *The Poetics of Imperialism: Translation and Colonization from "The Tempest" to "Tarzan"* (New York: Oxford University Press, 1991), 152.

and vengeful power, as a redemptive sacrifice; and of transposing the desiring and sacrificed other to an other world, ritualized and reduced to language, to a lyric of patrimony.

We will get the worst over first and look at the execution of George Sechel in "Couardise mère de la cruauté." The description of Sechel's death is graphic and disturbing. Cruelty disperses and subverts the subject; it is designed to incite despair. Cannibalism manifests, reduces, and corrects the rebellious subjectivity that incited Sechel's peasant uprising; it is a symbolic and material representation of relations of identification, desire, delegation, and redemption. Montaigne's account invites our identification with Sechel's followers and then implicates us in the sensations of their enforced feeding on him. Sechel appears as a sacrificial savior, consumed in two elements, and "drawing upon himself all the hatred for their misdeeds." The story contains a submerged identification of the Eucharist with cannibalism, although it is difficult to locate the source of that identification—the Polish executioners? Montaigne? Sechel himself? It makes us queasy, and would have had additional disturbing resonances for a Renaissance audience. These resonances would only have been heightened for those of Montaigne's readers who knew that after the St. Bartholomew's Day Massacre (1572), limbs of the Huguenots were sold in Paris and Lyon.[34]

The spectacle of cannibalism organized by Sechel's death is sequestered from language. The body that is—and was for Montaigne—articulated, constrained, and inserted into the relations of family and society is broken, separated and articulated, divided into parts, and painfully traversed by the social. Sechel's body is divided into nameless pieces, *"morceaux,"* and swallowing these morsels cancels the transgression that formed a rebellious popular body. Since that uprising was organized "under pretext of a crusade," it is punished under the pretext of a passion: Sechel, the only speaker in this story, takes on himself the guilt of his followers. Their consumption acts as a bar, a mark of separation: their identification is fixed at the moment when their affiliation with Sechel removed them from symbolic membership in the royal body of the prince to a wholly material consumption of Sechel's dead body. This is the horror story of a society that has forgotten the differences among the word *elephant,* an elephant, and a small figure of an elephant.

34. Natalie Zemon Davis, *Society and Culture in Early Modern France* (Stanford: Stanford University Press, 1975), 324.

Finally, the relation imposed on the rebel leader and his transgressive followers is absolutely nonreciprocal: they eat him; he does not eat them. It is final and nonrepeatable—an episode, not a story. Cannibalism, in this instance, is a form of the social that can never be stabilized in the symbolic, never articulated in the narrative of history. It is a version of intersubjectivity without exchange, without the circulation of meanings, without stable hierarchy. No language, no refusal of language, is too extreme a safeguard against this bad dream—neither suicide, Stoic detachment, absolute doubt, profound retirement, nor the obsessive composition and revision of essays.

Over against the nightmare of Sechel's execution, let us place the happy dream of union with La Boétie, of a friendship in which both rivalry and eros are contained so that intersubjectivity takes the form of an intense, linguistically mediated, and reciprocal cannibalism: their wills eat each other up.

Like the cruel execution of Sechel, motivated by "cowardice, the mother of cruelty," friendship is marked by gender. It excludes women and therefore procreation and therefore patrimony. Instead, friends have language. La Boétie's essay "De la servitude voluntaire" introduced him to Montaigne. Theirs was an inscribed and textual friendship; Montaigne insists that we "hardly read of the like" (136), that "we embraced each other by our names" (141), and refers the reader more than once to La Boétie's poetry (137, 139). The tribute to La Boétie is ornamented with exempla and quotations from classical authors, acknowledged quotations from Terence, Horace, Virgil, and Catullus and unacknowledged paraphrases of Cicero, Xenophon, and Menander (Villey, 1247–48).

Their friendship is also marked by absences of language: they have no need of "these words of separation and distinction: benefit, obligation, gratitude, request, thanks, and the like" (141), a lexicon of terms describing reciprocal relations. Indeed, since Butor, absence has been seen as a central concern of the essay. To embrace a name is to be friends with someone you have not met. Even the specific text that introduced La Boétie to Montaigne is absent, excised from the *Essais* (144). Not only La Boétie's text, but all possessions and all questions of property are excluded from their relation, including especially patrimony. "De l'amité," therefore, records the absence of the father whose patrimonial experiment in Latin haunts the vernacular rhythms of the *Essais*.

Even though "the name of brother is a beautiful name and full of affection" (137), brotherhood is a zero-sum game. Inheritance makes "the richness of one the poverty of the other" (136). Montaigne prefers friendship, in which sociality is taken up entirely within the symbolic. The commonwealth of friends reverses the terrifying reduction to the material that marked Sechel's execution. There is no need for reciprocity, because there is no possible separation of interests, even in absence. Friends are brothers without patrimony, without the father's vexing authority or deeply ambiguous mortality, without that mysterious transmission of qualities that troubled Montaigne in "De la ressemblance des enfans aux peres."

Friends contain each other even in absence and find there a kind of doubling of their powers ("De la vanité," 3, essay 9; Frame, 746). Separation and absence create a rupture in the fused being Montaigne/La Boétie, and restore to each of them their full faculties, giving them each access to an experience that is doubled by being inscribed, so that Montaigne and La Boétie carry each other as quotations. The friend who, present, is a benign cannibal, in absence provokes a discourse that carries and preserves you, that enables reflexivity.

Reflexivity, yes, but not narration, not the array and articulation of experience in time which the extension of prose can support. Friendship is not articulated into episodes. It cannot be narrated: its pleasures are "a general and universal warmth . . . constant and settled" (137). This particular friendship has no story; like death, it does not happen in narratable time. The two men meet, and because of who they are, they instantly become friends until La Boétie's death. Such a friendship drains the narrative energy from the rest of Montaigne's life:

> If I compare all [the rest of my life] . . . with the four years which were granted to me to enjoy the sweet company and society of that man, it is nothing but smoke, nothing but dark and dreary night (ce n'est que fumée, ce n'est qu'une nuit obscure et ennuyeuse). (143; Villey, 193)

The sociality formed in pure will, the innocence of temporality and exchange, the erotic vertigo of this state, all suggest a utopian project. La Boétie, for his part, also imagined a social utopia, without history or the exercise of power, if in a different key. Writing about the unjust ways that tyrants come to power in "De la servitude voluntaire," La Boétie observed that an "entirely new people" would follow neither the customs of liberty nor those of servitude, but obey reason rather than men.[35] And Montaigne was to imagine, in his turn, just such a race of newborn men, for whom "the very words that signify lying, treachery, dissimulation, avarice, envy, belittling, pardon" are "unheard of" (153; Villey, 206). That dubious utopia is in Brazil, intractably placed within history; there, intersubjectivity confronts language, time, the narrative of patrimony—and its nightmare, cannibalism.

How can we read Montaigne's image of the social in "Des cannibales?" Montaigne organizes his account as a quotation: he tells us that he knows about the cannibals by report of a simple, and therefore reliable, sailor. In its foregrounding of quotation, the essay resembles "De la force de l'imagination": both essays call into question the information they present.[36] The essay on cannibals is also marked by unacknowledged quotations, in this case from Montaigne's extensive collection of the literature of conquest and colonization.[37] Montaigne takes from these reports such terms as *sauvage* and *barbare,* but not their contempt for the Brazilians.

The initial description of the Brazilians, concrete and laconic, is of a piece with Montaigne's discussion of the diversity of social forms in "De la coustume" (1, essay 23). Both essays are performances of *copia,* multiplying examples and diverse accidents to shore up an argument or the writer's authority.[38] Montaigne's first quotation from the cannibals is an account of their "whole ethical science" (154; Villey, 208), the daily

35. La Boétie, *Oeuvres completes,* 20–21.

36. For a full comparison, see John O'Neill, *Essaying Montaigne: A Study of the Renaissance Institution of Writing and Reading* (London: Routledge and Kegan Paul, 1982).

37. For sources of these essays, see Michael Giordano, "Re-reading 'Des cannibales': 'Veritable tesmoignage' and the Chain of Supplements," *Neophilologus* 69, no. 1 (Jan. 1985): 25–33; and Edwin M. Duval, "Lessons of the New World: Design and Meaning in Montaigne's 'Des cannibales' (I, 31) and 'Des coches' (III, 6)," *YFS* 64 (1983): 95–113; and Michel de Certeau, *Heterologies: Discourse on the Other* (Minneapolis: University of Minnesota Press, 1986), 67–79. Other recent works on Montaigne's treatment of the New World are Myra Jehlen, "The Civilizations of the New World and the State of Nature," *Revue Française d'Études Americaines* 16 (Apr.–July 1991): 48–49; Cheyfitz, *Poetics of Imperialism,* 142–73; Moishe Black, "When Montaigne Conducts You on a Visit to His Cannibals, Take Care Not to Get Eaten by the Guide," *Dalhousie French Studies* 16 (spring–summer 1989): 15–36; and Tom Conley, "Montaigne and the Indies: Cartographies of the New World in the *Essais,* 1580–88," in *Re/Discovering Colonial Writing,* ed. Rene Jara and Nicholas Spadacci (Minneapolis: Prisma Institute, 1989), 225–62.

38. Cave, *The Cornucopian Text.*

admonition to be brave against their enemies and affectionate to the wives who prepare their drink. They have religion and kill false prophets, carry out war and eat their prisoners. After Montaigne praises the courage of the prisoners, "not one [of whom] but would rather be killed and eaten than so much as ask not to be" (156), and the courage of their armies, he quotes a death song, embedding the prisoner's words in his own paraphrase:

> J'ay une chanson faicte par un prisonnier, où il y a ce traict: qu'ils viennent hardiment trétous et s'assemblent pour disner de luy: car ils mangeront quant et quant leurs peres et leurs ayeux, qui ont servy d'aliment et de nourriture à son corps. Ces muscles, dit-il, cette cher et ces veines, ce sont les vostres, pauvres fols que vous estes; vous ne recognoissez pas que la substance des membres de vos ancestres s'y tient encore: savourez les bien, vous y trouverez le goust de vostre propre chair. (212)

> I have a song composed by a prisoner which contains this challenge, that they should all come boldly and gather to dine off him, for they will be eating at the same time their own fathers and grandfathers, who have served to feed and nourish his body. "These muscles," he says, "this flesh and these veins are your own, poor fools that you are. You do not recognize that the substance of your ancestors' limbs is still contained in them. Savor them well; you will find in them the taste of your own flesh. (158)

Montaigne comments that the idea of this song "does not smack [*ne sent*] of barbarity" (158; Villey, 212). We taste the song that invites us to taste the prisoner's flesh.

Cannibalism is a form of inheritance, the only form available to the Brazilians, who live under conditions of permanent surplus, and who leave everything in common to all their heirs. By encountering the father in the veins and flesh of an enemy, the cannibal comes into an inheritance, delegating to another the death of the father. Cannibalism delays and deflects patrimony, serving as a swerve or lateral detour in the connection between fathers and sons. And indeed, the hidden continuation of the "substance des membres" (212), of the victors' ancestors in the flesh of the captive, is homologous to the mysterious transmission of the stone from his father to Montaigne through "cette legere piece de sa substance" (764). In both cannibalism and common inheritance, the rivalry so tellingly described in "De l'amité" is deflected: "There have been nations where by custom the children killed their fathers, and others where the fathers killed their children, to avoid the interference that they can sometimes cause each other; and by nature one depends on the destruction of the other" (136). In both the consumption of their enemies and the transmission of property, the Brazilians follow a logic complementary to that of the atrocious executions in "Couardise mere de la cruauté": the object—body or inheritance—is confounded, dispersed into unnameable parts. For the Brazilians, this dispersal is presented not as a bloody morcellation but as the dissolution of one substance into another, of ancestor into enemy, of surplus property into the community. In both cannibalism and inheritance, language is erased: the blood of their forebears and their property are distributed without divisions, names, or titles. Unlike Sechel's execution, Brazilian cannibalism does not reduce the social to a permanent and painful presymbolic relation; it generates another form of language; something appears in the gap of absence. What appears in the place of patrimony is a system of nomenclature: "They generally call those of the same age, brothers; those who are younger, children; and the old men are fathers to all the others" (156). Brotherhood is reconfigured without inheritance, realizing in the social the utopian election of friendship.

Cannibalism produces a different discourse—a lyric, an epideictic expression of praise and blame. The lyric is embedded within the structures of prose and serves as doubled evidence of a courage which is remote and exotic and of a linguistic skill which establishes intersubjectivity and demands respect.

The experience of cannibalism is presented as self-referential: "Savor them well; you will find in them the taste of your own flesh" (158). And that self-reference is both a deflection of desire—reminding us of the interrupted arc of desire in "De la force de l'imagination"—and a cure for ignorance. Those who are about to consume the captive are poor fools who do not recognize his limbs as their own; the taste of themselves will disabuse them. Montaigne demystifies the search for an object and demonstrates that the desired object—including especially the object we desire to obliterate—already carries the taste of our own limbs, the taste of our ancestors. We find ourselves in the interrupted vector of desire, disrupting the narrative of revenge by turning it inward. And what we find there is a text. The quotation of the song is a demonstration of the central paradox of textuality, the paradox we have seen

in the interpolated letter to Mme. Duras. Montaigne cannot bring into
his text the Brazilian artifacts he collected—the bread tasting of cori-
ander or the bed—but he can bring in, materially, the prisoner's song,
or at least a translation of it.

Montaigne moves from indirect quotation of the song to the direct
representation of the prisoner's words without a marked transition. The
break between indirect and direct quotation occurs as the text names,
segments, and establishes proprietorship over the captive's body: "ces
muscles, dit-il, cette cher et ces veines, ce sont les vostres" (212).
"These muscles," he says, "this flesh, and these veins, are your own,"
since they were nourished by the flesh of the captor's ancestors. We
move from the cabinet of curiosities to the field of the captive's demonstration; like the captive's original audience, we are summoned and
placed by his "ces, cette, ces"; we own "les vostres." The untouched
body of the captive is refunctioned to display the wounds of his audience's ancestors. The display of wounds, a textbook example of an "inartistic proof," has been transformed in a practice of language that invokes time only to negate it.[39]

Montaigne's designation for that skill is *"invention"* (212), a term of
art in the despised science of rhetoric, commonly extended in the Renaissance to literary texts. Invention was a facility in finding things to
say, or as the English rhetorician Thomas Wilson put it, "the findyng
out of apte matter, called otherwise Invencion, is a searchyng out of
thynges true or thynges likely, the whiche maie reasonably sett furth
a matter and make it appere probable."[40] In literary contexts "invention" referred variously to the theme of the poem, to its originality and
expressiveness of figurative language, and to the poet's power over language. As George Gascoigne puts it, with his usual exasperating redun-
dancy, a poem is not good "unless the invention have in it also *aliquid
salis*. By this *aliquid salis* I mean some good and fine devise shewing the
quick capacity of a writer; and where I say some good and fine invention
I mean that I would have it both fine and good."[41] Invention, then,
refers to logic, to energy, and to trope or "devise": in all of these, the

39. For the display of wounds, see among many others Cicero, *De oratore*, 2:29.
40. Thomas Wilson, *The arte of Rhetorique, for the use of all suche as are studious
of Eloquence* (1553; New York: Garland, 1982), book 1, "Invencion, what it is."
41. George Gascoigne, *Certain Notes of Instruction Concerning the Making of
Verse or Rime in English* (1575), in *Complete Works of George Gascoigne*, ed. J. W.
Cunliffe, vol. 1 (Oxford: Oxford University Press, 1907).

captive's song is exemplary. He finds in his situation of weakness and approaching victimization a pretext for taunting and boasting; the material fact of being eaten is reflexively turned upon his captors. The song presents them with limbs, with muscles, refunctioned as members of their own lost ancestors, who will now not be vindicated or avenged but rather dismembered and dishonored once more.

Bringing together "things true or things likely," the poem's invention is analogous to the discursive "proof of reason." Good invention is the production of a text which seems probable, which is convincing.[42] The text does not operate through correspondence to the natural or social worlds but through intersubjective agreement, establishing a relation to the audience which is not at all cordial but which supports the construction of propositions, metaphors, speech acts. The lyric, specifically, vindicates claims of reason through the speaker's work with the materiality of language; the "devises" effected by the writer, the energy and acuity of quite contingent elements of language—nuances of lexicon, rhythm, figures of sound—are saturated with meaning.

For Montaigne's audience, the lyric was also an argument in the complex discussion about New World civilizations. For European readers of conquest literature, cannibalism was not simply exotic. With human sacrifice, it was specific proof that the Indians, despite their large cities, orderly government, stable family structure, and complex institutions, were nonetheless incapable of ruling themselves. They were either innately evil—perhaps even diabolically ruled—or dehumanized by their perverse diet.[43] Montaigne's essay does not argue that cannibalism is not cruel, or that it is not a sign of savagery; rather, he claims that it is not more cruel than European practices of executing criminals, and that savagery is a complex state, including vigor, reason, and kindliness as well as cruelty and irrationality. The operational conclusion from Montaigne's argument is drawn more explicitly in "Des coches" (3, essay 6):

> Why did not such a noble conquest fall to Alexander or to those ancient Greeks and Romans? Why did not such a great change and alteration of so many empires and peoples fall into hands that would have gently polished and cleared away whatever was

42. Margaret McGowan, *Montaigne's Deceits: The Art of Persuasion in the "Essais"* (London: University of London Press, 1974).

43. Anthony Pagden, *The Fall of Natural Man: The American Indian and the Origins of Comparative Ethnology* (Cambridge: Cambridge University Press, 1982), 79–90.

> barbarous in them, and would have strengthened and fostered
> the good seeds that nature had produced in them, not only
> adding to the cultivation of the earth and the adornment of
> cities the arts of our side of the ocean, in so far as they would
> have been necessary, but also adding the Greek and Roman vir-
> tues to those originally in that region? (694–95)

Montaigne concedes that the Brazilians certainly should have been con-
quered, but not by us, at least as we are now.

This argument is entirely counterfactual and critical. It deploys the
commonplace that the moderns are inferior to the ancients to argue that
only the ancients would have been worthy to conquer the cannibals.
The troops of the conquest, in a reversal of the captive's song, are de-
voured by their fathers. The conqueror is like the cannibal, equally cruel
and irrational: "I am not sorry that we notice the barbarous horror of
such acts, but I am heartily sorry that, judging their faults rightly, we
should be so blind to our own" (155). Not only is the Christian as bad
as the cannibal; the cannibal is also as good as the Christian. We listen
to the captive's song, are moved by its power, consume his words and
approve them as "invention qui ne sent aucunement la barbarie" (212).
We cannot taste the cannibal's bread, but we can taste their words, and
so we become cannibals and lose the right to call them barbarians.

The essay becomes an act of interpretation, a labor of language that
locates the reader in a more complex world, organizing ideological
common sense into a new structure of identification, revulsion, and desire. Montaigne's essay translates those relations into their consequences
in the public sphere. If we taste the invention of a song whose logic
depends on the identification of cannibalism with patrimony, we cannot
then judge the Brazilians debased. No strategy of containment distances
us from this song and its resonant invitation to identify with what we
had defined as alien and inhuman, with the place where an other had
been located. We have become the objects of conquest; we have been
colonized.

Montaigne imagined, in the *Essais,* two versions of the public—there
was, as yet, no real public sphere. On the one hand, there is the dangerous and vexed space of government, in which the circulation of discourse is blocked by danger and deceit, where the extended narrative
of religious carnage unrolls. And then there is an expansive domain of
readers and writers, organized by multiple frames of reference, includ-

ing the language of the dead that passes for living through acknowledged and unacknowledged quotation, relentlessly frustrating any grand
narrative arc. Without the horrifying image of devouring flesh, the text
does the work of cannibalism, transforming violent rivalries into civil
inventions, establishing the powerless subject as the master of discourse.
The text recognizes the father as a source of language and understands
that the paternal inheritance includes disease, pain, and early death. The
written text provides a vehicle for the eroticized intersubjectivity that
marked Montaigne's friendship with La Boétie; it establishes between
writer and reader a relation that marks, demonstrates, and makes use of
time but that displaces the narrative of history into the work of writing.

Against the public life of readers and writers Montaigne counterposes
the vexations and divisions of the religious wars, a disaster which he
referred to as "ce notable spectacle de nostre mort publique" (1046)
(this notable spectacle of our public death). Montaigne confronted a
social collapse, a confrontation with an inassimilable other, and a spectacle of public cruelty as intractable as that which faced the MOVE commission. He responded by imagining, and working to represent, a discursive space in which these problems could be kept in play, heightening
and deepening their intractability, leaving no room at all for simple or
normalizing solutions.

Montaigne uses the story of our public death to reflect on individual
mortality: "Since I cannot retard it, I am glad to be destined to watch it
and learn from it" (800). What there is to learn is the common lot that
Montaigne rehearses so unflinchingly, so cheerfully: the difficulty of human relations, the limits and fragility of the subject, the uncertainty of
knowledge, the folly of entrenched notions of the good. That lot is enjoyed only in a space won back from death, the moment which textually
represents the paradox of our temporality, the ambiguity of our patrimony. The public space of readers and writers keeps all these ideas in
motion, renouncing melancholy and sentiment and representing both
the material world that relentlessly resists knowledge and the social
world that relentlessly resists order.

Equally uncompromising is Montaigne's reflexive understanding of
the limits of his own text. The *Essais* are necessary; they are important;
they are not redemptive. (Redemption is, after all, another invitation to
the cannibal's feast.) "Si cherchons nous avidement de recognoistre en
ombre mesme et en la fable des Theatres la montre des jeux tragiques

de l'humaine fortune" (1046), or as Florio has it: "Yet seeke we evidently to know in shadowes, and understand by fabulous representations upon Theaters, to shew of the tragicke revolutions of humane fortune," and in those shows we find a kind of pleasure, "we please our selves to rowze up our displeasure" (3:301). The knowledge represented in the *Essais* is promiscuous; its interpretation cannot be controlled or even educated but only directed or subverted. It is not even especially dignified in the pleasures it generates: there is nothing noble in rousing ourselves up to displeasure. In the essay "Des cannibales" Montaigne turns this dubious energy against itself, allowing us to rouse our displeasure, permitting us a reassuring obbligato of compassion, and then returning our reflection upon ourselves. The theater moves inside: human fortune is no longer an empty abstraction but a figure for that temporality and location in history that no one inhabits happily.

Montaigne ends the essay with a final quotation from the Brazilians, a report of the remarks of three Brazilian visitors to Rouen. The Brazilians are asked what in Europe they find "most amazing" (159). Montaigne confesses to having forgotten their first remark (and he has complained, often enough, of his bad memory). The Brazilians did say that it was strange to see grown men guard the boy king. And then they remark:

> (They have a way in their language of speaking of men as halves of one another), they had noticed that there were among us men full and gorged with all sorts of good things, and that their other halves were beggars at their doors, emaciated with hunger and poverty; and they thought it strange that these needy halves could endure such an injustice, and did not take the others by the throat, or set fire to their houses. (159)

This quotation recalls Aristophanes' myth of the original human nature from the *Symposium*. In that privileged text, human beings were at first of a double nature, androgynous, and therefore powerful and dangerous. Zeus divided men to humble their pride; sexuality is therefore the "desire of one another which is implanted in us, reuniting our original nature, making one of two, and healing the state of man."[44] Montaigne's earlier reference to forming, with La Boétie, one being, refers to the *Symposium*, barely submerging its erotic resonances. On one level, then,

---

44. *Symposium,* in *The Works of Plato* (New York: Modern Library, 1928), 354.

the Tupis speak of a hope that the erotic relations among friends and lovers, dispersed, could regulate the reciprocal relations among social ranks and orders. The bodies of rich and poor, gorged and emaciated, are very physically brought before us, and we are invited to imagine an erotic practice of the social that could not tolerate this disparity. The erotic merger that shaped Montaigne's text would also organize social life.

The Tupis' observation, however, is not at all erotic but simply a cool speculation: why do not the poor rise against the rich? This speculation corresponds with their equally unlikely, equally counterfactual, critique of patrimonial rule: why do all these grownups consent to serve a child? The extension of the erotic to social relations is imagined as an act of simple appetitive violence, or, as Montaigne puts it earlier in the essay, "extreme revenge." Cannibalism has entered deeply into the structure of our sociality, placing the hungry generally at the disposal of the full. There is no escape from it. It can only be reciprocated or reversed. The Brazilians enter into the discourse of the *Essais* as a voice of reason, La Boétie's alternative to tyranny: they draw the probable conclusion from the evidence presented to them.

In private conversation with one of the Brazilians, who was the leader of four or five thousand soldiers, Montaigne asked the Tupi "what remains" for him after he retired from war. The Tupi replied that paths are cut for him through the underbrush so that he can visit dependent villages (159).

This speech, presented to us as a mangled translation, imagines sociality that reproduces the deflected desire of the *Essais* without violence. What is reasonable—the successful captain deserves a moderate reward—also traces the path traced for a desired encounter. The path, the prolonged narrative, associated elsewhere in the *Essais* with avarice and a thirst for power, here represents a tempered and contained ambition, a directed and temporary exercise of authority. The path does not deny reflexivity or draw the speaker into the vectors of desire which Montaigne has so consistently associated with ignorance and cruelty. Against that path, let us invoke the image of enclosure, of the careful frame that Montaigne constructs for the captain's speech, placing it in the context of his loss, his anticipated remorse, and his ignorance of his future. The image of a cleared path, an image of socialized desire open to rationality, comes to us at the price of the speaker's tranquility. It suggests to us both the convenience and the danger of following paths another has cut, lines that divide the forest of letters, tracing out the routes taken to visit dependent villages, to survey "qu'il en restoit" (214). The Tupis, and Montaigne, speak to us at the borders of the discourses of modernity, of a discursive terrain marked by paths rather than boundaries; such a speech was for them inexpressibly costly. We are only now learning the cost of reading it.

WORKS CITED   •   •   •   •

Abraham, Nicholas, and Maria Torok. *The Wolf Man's Magic Word: A Cryptonomy.* Minneapolis: University of Minnesota Press, 1986.

Ad C. Herennium de ratione dicendi (Rhetorica ad Herennium). Trans. Harry Caplan. Loeb Classical Library. Cambridge: Harvard Univ. Press, 1954.

Adorno, T. W. "Constellation in Science." In *Negative Dialectics,* trans. E. B. Ashton. New York: Seabury Press, 1973.

———. *Negative Dialectics.* Trans. E. B. Ashton. New York: Seabury Press, 1973.

Agger, Ben. *Socio(Onto)Logy: A Disciplinary Reading.* Champaign: University of Illinois Press, 1989.

Allen, Michael B. *Marsilio Ficino and the Phaedran Charioteer.* Berkeley and Los Angeles: University of California Press, 1981.

Anderson, John, and Hilary Hevenor. *Burning down the House: MOVE and the Tragedy of Philadelphia.* New York: Norton, 1987.

Anderson, Paul V., R. John Brockmann, and Carolyn R. Miller, eds. *New Essays in Technical and Scientific Communication: Research, Theory, Practice.* Baywood Series in Technical and Scientific Communication. Farmingdale, N.Y.: Baywood Publishing, 1983.

Appel, Karl-Otto. "Normatively Grounding 'Critical Theory' through Recourse to the Lifeworld? A Transcendental-Pragmatic Attempt to Think with Habermas against Habermas." In *Philosophical Interventions in the Unfinished Project of Enlightenment,* ed. Axel Honneth and others. Cambridge: MIT Press, 1992.

Aristotle. *Rhetoric: A Theory of Civic Discourse.* Trans. George A. Kennedy. New York: Oxford University Press, 1991.

Atwill, Janet. "Instituting the Art of Rhetoric: Theory, Practice, and Productive Knowledge in Interpretations of Aristotle's *Rhetoric.*" In *Rethinking the History of Rhetoric: Multidisciplinary Essays on the Rhetorical Tradition,* ed. Takis Poulakos. Boulder: Westview Press, 1993.

Avery, Linda Wright, Burton Caine, William R. Meek, and Rev. Paul Matthews Washington. *Voices from the Community.* Philadelphia: American Friends Service Committee, 1986.

Baker, Keith Michael. "Defining the Public Sphere in Eighteenth-Century France: Variations on a Theme by Habermas." In *Habermas and the Public Sphere,* ed. Craig Calhoun. Cambridge: MIT Press, 1992.

Bakhtin, Mikhail M. *The Dialogic Imagination.* Ed. Michael Holquist and trans. C. Emerson. Austin: University of Texas Press, 1981.

Baron, Dennis. *Grammar and Gender.* New Haven: Yale University Press, 1986.

Bauer, Henry H. *Scientific Literacy and the Myth of the Scientific Method.* Urbana: University of Illinois Press, 1992.

Bauman, Zygmunt. *Intimations of Postmodernity.* London and New York: Routledge, 1992.

Bazerman, Charles. "How Natural Philosophers Can Cooperate: The Literary Technology of Coordinated Investigation in Joseph Priestley's *History and Present State of Electricity* (1767)." In *Textual Dynamics of the Professions: Historical and Contemporary Studies of Writing in Professional Communities,* ed. Charles Bazerman and James Paradis. Madison: University of Wisconsin Press, 1991.

———. "Physicists Reading Physics: Schema-Laden Purposes and Purpose-Laden Schema." *Written Communication* 2 (1985): 3–23.

———. *Shaping Written Knowledge: The Genre and Activity of the Experimental Article in Science.* Madison: University of Wisconsin Press, 1988.

Bazerman, Charles, and James Paradis, eds. *Textual Dynamics of the Professions: Historical and Contemporary Studies of Writing in Professional Communities.* Madison: University of Wisconsin Press, 1991.

Beer, Gillian. *Darwin's Plots: Evolutionary Narrative in Darwin, George Eliot, and Nineteenth Century Fiction.* London: Routledge, 1983.

Belenky, Mary Filed, Blythe McVicker Clinchy, Nancy Rule Goldberger, and Jill Mattuck Tarule. *Women's Ways of Knowing.* New York: Basic Books, 1986.

Benhabib, Seyla. *Critique, Norm, and Utopia: A Study of the Foundations of Critical Theory.* New York: Columbia University Press, 1986.

———. "Models of Public Space: Hannah Arendt, the Liberal Tradition, and Jürgen Habermas." In *Habermas and the Public Sphere,* ed. Craig Calhoun. Cambridge: MIT Press, 1992.

Berlin, James. "Rhetoric and Ideology in the Writing Class." *College English* 50 (1988): 477–94.

———. *Rhetoric and Reality: Writing Instruction in American Colleges, 1900–85.* Carbondale: Southern Illinois University Press, 1987.

Berthoff, Ann. *Forming/Thinking/Writing: The Composing Imagination.* Upper Montclair, N.J.: Boynton/Cook, 1978.

Black, Maria, and Rosalind Coward. "Linguistic, Social, and Sexual Relations: A Review of Dale Spender's *Man Made Language.*" In *The Feminist Critique of Language: A Reader,* ed. Deborah Cameron. London: Routledge, 1990.

Black, Moishe. "When Montaigne Conducts You on a Visit to His Cannibals, Take Care Not to Get Eaten by the Guide." *Dalhousie French Studies* 16 (spring–summer 1989): 15–36.

Bloom, Lynn. "Anxious Writers in Context." In *When a Writer Can't Write,* ed. Michael Rose. New York: Guilford, 1985.

Bludman, S. A. "Thermodynamics and the End of a Closed Universe." *Nature* 308 (Mar. 22, 1984): 319–22.

Blumenthal, George R., S. M. Faber, Joel R. Primack, and Martin J. Rees. "Formation of Galaxies and Large-Scale Structure with Cold Dark Matter" (review article). *Nature* 311 (Oct. 11, 1984): 517–25.

Bowser, Charles. *Opinion of Charles Bowser, Esq.* Typescript bound with *The Findings, Conclusions, and Recommendations of the Philadelphia Special Investigation Commission* (Philadelphia, Mar. 6, 1986). Paley Library, Temple University, Philadelphia, Pa.

Bracher, Mark. *Lacan, Discourse, and Social Change: A Psychoanalytic Cultural Criticism.* Ithaca: Cornell University Press, 1993.

Braverman, Harry. *Labor and Monopoly Capital: The Degradation of Work in the Twentieth Century.* New York: Monthly Review Press, 1974.

Britton, James. *The Development of Writing Abilities, 11–18.* London: Macmillan, 1975.

Brockmann, John, Barbara Couture, Jone Goldstein, Susan Feinberg, Marcus Green, and Charles Sides, eds. *The Case Method in Technical Communication: Theory and Models.* N.p.: Association of Teachers of Technical Writing, 1984.

Brodsky, Claudia. *The Imposition of Form: Studies in Narrative Representation and Knowledge.* Princeton: Princeton University Press, 1987.

Brooks, Peter. *Reading for the Plot: Design and Intention in Narrative.* Cambridge: Harvard University Press, 1991.

Brouwer, Dede, and D. de Haan, eds. *Women's Language, Socialization, and Self-Image.* Providence, R.I.: Foris, 1987.

Bubner, Rüdiger. "Habermas' Concept of Critical Theory." In *Habermas: Critical Debates,* ed. John Thompson and David Held. Cambridge: MIT Press, 1982.

Bullock, Richard, and John Trimbur. *The Politics of Writing Instruction: Postsecondary.* Portsmouth: Boynton/Cook, 1990.

Burger, Ronna. *Plato's "Phaedrus": A Defense of a Philosophic Art of Writing.* University: University of Alabama Press, 1980.

Burke, Kenneth. *A Grammar of Motives.* New York: Prentice-Hall, 1945. Reprint, Berkeley and Los Angeles: University of California Press, 1969.

———. *Language as Symbolic Action.* Berkeley and Los Angeles: University of California Press, 1969.

———. *A Rhetoric of Motives.* Berkeley and Los Angeles: University of California Press, 1950. Reprint, 1969.

Burton, Frank, and Pat Carlen. *Official Discourse: On Discourse Analysis, Government Publications, Ideology and the State.* London: Routledge and Kegan Paul, 1979.

Butor, Michel. *Essais sur "Les Essais."* Paris: Gallimard, 1968.

Calhoun, Craig, ed. *Habermas and the Public Sphere.* Cambridge: MIT Press, 1992.

Cameron, Deborah, ed. *The Feminist Critique of Language: A Reader.* London: Routledge, 1990.

Campbell, John A. "The Polemical Mr. Darwin." *Quarterly Journal of Speech* 61 (1975): 375–90.

Cave, Terence. *The Cornucopian Text: Problems of Writing in the French Renaissance.* Oxford: Oxford University Press, 1979.

———. "Problems of Reading in the *Essais.*" In *Montaigne: Essays in Honor of Richard Sayce,* ed. I. D. McFarlane and Ian Maclean. Oxford: Clarendon, 1982.

Certeau, Michel de. *Heterologies: Discourse on the Other.* Minneapolis: University of Minnesota Press, 1986.

Chatman, Seymour. *Coming to Terms: The Rhetoric of Narrative in Fiction and Film.* Ithaca: Cornell University Press, 1990.

———. *Story and Discourse: Narrative Structure in Fiction and Film.* Ithaca: Cornell University Press, 1978.

Cheyfitz, Eric. *The Poetics of Imperialism: Translation and Colonization from "The Tempest" to "Tarzan."* New York: Oxford University Press, 1991.

Cicero. *De oratore, Books I–II.* Trans. E. W. Sutton and H. Rackham. Loeb Classical Library. Cambridge: Harvard University Press, 1959.

Cixous, Helene. *La jeune née.* Paris: Union Générale d'Éditions, 1975.

Clifford, James. "On Ethnographic Allegory." In *Writing Culture: The Poetics and Politics of Ethnography,* ed. James Clifford and George E. Marcus. Berkeley and Los Angeles: University of California Press, 1986.

Clifford, James, and George E. Marcus, eds. *Writing Culture: The Poetics and Politics of Ethnography.* Berkeley and Los Angeles: University of California Press, 1986.

Coates, J., and D. Cameron, eds. *Women in Their Speech Communities: New Perspectives on Language and Sex.* London: Longman, 1989.

Collins, Harry, and Trevor Pinch. *Frames of Meaning: The Social Construction of Extraordinary Science.* London: Routledge and Kegan Paul, 1982.

Con Davis, Robert. *Lacan and Narration: The Psychoanalytic Difference in Narrative Theory.* Baltimore: Johns Hopkins University Press, 1984.

———, ed. *The Fictional Father: Lacanian Readings of the Text.* Amherst: University of Massachusetts Press, 1981.

Conley, Tom. "Institutionalizing Translation: On Florio's Montaigne." In *Demarcating the Disciplines: Philosophy, Literature, Art,* ed. Samuel Weber. Glyph Textual Studies 1. Minneapolis: University of Minnesota Press, 1986.

———. "Montaigne and the Indies: Cartographies of the New World in the *Essais,* 1580–88." In *Re/Discovering Colonial Writing,* ed. Rene Jara and Nicholas Spadacci. Minneapolis: Prisma Institute, 1989.

Cooper, Marilyn, and Michael Holzman. *Writing as Social Action.* Portsmouth: Boynton/Cook, 1989.

Corbett, Edward P. J. *Classical Rhetoric for the Modern Student.* 2d ed. New York: Oxford University Press, 1971.

Cottrell, Robert. *Sexuality/Textuality: A Study of the Fabric of Montaigne's "Essais."* Columbus: Ohio State University Press, 1981.

Couture, Barbara, ed. *Professional Writing: Toward a College Curriculum.* N.p.: Association of Teachers of Technical Writing, 1987.

Daly, Mary, in cahoots with Jane Caputi. *Websters' First New Intergalactic Wikedary of the English Language*. Boston: Beacon, 1987.

Darwin, Charles. *The Origin of Species*. Ed. Philip Appleman. New York: Norton, 1979.

Davis, Natalie Zemon. *Society and Culture in Early Modern France*. Stanford: Stanford University Press, 1975.

Dear, Peter, ed. *The Literary Structure of Scientific Argument*. Philadelphia: University of Pennsylvania Press, 1991.

Defaux, Gerard, ed. *Montaigne: Essays in Reading*. *YFS* 64 (1983).

de Man, Paul. *Allegories of Reading: Figural Language in Rousseau, Nietzsche, Rilke, and Proust*. New Haven: Yale University Press, 1979.

———. "Semiology and Rhetoric." In *Textual Strategies*, ed. Josue Harari. Ithaca: Cornell University Press, 1979.

Demianski, M. "Large Anisotropy in the Universe Does Not Prevent Inflation" (letter). *Nature* 307 (Jan. 12, 1984): 140–41.

Derrida, Jacques. *Dissemination*. Trans. Barbara Johnson. Chicago: University of Chicago Press, 1981.

———. "Limited Inc abc." *Glyph II* (1977).

———. *Of Grammatology*. Trans. Gayatri Spivack. Baltimore: Johns Hopkins University Press, 1974.

———. "Signature Event Context." Trans. Samuel Weber and Jeffrey Mehlman. *Glyph I* (1977).

De Vries, Gerrit J. *A Commentary on the "Phaedrus" of Plato*. Amsterdam: Hakkert, 1969.

Dews, Peter. *Logics of Disintegration: Post-structuralist Thought and the Claims of Critical Theory*. London: Verso, 1987.

———, ed. *Habermas: Autonomy and Solidarity: Interviews*. London: Verso, 1986.

———. "Ideologies and Society in the Post-war World." In *Habermas: Autonomy and Solidarity: Interviews*. London: Verso, 1986. Interview with Gad Freudenthal, 1977.

Dickens, Charles. *Little Dorrit*. Oxford: Oxford University Press, 1987.

duBois, Page. "Violence, Apathy, and the Rhetoric of Philosophy." In *Rethinking the History of Rhetoric Multidisciplinary Essays on the Rhetorical Tradition*, ed. Takis Poulakos. Boulder: Westview Press, 1993.

Duval, Edwin M. "Lessons of the New World: Design and Meaning in Montaigne's 'Des cannibales' (I, 31) and 'Des coches' (III, 6)." *YFS* 64 (1983): 95–113.

Ehrenreich, Barbara. *Fear of Falling: The Inner Life of the Middle Class*. New York: Pantheon, 1989.

Ehrenreich, Barbara, and John Ehrenreich. "The Professional-Managerial Class." In *Between Labor and Capital: The Professional-Managerial Class*, ed. Pat Walker. Boston: South End Press, 1979.

Elbow, Peter. *Embracing Contraries: Explorations in Learning and Teaching*. New York: Oxford University Press, 1986.

———. *Writing without Teachers*. New York: Oxford University Press, 1973.

———. *Writing with Power*. New York: Oxford University Press, 1981.

Eley, Geoff. "Nations, Publics, and Political Cultures: Placing Habermas in the Nineteenth Century." In *Habermas and the Public Sphere*, ed. Craig Calhoun. Cambridge: MIT Press, 1992.

Elgin, Suzette Hayden. *The Judas Rose*. New York: DAW, 1987.

———. *Native Tongue*. New York: DAW, 1984.

Erasmus, Desiderius. *Collected Works of Erasmus*. Ed. Craig R. Thompson. Vol. 24, *Literary and Educational Writings*. Bk. 2, *De Copia: De Ratione Studii*. Trans. Betty Knott. Toronto: University of Toronto Press, 1978.

Fabian, A. C., P. E. J. Nulsen, and C. R. Canizares. "Cooling Flows in Clusters of Galaxies" (review article). *Nature* 310 (Aug. 30, 1984): 733–40.

Faigley, Lester, and Thomas Miller. "What We Learn from Writing on the Job." *College English* 44 (Oct. 1982): 557–69.

Farrell, Thomas. *Norms of Rhetorical Culture*. New Haven: Yale University Press, 1993.

Felman, Shoshana. *Jacques Lacan and the Adventure of Insight: Psychoanalysis and Contemporary Culture*. Cambridge: Harvard University Press, 1987.

Ferrari, G. R. F. *Listening to the Cicadas: A Study of Plato's "Phaedrus."* Cambridge: Cambridge University Press, 1987.

Feyerabend, Paul. *Realism, Rationalism and the Scientific Method: Philosophical Papers*. Vol. 1. Cambridge: Cambridge University Press, 1981.

Fineman, Joel. *The Subjectivity Effect in Western Literary Tradition: Essays toward the Release of Shakespeare's Will*. Cambridge: MIT Press, 1991.

Finke, Laurie. "Knowledge as Bait: Feminism, Voice, and the Pedagogical Unconscious." *College English* 55 (Jan. 1993): 7–27.

Fish, Stanley. *Doing What Comes Naturally: Change, Rhetoric, and the Practice of Theory in Literary and Legal Studies*. Durham, N.C.: Duke University Press, 1989.

Fishman, Stephen, and Lucille McCarthy. "Is Expressivism Dead? Reconsidering Its Romantic Roots and Its Relation to Social Constructionism." *College English* 54 (1992): 647–61.

Fleck, Ludwig. *Genesis and Development of a Scientific Fact*. Ed. Thaddeus Trenn and Robert Merton, trans. F. Bradley and T. Trenn. Chicago: University of Chicago Press, 1979. Originally published in 1935.

Fleischman, Suzanne. *Tense and Narrativity: From Medieval Performance to Modern Fiction*. Austin: University of Texas Press, 1990.

Flower, Linda, John Hayes, and Heidi Swarts. "Reader-Based Revision of Functional Documents: The Scenario Principle." In *New Essays in Technical and Scientific Communication: Research, Theory, Practice*, ed. Paul V. Anderson, R. John Brockmann, and Carolyn R. Miller. Baywood Series in Technical and Scientific Communication. Farmingdale, N.Y.: Baywood Publishing, 1983.

Foster, Hal, ed. *The Anti-aesthetic: Essays on Postmodern Culture*. Seattle: Bay Press, 1983.

Foucault, Michel. *The Birth of the Clinic: An Archeology of Medical Perception*. Trans. A. M. Sheridan-Smith. New York: Vintage, 1973.

———. *The History of Sexuality*. 3 vols. New York: Pantheon, 1978–86.

————. *The Order of Things: An Archeology of the Human Sciences.* New York: Random House, 1970.

————. *Power/Knowledge.* New York: Vintage, 1980.

————. *Technologies of the Self: A Seminar with Michel Foucault.* Ed. Luther Martin, Huck Gutman, and Patrick Hutton. Amherst: University of Massachusetts Press, 1988.

Frame, Donald. "Considerations on the Genesis of Montaigne's *Essais.*" In *Montaigne: Essays in Memory of Richard Sayce,* ed. I. D. McFarlane and Ian Maclean. Oxford: Clarendon, 1982.

————. *Montaigne: A Biography.* New York: Harcourt, Brace, and World, 1965.

Fraser, Nancy, "Rethinking the Public Sphere: A Contribution to the Critique of Actually Existing Democracy." In *Habermas and the Public Sphere,* ed. Craig Calhoun. Cambridge: MIT Press, 1992.

————. *Unruly Practices: Power, Discourse, and Gender in Contemporary Social Theory.* Minneapolis: University of Minnesota Press and Polity Press, 1989.

————. "What's Critical about Critical Theory? The Case of Habermas and Gender." In *Unruly Practices: Power, Discourse, and Gender in Contemporary Social Theory.* Minneapolis: University of Minnesota Press and Polity Press, 1989.

Freud, Sigmund. "Analysis Terminable and Interminable." In *The Standard Edition of the Complete Psychological Works of Sigmund Freud,* ed. James Strachey, vol. 23. London: Hogarth Press and Institute of Psychoanalysis, 1975. Originally published in 1937.

————. *Dora: An Analysis of a Case of Hysteria.* Ed. Phillip Rieff and trans. Douglas Bryan. New York: Macmillan, 1963.

————. *The Interpretation of Dreams.* Trans. James Strachey. New York: Avon, 1965. Reprint of *Standard Edition,* vols. 4 and 5. London: Hogarth Press, 1975.

————. "Three Essays on Sexuality." In *The Standard Edition of the Complete Psychological Works of Sigmund Freud,* ed. James Strachey, vol. 7. London: Hogarth, 1953.

Gallop, Jane. *Reading Lacan.* Ithaca: Cornell University Press, 1985.

Gaonkar, Dilip Parameshwar. "The Idea of Rhetoric in the Rhetoric of Science." *Southern Communication Journal* 58 (1993): 258–95.

————. "Reflections on the Rhetorical Turn in the Human Sciences." In *The Rhetorical Turn: Invention and Persuasion in the Conduct of Inquiry,* ed. Herbert W. Simons. Chicago: University of Chicago Press, 1990.

Gascoigne, George. *Certain Notes of Instruction Concerning the Making of Verse or Rime in English.* In *Complete Works of George Gascoigne,* ed. J. W. Cunliffe, vol. 1. Oxford: Oxford University Press, 1907. Originally published in 1575.

Gennette, Gerard. *Narrative Discourse: An Essay in Method.* Ithaca: Cornell University Press, 1983.

————. *Narrative Discourse Revisited.* Ithaca: Cornell University Press, 1990.

Gibbon, Edward. *The Decline and Fall of the Roman Empire.* 3 vols. London: J. M. Dent, 1910.

Giddens, Anthony. *Central Problems in Social Theory: Action, Structure, and*

Contradiction in Social Analysis. Berkeley and Los Angeles: University of California Press, 1983.

——. "Labour and Interaction." In *Habermas: Critical Debates,* ed. J. Thompson and D. Held. Cambridge: MIT Press, 1982.

——. *New Rules of Sociological Method.* London: Hutchison, 1976.

Gilbert, G. Nigel, and Michael Mulkay. *Opening Pandora's Box: A Sociological Analysis of Scientists' Discourse.* Cambridge: Cambridge University Press, 1984.

Gilligan, Carol. *In a Different Voice.* Cambridge: Harvard University Press, 1982.

Giordano, Michael. "Re-reading 'Des cannibales': 'Veritable tesmoignage' and the Chain of Supplements." *Neophilologus* 69, no. 1 (Jan. 1985): 25–33.

Goode, W. Wilson. "Executive Order No. 5–85 Establishing the Philadelphia Special Investigation Commission." Unnumbered first page of the *Philadelphia Special Investigation Commission Report.* Philadelphia, Mar. 7, 1986.

Görtzen, Rene. *Jürgen Habermas: Eine Bibliographie seiner Schriften und der Sekundarliteratur, 1952–81.* Frankfurt: Suhrkamp, 1982.

Gould, Stephen J. *Hen's Teeth and Horse's Toes.* New York: Norton, 1983.

Gould, Stephen J., and R. C. Lewontin. "The Spandrels of San Marco and the Panglossian Paradigm: A Critique of the Adaptationist Programme." *Proceedings of the Royal Society of London,* 1979. Reprinted in J. Selzer, ed., *Understanding Scientific Prose* (Madison: University of Wisconsin Press, 1993).

Grady, Hugh. *The Modernist Shakespeare: Critical Texts in a Material World.* Oxford: Clarendon, 1991.

Gramsci, Antonio. *Selections from the Prison Notebooks of Antonio Gramsci.* Ed. and trans. Quintin Hoare and G. N. Smith. New York: International, 1971.

Griswold, Charles L. *Self-Knowledge in Plato's "Phaedrus."* New Haven: Yale University Press, 1986.

Gross, Alan. *The Rhetoric of Science.* Cambridge: Harvard University Press, 1990.

Habermas, Jürgen. *Communication and the Evolution of Society.* Boston: Beacon, 1979.

——. "The Entwinement of Myth and Enlightenment: Rereading *The Dialectic of Enlightenment.*" *New German Critique* 26 (spring–summer 1982): 13–20.

——. "Further Reflections on the Public Sphere." In *Habermas and the Public Sphere,* ed. Craig Calhoun. Cambridge: MIT Press, 1992.

——. "Historical Materialism and the Development of Normative Structures." In *Communication and the Evolution of Society.* Boston: Beacon, 1979.

——. *Justification and Application: Remarks on Discourse Ethics.* Trans. C. Cronin. Cambridge: MIT Press, 1993.

——. *Knowledge and Human Interests.* Trans. J. J. Shapiro. Boston: Beacon, 1971.

——. *Legitimation Crisis.* Trans. T. McCarthy. Boston: Beacon, 1975.

——. "Modernity—an Incomplete Project." In *The Anti-aesthetic: Essays on Postmodern Culture,* ed. Hal Foster. Seattle: Bay Press, 1983.

——. *Moral Consciousness and Communicative Action.* Trans. Christian Lenhardt and Shierry Weber Nicholsen. Cambridge: MIT Press, 1990.

————. *The Philosophical Discourse of Modernity.* Trans. Frederick Lawrence. Cambridge: MIT Press, 1987.

————. *Postmetaphysical Thinking: Philosophical Essays.* Trans. William Mark Hohengarten. Cambridge: MIT Press, 1992.

————. "A Reply to My Critics." In *Habermas: Critical Debates,* ed. John Thompson and David Held. Cambridge: MIT Press, 1982.

————. *The Structural Transformation of the Public Sphere.* Trans. Thomas Burger with Frederick Lawrence. Cambridge: MIT Press, 1989.

————. "Struggles for Recognition in the Democratic Constitutional States." In *Multiculturalism: Examining the Politics of Recognition,* ed. Charles Taylor and others. Princeton: Princeton University Press, 1994.

————. *Theory and Practice.* Trans. J. Viertel. Boston: Beacon, 1973.

————. *The Theory of Communicative Action,* 2 vols. Trans. Thomas McCarthy. Vol. 1, *Reason and the Rationalization of Society.* Vol. 2, *Lifeworld and System: A Critique of Functionalist Reason.* Boston: Beacon, 1981–83.

————. *Toward a Rational Society: Student Protest, Science, and Politics.* Trans. J. J. Shapiro. Boston: Beacon, 1970.

Halliday, M. A. K., and J. R. Martin. *Writing Science: Literacy and Discursive Power.* Pittsburgh: University of Pittsburgh Press, 1993.

Halloran, Michael. "The Birth of Molecular Biology: An Essay in the Rhetorical Criticism of Scientific Discourse." *Rhetoric Review* 3 (1984): 70–83.

Haraway, Donna. "A Cyborg Manifesto: Science, Technology, and Socialist-Feminism in the Late Twentieth Century." In *Simians, Cyborgs, and Women: The Reinvention of Nature.* New York: Routledge, 1991.

————. *Primate Visions: Gender, Race, and Nature in the World of Modern Science.* New York: Routledge, 1989.

————. *Simians, Cyborgs, and Women: The Reinvention of Nature.* New York: Routledge, 1991.

————. "Teddy Bear Patriarchy: Taxidermy in the Garden of Eden, New York City, 1908–36." *Social Text* 11 (1984–85): 20–64.

Harding, Sandra. *The Science Question in Feminism.* Ithaca: Cornell University Press, 1988.

Harkin, Patricia, and John Schilb, ed. *Contending with Words: Composition and Rhetoric in a Postmodern Age.* New York: MLA, 1991.

Hawking, Stephen. *A Brief History of Time: From the Big Bang to Black Holes.* New York: Bantam, 1988.

Held, David. *Introduction to Critical Theory.* Berkeley and Los Angeles: University of California Press, 1980.

Hermogenes. "Hermogenes's *On Stasis:* A Translation with an Introduction and Notes." Trans. Ray Nadeau. *Speech Monographs* 31 (Nov. 1964): 361–424.

Herndl, Carl, Barbara Fennell, and Carolyn Miller. "Understanding Failures in Organizational Discourse: The Accident at Three Mile Island and the Shuttle Challenger Disaster." In *Textual Dynamics of the Professions,* ed. Charles Bazerman and James Paradis. Madison: University of Wisconsin Press, 1991.

Hoffman, George. "The Montaigne Monopoly: Revising the *Essais* under the French Privilege System." *PMLA* 108, no. 2 (Mar. 1993): 308–19.

Hogan, C. J., and M. J. Rees. "Gravitational Interactions of Cosmic Strings." *Nature* 311 (Sept. 13, 1984): 109–14.

Holub, Robert C. *Jürgen Habermas: Critic in the Public Sphere.* London and New York: Routledge, 1991.

Honneth, Axel, and Hans Joas, eds. *Communicative Action: Essays on Jürgen Habermas's "The Theory of Communicative Action."* Cambridge: Polity Press, 1991.

Honneth, Axel, Thomas McCarthy, Claus Offe, and Albrecht Wellmer, eds. *Philosophical Interventions in the Unfinished Project of Enlightenment.* Cambridge: MIT Press, 1992.

Horkheimer, Max. "Notes on Science and the Crisis." In *Critical Theory: Selected Essays.* New York: Seabury, 1972.

Horkheimer, Max, and T. W. Adorno. *The Dialectic of Enlightenment.* New York: Seabury, 1969.

Hut, Piet, and Simon D. M. White, "Can a Neutrino-Dominated Universe Be Rejected?" (review article). *Nature* 310 (Aug. 23, 1984): 637–40.

Hutcheon, Linda. *A Poetics of Postmodernism: History, Theory, Fiction.* New York: Routledge, 1988.

Iragaray, Luce. *Speculum of the Other Woman.* Trans. Gillian Gill. Ithaca: Cornell University Press, 1985.

———. *This Sex Which Is Not One.* Trans. Catherine Porter. Ithaca: Cornell University Press, 1985.

Jakobsen, Roman. "Closing Statement: Linguistics and Poetics." In *Style in Language,* ed. Thomas Sebeok. Cambridge: MIT Press, 1960.

Jameson, Fredric. *Marxism and Form: Twentieth Century Dialectical Theories of Literature.* Princeton: Princeton University Press, 1971.

———. *The Political Unconscious.* Ithaca: Cornell University Press, 1982.

Jamieson, Kathleen Hall. *Eloquence in an Electronic Age: The Transformation of Political Speechmaking.* New York: Oxford University Press, 1988.

Jarratt, Susan C. *Rereading the Sophists: Classical Rhetoric Refigured.* Carbondale: Southern Illinois University Press, 1991.

Jay, Martin. *Marxism and Totality: The Adventures of a Concept from Lukacs to Habermas.* Berkeley and Los Angeles: University of California Press, 1984.

Jehlen, Myra. "The Civilizations of the New World and the State of Nature." *Revue Française d'Études Americaines* 16 (Apr.–July 1991): 48–49.

Kalinich, Lila. "Some Reflections on the Wolf-Man." In *Lacan and the Subject of Language,* ed. Ellie Ragland-Sullivan and M. Bracher. New York: Routledge, 1991.

Keller, Evelyn Fox. *Reflections on Gender and Science.* New Haven: Yale University Press, 1985.

Kennedy, George A. *Classical Rhetoric and Its Christian and Secular Tradition from Ancient to Modern Times.* Chapel Hill: University of North Carolina Press, 1980.

Kinneavy, James. *A Theory of Discourse.* Englewood Cliffs, N.J.: Prentice Hall, 1971.

Kittay, Jeffrey, and Wlad Godzich. *The Emergence of Prose: An Essay in Prosaics.* Minneapolis: University of Minnesota Press, 1987.

Knoblauch, C. H., and Lil Brannon. *Rhetorical Traditions and the Teaching of Writing.* Upper Montclair, N.J.: Boynton/Cook, 1984.

Kraemer, Don. "Gender and the Autobiographical Essay: A Critical Extension of the Research." *College Composition and Communication* 43 (Oct. 1992): 32–39.

Kramarae, Cheris. *Women and Men Speaking.* Rowley, Mass.: Newbury House, 1981.

Kramer, Lloyd. "Habermas, History, and Critical Theory." In *Habermas and the Public Sphere,* ed. Craig Calhoun. Cambridge: MIT Press, 1992.

Krauss, Lawrence, M. Sheldon, L. Glashow, and David N. Schramm. "Antineutrino Astronomy and Geophysics" (review article). *Nature* 310 (July 19, 1984): 191–98.

Kristeva, Julia. *The Revolution in Poetic Language.* New York: Columbia University Press, 1984.

Kuhn, T. S. *The Structure of Scientific Revolutions.* Chicago: University of Chicago Press, 1962.

La Boétie, Étienne de. *Oeuvres completes.* Ed. Paul Bonnefon. Geneva: Slatkine Reprints, 1967.

———. *The Politics of Obedience: The Discourse of Voluntary Servitude.* Introduction by Murray Rothbard. New York: Free Life Editions, 1975.

Labov, William. "The Transformation of Experience in Narrative Syntax." In *Language in the Inner City.* Philadelphia: University of Pennsylvania Press, 1972.

Lacan, Jacques. "L'agressivité en psychanalyse." In *Écrits.* Paris: Seuil, 1966.

———. *Écrits.* Paris: Seuil, 1966.

———. *Écrits: A Selection.* Trans. A. Sheridan. New York: Norton, 1977.

———. *Encore, 1972–73. Le seminaire, 20.* Ed. Jacques-Alain Miller. Paris: Seuil, 1975.

———. *Feminine Sexuality: Jacques Lacan and the École Freudienne.* Ed. Juliet Mitchell and Jacqueline Rose. New York: Norton, 1982.

———. *The Four Fundamental Concepts of Psycho-analysis.* Ed. J.-A. Miller and trans. Alan Sheridan. New York: Norton, 1978.

———. "Intervention on Transference." In *Feminine Sexuality: Jacques Lacan and the École Freudienne.* Ed. Juliet Mitchell and Jacqueline Rose. New York: Norton, 1985.

———. *Le seminaire XVII.* Paris: Seuil, 1991.

———. "Seminar on 'The Purloined Letter.'" In *The Purloined Poe: Lacan, Derrida, and Psychoanalytic Reading.* Ed. John Muller and William Richardson. Baltimore: Johns Hopkins University Press, 1988.

———. *Seminars.* Ed. Jacques-Alain Miller. Vol. 1, 1953–54, *Freud's Papers on Technique.* Trans. John Forrester. New York: Norton, 1988. First published Paris: Seuil, 1975. Vol. 2, 1954–55, *The Ego in Freud's Theory and in the Technique of Psychoanalysis.* Trans. S. Tomaselli. New York: Norton, 1988.

First published Paris: Seuil, 1978. Vol. 7, 1959–60, *The Ethics of Psychoanalysis*. Trans. Dennis Porter. New York: Norton, 1992. First published Paris: Seuil, 1986.

Lakoff, Robin. *Language and Women's Place*. New York: HarperCollins, 1975.

Landau, Misia. *Narratives of Human Evolution*. New Haven: Yale University Press, 1991.

Laplanche, Jean. *Life and Death in Psychoanalysis*. Trans. Jeffrey Mehlman. Baltimore: Johns Hopkins University Press, 1976.

Larson, Magali Sarfatti. *The Rise of Professionalism: A Sociological Analysis*. Berkeley and Los Angeles: University of California Press, 1977.

Latour, Bruno, and Steven Woolgar. *Laboratory Life: The Social Construction of Scientific Facts*. Sage Library of Social Research 80. Beverly Hills: Sage, 1979.

Lebeck, Anne. "The Central Myth of Plato's *Phaedrus*." *Journal of Greek, Roman, and Byzantine Studies* 13 (1972): 267–70.

Leitch, Thomas. *What Stories Are: Narrative Theory and Interpretation*. College Station: Penn State University Press, 1986.

Longino, Helen. *Science as Social Knowledge*. Princeton: Princeton University Press, 1990.

Lynch, Michael. *Art and Artifact in Laboratory Science: A Study of Shop Work and Shop Talk in a Research Laboratory*. London: Routledge and Kegan Paul, 1985.

Lyne, John, and Henry Howe. "'Punctuated Equilibria': Rhetorical Dynamics of a Scientific Controversy." *Quarterly Journal of Speech* 72 (1986): 132–47.

Lyotard, Jean-François. *The Postmodern Condition: A Report on Knowledge*. Trans. Geoff Bennington and Brian Massumi. Minneapolis: University of Minnesota Press, 1984.

Margolis, Joseph. *Texts without Referents: Reconciling Science and Narrative*. Oxford: Blackwell, 1989.

Mariani, James. "The New SSTG Microbalance System." Dec. 1990. Typescript.

Maskell, David. "Evolution of the *Essais*." In *Montaigne: Essays in Memory of Richard Sayce*, ed. I. D. McFarlane and Ian Maclean. Oxford: Clarendon, 1982.

McCarthy, Thomas. *The Critical Theory of Jürgen Habermas*. Cambridge: MIT Press, 1978.

———. *Ideals and Illusions: On Reconstruction and Deconstruction in Contemporary Critical Theory*. Cambridge: MIT Press, 1993.

McConnell-Ginet, S., R. Borker, and N. Furman. *Women and Language in Literature and Society*. New York: Praeger, 1980.

McFarlane, I.D., and Ian Maclean. *Montaigne: Essays in Honor of Richard Sayce*. Oxford: Clarendon, 1982.

McGowan, Margaret. *Montaigne's Deceits: The Art of Persuasion in the "Essais."* London: University of London Press, 1974.

Mellard, James M. *Using Lacan, Reading Fiction*. Urbana: University of Illinois Press, 1991.

Melville, Steven. "Psychoanalysis and the Place of Jouissance." In *The Trial(s) of Psychoanalysis,* ed. Françoise Meltzer. Chicago: University of Chicago Press, 1987.

Miller, Jacques-Alain. "The Analytic Experience." In *Lacan and the Subject of Language,* ed. E. Ragland-Sullivan and M. Bracher. New York: Routledge, 1991.

Miller, Richard. "Fault Lines in the Contact Zone." *College English* 65, no. 4 (Apr. 1994): 389–408.

Minto, Barbara. *The Pyramid Principle: Logic in Writing and Thinking.* London: Minto International, 1982.

Montaigne, Michel de. *The Complete Essays of Montaigne.* Trans. Donald Frame. Stanford: Stanford University Press, 1943.

———. *Les essais.* 3 vols. Ed. Pierre Villey. Paris: Presses Universitaires de France, 1965.

———. *The Essays of Montaigne, Done into English by John Florio.* 3 vols. New York: AMS Press, 1967.

Moran, Emerson. "Should the Mayor Resign?" *Philadelphia Magazine,* May 1987.

Muller, John P., and William Richardson, eds. *The Purloined Poe: Lacan, Derrida, and Psychoanalytic Reading.* Baltimore: Johns Hopkins University Press, 1988.

Myers, Greg. *Writing Biology: Texts in the Social Construction of Scientific Knowledge.* Madison: University of Wisconsin Press, 1990.

Nadeau, Ray. "Classical Systems of Stases." *Greek, Roman, and Byzantine Studies* 2 (1959): 51–71.

Narayan, Ramesh, Roger Blandford, and Rajaram Nityananda. "Multiple Imaging of Quasars by Galaxies and Clusters." *Nature* 310 (July 12, 1984): 112–15.

Neel, Jasper. *Plato, Derrida, and Writing.* Carbondale: Southern Illinois University Press, 1988.

Negt, Oskar, and Alexander Kluge. *The Public Sphere and Experience: Toward an Analysis of the Bourgeois and the Proletarian Public Sphere.* Minneapolis: University of Minnesota Press, 1993.

North, Stephen M. *The Making of Knowledge in Composition: Portrait of an Emerging Field.* Portsmouth: Boynton/Cook, 1987.

Nussbaum, Martha. *The Fragility of Goodness: Luck and Ethics in Greek Thought and Philosophy.* Cambridge: Cambridge University Press, 1986.

Odell, Lee, Dixie Goswami, Anne Herrington, and Doris Quick. "Studying Writing in Non-academic Settings." In *New Essays in Technical and Scientific Communication: Research, Theory, Practice,* ed. Paul V. Anderson, R. John Brockmann, and Carolyn R. Miller. Baywood Series in Scientific and Technical Communication. Farmingdale, N.Y.: Baywood Publishing, 1983.

Ohmann, Richard. *English in America: A Radical View of the Profession.* New York: Oxford University Press, 1976.

O'Neill, John. *Essaying Montaigne: A Study of the Renaissance Institution of Writing and Reading.* London: Routledge and Kegan Paul, 1982.

Pagden, Anthony. *The Fall of Natural Man: The American Indian and the Origins of Comparative Ethnology*. Cambridge: Cambridge University Press, 1982.

Parker, Patricia. "Gender, Ideology, and Gender Change: The Case of Marie Germaine." *Critical Inquiry* 19, no. 2 (winter 1993): 337–64.

Pearsall, Thomas E. "The State of Technical Writing." Paper presented at the annual meeting of the Midwest Regional Conference on English in the Two-Year College, Minneapolis, Minn., Feb. 1981.

Penley, Constance. "Teaching in Your Sleep: Feminism and Psychoanalysis." In *Theory in the Classroom*, ed. Cary Nelson. Urbana: University of Illinois Press, 1986.

Perelman, Chaim, and Lynn Olbrechts-Tyteca. *The New Rhetoric: A Treatise on Argumentation*. Trans. John Wilkinson and Purcell Weaver. Notre Dame: University of Notre Dame Press, 1969.

Peterson, Linda. "Gender and the Autobiographical Essay: Research Perspectives, Pedagogical Practices." *College Composition and Communication* 42 (May 1991): 170–83.

Phelan, James, ed. *Reading Narrative: Form, Ethics, Ideology*. Columbus: Ohio State University Press, 1989.

Philadelphia Special Investigation Commission. "Findings, Conclusions, and Recommendations." *Temple Law Quarterly* 59, no. 2 (1986).

———. *The Findings, Conclusions, and Recommendations of the Philadelphia Special Investigation Commission*. Philadelphia, Mar. 6, 1986.

———. *Hearings of the Philadelphia Special Investigation Commission*. Philadelphia, 1985.

Plato. *Phaedrus*. Trans. H. N. Fowler. Cambridge: Harvard University Press, 1914.

———. *Phaedrus*. Trans. W. C. Helmbold and W. G. Rabinowitz. Indianapolis: Bobbs-Merrill, 1956.

———. *Phaedrus*. Trans. R. Hackforth. Indianapolis: Bobbs-Merrill, 1960.

———. *Symposium*. In *The Works of Plato*. New York: Modern Library, 1928.

Platt, Anthony. *The Politics of Riot Commissions, 1917–70: A Collection of Official Reports and Critical Essays*. New York: Macmillan, 1971.

Popper, Karl. *The Logic of Scientific Discovery*. New York: Harper and Row, 1934. Reprint, 1968.

Poulakos, Takis. "Human Agency in the History of Rhetoric: Gorgias's *Encomium of Helen*." In *Writing Histories of Rhetoric*, ed. Victor Vitanza. Carbondale: Southern Illinois University Press, 1994.

———, ed. *Rethinking the History of Rhetoric: Multidisciplinary Essays on the Rhetorical Tradition*. Boulder: Westview Press, 1993.

Prelli, Lawrence. *A Rhetoric of Science: Inventing Scientific Discourse*. Columbia: University of South Carolina Press, 1989.

Prince, Gerald. *Narrative as Theme: Studies in French Fiction*. Lincoln: University of Nebraska Press, 1992.

———. *Narratology: The Form and Function of Narrative*. The Hague: Mouton, 1982.

Quintilian. *The Institutio oratoria of Quintilian.* 4 vols. Trans. H. E. Butler. Cambridge: Loeb Classical Library, 1921.

Rabinow, Paul, ed. *Foucault Reader.* New York: Pantheon, 1984.

Ragland-Sullivan, Ellie. *Jacques Lacan and the Philosophy of Psychoanalysis.* Urbana and Chicago: University of Illinois Press, 1987.

Ragland-Sullivan, Ellie, and M. Bracher, ed. *Lacan and the Subject of Language.* New York: Routledge, 1991.

Rasmussen, David. *Reading Habermas.* Cambridge, Mass.: Blackwell, 1990.

Reiss, Timothy. "Montaigne and the Subject of Polity." In *Literary Theory and Renaissance Texts,* ed. P. Parker and D. Quint. Baltimore: Johns Hopkins University Press, 1986.

Richards, I. A. *The Philosophy of Rhetoric.* New York: Oxford, 1936. Reprint, 1965.

Ricoeur, Paul. *Time and Narrative.* 3 vols. Trans. Kathleen Blamey and David Pellauer. Chicago: University of Chicago Press, 1984–88.

Rigolot, François. "Montaigne's Purloined Letters." In *Montaigne: Essays in Reading,* ed. Gerard Defaux, *YFS* 64 (1983): 145–67.

Rimmon-Kenan, Shlomin. *Narrative Fiction: Contemporary Poetics.* London: Routledge and Kegan Paul, 1983.

Riordan, Michael, and David N. Schramm. *The Shadows of Creation: Dark Matter and the Structure of the Universe.* New York: Freeman, 1991.

Robbins, Bruce, ed. *The Phantom Public Sphere.* Minneapolis: University of Minnesota Press, 1993.

Roe, Emery. *Narrative Policy Analysis: Theory and Practice.* Durham, N.C.: Duke University Press, 1994.

Rorty, Richard. *Philosophy and the Mirror of Nature.* Princeton: Princeton University Press, 1979.

Rosaldo, Renato. *Culture and Truth: The Remaking of Social Analysis.* Boston: Beacon, 1989.

Ryan, Mary. "Gender and Public Access: Women's Politics in Nineteenth-Century America." In *Habermas and the Public Sphere,* ed. Craig Calhoun. Cambridge: MIT Press, 1992.

Saussure, Ferdinand de. *Course in General Linguistics.* Ed. C. Bally and A. Sechehaye, trans. Wade Baskin. New York: Philosophical Library, 1959. First published in 1916.

Schafer, Roy. *Retelling a Life: Narration and Dialogue in Psychoanalysis.* New York: Basic, 1992.

Schama, Simon. *Dead Certainties (Unwarranted Speculations).* New York: Vintage, 1991.

Schiebinger, Londa. *Nature's Body: Gender in the Making of Modern Science.* Boston: Beacon, 1993.

Schneiderman, Stuart. *Returning to Freud: Clinical Psychoanalysis in the School of Lacan.* New Haven: Yale University Press, 1980.

Schramm, David, and Michael Turner. "Universal Truths." *Scientific American* 263, no. 4 (Oct. 1990): 111–17.

Sedgwick, Eve. *Epistemology of the Closet*. Berkeley and Los Angeles: University of California Press, 1990.

Selzer, Jack, ed. *Understanding Scientific Prose*. Madison: University of Wisconsin Press, 1993.

Shapin, Steven. "The Politics of Observation: Cerebral Anatomy and Social Interests in the Edinburgh Phrenology Disputes." In *On the Margins of Science: The Social Construction of Rejected Knowledge*, ed. Roy Wallis. Sociological Review Monograph 27. Keele: University of Keele, 1979.

Shapin, Steven, and Simon Schaffer. *Leviathan and the Air-Pump: Hobbes, Boyle, and the Experimental Life*. Princeton: Princeton University Press, 1985.

Shweder, Richard. "Post-Nietzschian Anthropology: The Idea of Multiple Objective Worlds." In *New Essays on Human Development*, ed. Michael Krausz. Notre Dame: Notre Dame University Press 1991.

Simons, Herbert W. "The Rhetoric of Inquiry as an Intellectual Movement." In *The Rhetorical Turn: Invention and Persuasion in the Conduct of Inquiry*, ed. Herbert W. Simons. Chicago: University of Chicago Press, 1990.

———, ed. *The Rhetorical Turn: Invention and Persuasion in the Conduct of Inquiry*. Chicago: University of Chicago Press, 1990.

Spender, Dale. *Man Made Language*. London: Routledge and Kegan Paul, 1985.

Starobinski, Jean. *Montaigne in Motion*. Chicago: University of Chicago Press, 1985.

Stewart, Susan. *Crimes of Writing: Problems in the Containment of Representation*. New York: Oxford University Press, 1991.

Stone, Lawrence. *The Past and the Present*. London: Routledge, 1988.

Struever, Nancy. *Theory as Practice: Ethical Inquiry in the Renaissance*. Chicago: University of Chicago Press, 1992.

Sutton, Jane. "The Marginalization of Sophistical Rhetoric and the Loss of History." In *Rethinking the History of Rhetoric: Multidisciplinary Essays on the Rhetorical Tradition*, ed. Takis Poulakos. Boulder: Westview Press, 1993.

Swearingen, C. Jan. *Rhetoric and Irony: Western Literacy and Western Lies*. New York: Oxford University Press, 1991.

Taylor, Charles, K. Anthony Appiah, Jürgen Habermas, Steven Rockefeller, Michael Walzer, and Susan Wolf. *Multiculturalism: Examining the Politics of Recognition*. Princeton: Princeton University Press, 1994.

Thibaudet, Albert. *Montaigne*. Paris: Gallimard, 1963.

Thompson, John, and David Held, eds. *Habermas: Critical Debates*. Cambridge: MIT Press, 1982.

Todorov, Tzvetan. "L'Être et L'Autre: Montaigne." *YFS* 64 (1983): 113–44.

———. *The Poetics of Prose*. Ithaca: Cornell University Press, 1977.

Tönnies, Ferdinand. *Community and Society*. New York: Harper Torchbooks, 1957.

Toulmin, Stephen. *The Return to Cosmology: Postmodern Science and the Theology of Nature*. Berkeley and Los Angeles: University of California Press, 1982.

Turkle, Sherry. *Psychoanalytic Politics: Jacques Lacan and Freud's French Revolution*. 2d ed. New York: Guilford, 1992.

Vickers, Brian. *In Defense of Rhetoric.* Oxford: Clarendon, 1988.

Villey, Pierre. *Les sources et l'evolution des "Essais" de Montaigne.* 2d ed. 2 vols. Paris: Hachette, 1908. Reprint, 1938.

Vitanza, Victor J. "'Notes' toward Historiographies of Rhetorics; Or, Rhetorics of the Histories of Rhetorics: Traditional, Revisionary, and Sub/Versive." *PRE/TEXT* 8, nos. 1–2 (1987): 63–125.

———, ed. *Writing Histories of Rhetoric.* Carbondale: Southern Illinois University Press, 1994.

Wagner-Pacifici, Robin. *Discourse and Destruction: The City of Philadelphia versus MOVE.* Chicago: University of Chicago Press, 1994.

———. "The Text of Transgression: The City of Philadelphia versus MOVE." Philadelphia, 1987. Typescript.

Wallis, Roy, ed. *On the Margins of Science: The Social Construction of Rejected Knowledge.* Sociological Review Monograph 27. Keele: University of Keele, 1979.

Warner, Michael. "The Mass Public and the Mass Subject." In *Habermas and the Public Sphere,* ed. Craig Calhoun. Cambridge: MIT Press, 1992.

Weber, Max. *The Protestant Ethic and the Spirit of Capitalism.* Trans. Talcott Parsons. New York: Scribners, 1958.

———. "Science as a Vocation." In *From Max Weber: Essays in Sociology.* Ed. and trans. H. H. Gerth and C. W. Mills. New York: Oxford University Press, 1974.

Welch, Kathleen Ethel. "Intepreting the Silent 'Aryan Model' of Histories of Classical Rhetoric: Martin Bernal, Terry Eagleton, and the Politics of Rhetoric and Composition Studies." In *Writing Histories of Rhetoric,* ed. V. Vitanza. Carbondale: Southern Illlinois University Press, 1994.

Wells, Susan. "Narrative Figures and Subtle Persuasions." In *The Rhetorical Turn: Invention and Persuasion in the Conduct of Inquiry,* ed. Herbert W. Simons. Chicago: University of Chicago Press, 1990.

White, David A. *Rhetoric and Reality in Plato's "Phaedrus."* Albany: SUNY Press, 1993.

White, Hayden. *Metahistory: The Historical Imagination in Nineteenth Century Europe.* Baltimore: Johns Hopkins University Press, 1973.

———. *Tropics of Discourse: Essays in Cultural Criticism.* Baltimore: Johns Hopkins University Press, 1978.

White, Stephen K. *The Recent Work of Jürgen Habermas: Reason, Justice and Modernity.* Cambridge: Cambridge University Press, 1988.

Wideman, John Edgar. *Philadelphia Fire.* New York: Vintage, 1991.

Wilden, Anthony. "Montaigne on the Paradoxes of Individualism." In *System and Structure: Essays in Communication and Exchange.* London: Routledge, 1980.

———. "Montaigne's *Essays* in the Context of Communication." *MLN* 85 (1970): 454–70.

———. "Pars divers moyens . . ." *MLN* 83 (1968): 577–97.

Wilson, Thomas. *The arte of Rhetorique, for the use of all suche as are studious of Eloquence.* New York: Garland, 1982. Originally published in 1553.

Woodward, Kathleen, ed. *The Myths of Information: Technology and Post-industrial Culture*. London: Routledge and Kegan Paul, 1980.

Zappen, James. "A Rhetoric for Research in Sciences and Technologies." In *New Essays in Technical and Scientific Communication: Research, Theory, Practice*, ed. Paul V. Anderson, R. John Brockmann, and Carolyn R. Miller. Baywood Series in Technical and Scientific Communication. Farmingdale, N.Y.: Baywood Publishing, 1983.

Žižek, Slavoj. *The Sublime Object of Ideology*. London: Verso, 1989.

———. *Tarrying with the Negative: Kant, Hegel, and the Critique of Ideology*. Durham, N.C.: Duke University Press, 1993.

INDEX

• • • •